EIGHT MILES
WITHOUT A POTHOLE

With my Best Wishes

Jim Klobuchar

EIGHT MILES
WITHOUT A POTHOLE
AS CLOSE TO HEAVEN AS I'M GOING TO GET

by

JIM KLOBUCHAR

VOYAGEUR PRESS

Published by Voyageur Press Inc.
212 North Second Street
Minneapolis, MN 55401

ISBN 0-89658-070-9 (hardbound)
ISBN: 0-89658-068-7 (paperback)

Printed in the United States of America.

To Bob
A friend and colleague who loved books and authors
and forgave columnists.

Contents

GIVE HER MATCHING JUMPER CABLES: MINNESOTA AND MINNESOTANS

THE SMALLEST TUG ON THE LINE: THE BUSINESS WORLD

YOU DON'T HAVE TO BE FAMOUS TO BE MEMORABLE: EXTRAORDINARY ORDINARY PEOPLE

COPING WITH CAESAR: POLITICS AND ITS PRACTITIONERS

A FEW MENTAL BURRS SHORT OF ABSOLUTE ECSTASY: THE HUMAN CONDITION

Foreword

TECHNOLOGY HAS REMADE the face of newspapering in ways that are wondrous to workaday newspaper folk. Today we compose on screens filled with dancing green figures and magically move paragraphs from top to bottom with the flick of a finger. We tell the machine to correct our spelling errors and we curdle when a disembodied voice warns the city room: "Store and dig in, the system is about to crash."

Almost nobody works a typewriter any more and reporters' pads are becoming extinct. Yet the rewards of this stubborn and still-absorbing craft are about what they used to be: There are days when the weave of the news permits the journalist to express what is in the heart or head of the reader, and other days when the writer is able to introduce or reacquaint the reader with a human being worth their shared time. That person may be attractive, dangerous, famous, or obscure, but uncommon enough to be memorable. And if the next day the newspaper's subscriber can ask a neighbor, "Did you read about . . . " then the lodge of newspapering is alive and flourishing.

I've been at it for enough years to plead maturity and also long enough, I suppose, not to blush at recycling some of my produce and serving it once more to an audience that may not necessarily be howling nonstop for encores. But I think a collection like this can be both fun and instructive. If there is any genuine artistic merit for exhuming yesterday's faces and scenes, I think it is this:

We all like to leaf through our memories. While we're doing it we can rekindle a moment or an interlude in our lives that may have been amusing, thrilling, or profound. So if that exercise has value, let me be your escort in the pages of this book, and let the stories in it renew for you a link with some old friends, a few old villains, and a lot of faces and times that simply deserve renewal.

I'm comfortable in that role by occupation. Somebody asked me once what I called myself as a newspaperman. I told him if I had to call myself anything it would probably be a minstrel. In the kind of column I write for the *Minneapolis Star and Tribune*, I'm a teller of stories, a witness, a foil, an advocate, and, as often as I can be, a friend. It's a free-floating charter that takes me and therefore the reader into the street, the government cubicles, locker rooms, wilderness and mountain, and living rooms. It's a daily perambulation that has brought me pictures and sounds of humanity I can never forget — the quiet indomitability of an old man looking after his wife in her last hours, the honest rage and happy absurdities inflicted on an innocent Sunday by millionaire athletes, the mixed enrichments of life at 20 below zero, the fears of the famous that they will cease to be famous, and the wisdom of some of the anonymous who know that being famous may be dangerous to the health.

The journalist's wanderings give him daily glimpses of the foolishness and nobility in the human spirit, the struggles, pain, and victories that mark its passage. The locale of most of the scenes in this book is Minnesota. But the people in it are pretty much everyone — except for the skier who found herself descending a slope with her pants at half-staff.

She could only have come from Minnesota.

Jim Klobuchar
August 1986

Faces in the Arena: Sports and Players

The Viking Amazons Accost Rush Street

OCTOBER 30, 1984

AT EIGHTEEN MINUTES to midnight Saturday night, the telephone rang in my room in the Bismarck Hotel in downtown Chicago and introduced me to strangled sounds of turmoil and amazement from a restaurant on Rush Street. "You got some kind of group here from Minninapolis?" a cheerless voice asked.

I said yes and no. I said I was in charge of 100 knowledge-craving women from my football clinic, in Chicago to meet the demands of scholarship with their annual field trip for the Vikings–Bears game. But by no twist of the language could this be described as a group.

"The women are individualists," I said. "They are pursuing independent study."

The voice at the restaurant grunted semiliterately, in the style of Chicago restaurateurs. I tried to put a face to his voice and mentally thumbed through post office bulletin boards. I picked a Turk galleymaster with gold earrings and pointed ears.

"The one I'm lookin' at ain't pursuing independent study," he said. "She's got this crazy rubber sword and she's trying to attack my customers like she's a matador.

"She said you taught them how to go hut-hut-hut. I told her to take her act back to the Halloween party, but she said she was just getting psyched up for the game and she gave me your name. No, it's not the one with the purple caterpillar antennae. If one like that comes through the door, the one in here is going through the window. Lemme tell you, buddy. If she drills somebody with that goofy little Viking sword, you're an accessory."

It was one of the more generous names I absorbed over the weekend.

Before he hung up he made a demand. "If you're in charge of these 100 women, how come you're not down here on Rush Street with them?" I told him that when the going starts to smart, the smart stay back in the hotel.

I would like to give you all of the gripping events of the weekend, but I can't because I have been under moderate sedation most of the day. I want my creditors to know that the prognosis is all right. Most of the quivering in my nostrils has subsided and I no longer look for falling chandeliers when I hear noises on the floor above. The therapy I have been receiving since the three buses got back is mostly covered by insurance, and the treatment is nonaddictive.

I want to make a public explanation, though, to the husband who hung up on me.

To do it I have to give a testimonial to the basic sense of commitment my student body carried into Rush Street Saturday night. Academicians will tell you that a test of scholarship is not only the zeal but also the ingenuity the seeker of wisdom carries into the field. My class for the last two sessions has been exploring the tactics and psychology of the 4–3 pass rush and the linebacker blitz. I explained that often a team takes on a behavioral tone from the environment in which it plays. The Pittsburgh Steelers, I said, used to reflect the iron-fisted mentality of the city of steel.

Kim Thompson, a computer programmer from Bloomington, stopped me at breakfast Saturday and said she represented a delegation of 100. "We believe the Bears get their desperation tactics on defense watching pedestrians trying to survive on Rush Street," she said. "We're all going down to do research."

Like the football coaches, I establish a curfew for the women on nights before the game. I set 3 a.m. as a reasonable time for the clinical urges to subside. I also cut off telephone service to the scholars' rooms so they won't be distracted from their field work by their husbands or boyfriends back in Minnesota. Instead, the calls ring on my phone.

I get at least one every year. The guy wanted to know why his wife's phone wasn't answering at 2 a.m. I said she was probably on Rush Street stopping traffic.

There was just no reason for him to get testy and bang the telephone.

Francis's Whirling Mind
Visualized a Game of Games

JANUARY 7, 1977

Los Angeles

THE CHATTER IN the bus had subsided. Freeway traffic streamed by and a half mile in the distance lay the Pacific Ocean. Francis Tarkenton stared at it, allowing himself some time for reflection.

A minute or so. Francis Tarkenton in a Super Bowl week measures his reflection time in spasms, fugitive retreats into a rare cosmos of calm. It is not that he is thinking or working football round the clock. His world, whether in early January three days before a championship football game or at a corporate pep rally in Macon, Georgia, is involvement. Get it on. Make things happen. If something is happening, what does it mean to Francis Tarkenton?

He turned from brief meditation and tapped the knee of a friend who had attended a gathering of Oakland Raider players. "How's Stabler handling it?" he asked. "The circus. How's he dealing with the newshawks?"

"Accommodating and pleasant," the friend said. "They ask him what he does an hour before the game and he says he goes into the john to relieve himself. Just like Tarkenton."

The quarterback howled. At least they were even going in. It was a snippet of intelligence he probably wouldn't have to pipe into the computer.

He wasn't preoccupied with Kenny Stabler, or even the Oakland Raiders for that matter. But his mind was in constant motion, whimsical, probing, gossipy, erudite.

He is naturally a restless man, but never so much as the week of Super Bowl XI. He has burned his defenses and made a concession not only to himself but to that part of the planet that cares about Super Bowl. It IS the pinnacle for him and for his football team, and he is reaching for it—unblushingly and brashly, profanely and devoutly.

If the Minnesota Vikings win the Super Bowl Francis A. Tarkenton will stand in the middle of a roomful of roaring, crying football players and say, "I love you, I love you, you big, bad, beautiful sons of bitches." They will dump the same endearments on his head, and they will embrace and pound each other with the delirium of grown, wealthy men for whom one football game has become both the anvil of their minds and their deliverance.

Could a football game mean all that to 43 people, most of whom have kids in their fashionable suburban houses in Bloomington or Lakeville or southern California, closets full of clothes and sports cars in the garage?

It could, for Nate Wright and Doug Sutherland no less than Francis A. Tarkenton. The imperatives of big-time athletics and the demands of the crowds' fantasies have made it so. If you play professional football, you must win a championship to establish your competitive manhood, and you have not won the championship—never mind divisions and NFCs—until you have won the Super Bowl.

Francis Tarkenton has heard it so many times and in so many tones (it has been poured on him derisively, jocularly, pontifically) that he of all people, the millionaire sophisticate of the nation's arenas, has come to believe it. And if the Minnesota Vikings should lose Sunday?

"We won't go skulking to Siberia," he said. "But it would be a blast in the can, wouldn't it?"

He comes into his third Super Bowl as the centerpiece of the action. He is a man who quite suddenly in the last 12 months has become one of the most famous in America, his face almost as familiar as presidents', his wealth surpassing that of industrial barons and far-off monarchs.

His antagonists in the Rose Bowl Sunday are diversified. One is Stabler, the nervy, disciplined left-handed quarterback who is capable of stampeding a football team.

The actual conflict between the two is indirect. The romanticists and hype artists can advertise it as a shootout. But Stabler and Tarkenton aren't competing against each other. If Tarkenton feels anything about the bearded Alabaman called Snake, aside from respect, it is an ever-so-faint resentment over the professional esteem Stabler has attracted while Tarkenton's own standing is frequently hung with asterisk. He is accorded reluctant praise and a kind of probationary immortality among the great quarterbacks.

Stabler is the classicist, ominously peering at unfolding patterns, unloading 20 yards downfield. Right out of the clinics. Tarkenton is the scurrier, operating a football flea market on his brains and gall.

"Okay, Tarkenton, you got all the statistics and the money, but where is the Super Bowl championship?"

Tarkenton used to laugh at that, or he ridiculed it. More frequently he simply ignored it. He tried all the antidotes and escapes. And this season, possibly because there were no more protections by which the civilized athlete can arm himself against the pain of failure, Tarkenton turned and confronted the detractors. And the braying myth.

"All right," he said, "the game matters something fierce to me. It is an obsession we have, to win it. An obsession I have. We will win it."

He knows you cannot talk your way through a first-rate defensive secondary, which is another problem for him Sunday.

But if the pressures both imposed and self-created are greater than ever for the 36-year-old athlete-executive, he would never claim any psychological hardship for that. He relishes them, and courts them. He is now so successful and so impervious to the second-guess that he actually expands the pressures by provoking his detractors. He says, in short, what he pleases. He used to think about being prudent and gracious. But now on television and in the press conference he has become one of the very same pundits he kids as an athlete.

Does the conflict bother him?

"Don't be silly. I love the life I have. I had a personal matter [his separation from his wife] and that concerned me, because of the lives it affected. But some people have tried to construct 1976 as a year of great trial for me. Injury as a player. The old Big One syndrome. Getting old. Gossip. All that. Well, if you'd like one word for how I look at my year, the word is *colossal*."

Not good, or very good, which as annual performance goes might not be considered shabby.

But colossal.

Francis A. Tarkenton simply thinks in those terms. And what could be better than colossal?

"The Super Bowl championship," he said, "might give you a start."

He makes that concession to all of the old goblins that the pro football fans have conjured for him. Winning the game would be an immense gratification, a burden shed, a glory earned. A bad dream exorcised?

"Okay, that."

But in the mind of Francis Tarkenton it can never truly define his right to greatness. He believes his record and performance have irrefutably defined that. Would a Super Bowl championship confirm it?

"That's a word game I don't have to play."

But football fans do, and he recognizes that, and so for a boy bubble-gum-card collector who understands the fan's inspirations and his obtuseness better than most, Sunday will be another day of exhilaration at the ballpark. He is out there throwing, shouting, conniving. He knows the game as well as any quarterback who ever played. The confidence and trust he carries on the team is total. He has a roughened style of talk now, in the locker-room environment, and he affects the old pro role with tobacco in his jaw, but all of that is his own personal imagery. What he does best in football is not posturing but thinking, gambling, striving, and leading. For the first time Sunday, he will wear his own grail-goal on his helmet, and it ought to be a spectacle.

Harry P. Grant's Most Outrageous Con Job

OCTOBER 17, 1977

WHY WAS NATE Allen kneeling on the end of the bench with his eyes shut and his lips mumbling a prayer? And why was Francis Tarkenton stalking the sideline indignantly, kicking huge divots in the grass and otherwise disturbing the Sabbath with a stream of pungent syllables? And what was the Minnesota Vikings offensive line doing in the huddle, the most automated creatures in pro football, renouncing their vows of silence and suddenly, in near mutiny, roaring in unison: "A fake WHAT?"

They shared a common grief.

Without exception they were convinced Harry P. (Bud) Grant was out of his gourd. And so young a man, outwardly so healthy and rational. It was a conviction that had already permeated thousands in Metropolitan Stadium who were stricken at the sight of Fred Cox waddling into the game halfway through the overtime, apparently bent on kicking a field goal to beat the Chicago Bears.

To appreciate the depth of the fieldside anguish — and to understand the breadth of the con job Harry Grant administered with the Paul Krause to Stu Voigt touchdown pass and the 22–16 victory it produced — you had to be on the floor of the arena. In the stands, the consternation may have been general. On the field, it was unanimous.

Consider:

The Vikings and Bears stood 16–16 with the Vikings on the Bears' 11-yard line, first down.

Enter Cox, Paul Krause, Jeff Siemon, Matt Blair, and Doug Dumler, principal agents of the Viking field goal team.

"No!" Tarkenton screamed.

He elaborated as Cox neared. "What do we need with a ------ ------ field goal. We come all the ---- ------ way, 70 ---- -- --- yards, and now this ---- -------- ----. It's a -- -- ------."

Cox said it was debatable but Tarkenton ought to get off the field. Tarkenton scanned the sky for moral support. In view of the ferocity of his language, none was available there. The eavesdropping Bears on the field, while not sympathetic, were enthralled. The field goal didn't make any more sense to them than it did to Tarkenton, but it was lovely to hear the purpleheads quarreling among themselves, a practice on which the Bears held the franchise for years.

Having eluded Tarkenton, Cox, Krause, and the others joined the huddle. Krause gave the play casually, almost flinging it over his shoulder.

"Fake field goal," he said.

Ron Yary, later: *"Nobody believed him. Everybody on the offensive line took one step forward and said 'What?' I thought [Chuck] Goodrum was going to swallow him. Krause said it again. It didn't sound any better the second time. Even Jeff Siemon, who came on with the field goal team, said something like 'But it's first down.'"*

Krause stepped out of the huddle. In his last official act before leaving the field, Tarkenton had called time out eight seconds before the Vikings would have been docked five yards for delay of game.

Cox, later: *"Tarkenton was beautiful. He was so mad he made the act better without knowing it. He felt kind of betrayed. He's like any other quarterback. He wanted the offense to take the ball in after it had come all the way from our 20. I'm sure he remembered the Rams game last year when he threw an interception near the goal line when we were looking at a field goal inside the 10. I don't blame him. But I thought I was going to have to get the National Guard to take him off the field."*

Even the wisest quarterback in pro football, Grant decided, should be sheltered from shocking news now and then. He let Tarkenton stew in his oblivion. When Harry Grant conceives a flimflam, not even pals, hunting dogs, and 38-year-old quarterbacks are immune. On the field Krause stood aloof from his baffled teammates, trying to avoid conversation which might have tipped the Bears. When they lined up, the ham instinct latent in all pro football players took over.

Kneeling to take the snap from Dumler, Krause elaborately counted the yards separating him from the center. He did it with his arm. The picture had to be obvious to the Bears. Krause was making sure he had the prescribed seven-yard distance behind the line of scrimmage. Yary, Goodrum, Ed White, and the others called out blocking assignments on the line, as they always do on field goal attempts.

Cox, later: *"I could have rubbed off the fake field goal by yelling 'Overshift.' It would have changed the play back to a field goal if the Bears were in a defensive formation that looked like they could cover all of our receivers. But I really didn't want to do that. I was thinking fake field goal from the moment Bud told me we might try it. He did that right after I came back from kicking off to open the overtime. Krause and I have been trying to talk Bud into using the play practically every week. Krause has really been lobbying: 'This week, Bud? This week?' I like it for selfish reasons. Showing a pass from a field goal formation means dividends for a long time ahead. They can't come with that all-out rush knowing we can pass. I was kicking well against the Bears and I had made these three field goals already, but I really didn't want to switch back to thinking field goal after thinking field goal fake on the sidelines. You have to get yourself ready psychologically. And the Bears defense looked good for the fake."*

So Paul Krause, 35-year-old rookie rollout quarterback, shouted, "Set," took the snap, rose, and began running toward his right, looking for Steve Craig or Jeff Siemon, who lined up as a blocking wingback. Craig appeared covered by Alan Ellis. Siemon seemed open, but a large body, belonging to lineman Jerry Meyers, was lunging toward the territory. Paul Krause, however, had no trouble avoiding panic. He was, in fact, luxuriating. Why shouldn't he? They said four months ago that Paul Krause was being phased out by the Vikings after 13 years of pro football and his 74 interceptions. Somebody gossiped that the coaching staff had already made the decision and Bill Bradley was being imported from Philadelphia to retire Paul Krause to his cattle ranches, his contracting companies, his investments, and his expanding coiffure.

They couldn't run Krause off the football team. And now he was running free with options galore. The Bears were no less befuddled than the crowd or Tarkenton. Krause could run toward the goal line. He could run out of bounds. He could throw the ball to a receiver or he could throw it away intentionally if danger loomed. The last time he threw the ball competitively was nine years ago, when he dropped a pass from center. The last time he threw it formally was nearly 20 years ago in Bendle High School in Flint, Michigan, where he played quarterback.

Stu Voigt materialized near the goal line. Good old Chainsaw. He came chugging off the left end, with nobody to block. He was, he said, "available." You don't spend years playing with Tarkenton without learning the cardinal rule of catching footballs from a scrambling quarterback: Go someplace where he can see you. Voigt ran toward the goal line crossfield, saw the others covered or bothered, and yelled, "Paul." He also waved. He could have stopped to brush his teeth, because nobody covered him. Krause considered Stu Voigt judiciously and then floated a spiral to him. Voigt gathered it in the robust style of a lumberjack spearing the pancakes.

He just didn't leave much for the Bears.

Voigt, later: *"I think the play looked simpler than it was. There's a lot of pressure on the passer in a situation like that. It was the kind of play that demanded a guy with a lot of savvy and a good head, and that's the best thing about the way Krause plays football. He threw that ball in there well, with just enough on it to make it a good pass but not too hard to risk putting it off line."*

And when it was over, Matt Blair hugged Stu Voigt as they romped off the field to the uproar of the 47,708, a sizeable number of whom had thundered their jeers at the broad-rumped arrival of Fred Cox with his kicking team a minute before.

"I loved it, just loved it," he said. "It was a perfect call, and Bud stuck with it. We practice that play, but we hadn't done it for a week, and it almost never works in practice because the defense knows it's coming."

On the sideline, Francis Tarkenton dug Bud Grant in the ribs. "You dog," he said. "You faked out the old quarterback."

Among a few million other souls.

He Rode the Wind to the Hall of Fame

DECEMBER 5, 1979

THE GAME JIM Marshall played was meant for adolescents, for Tom Sawyers who grappled barefooted in rutabaga fields and laughed through busted teeth when they unraveled themselves.

Its creators never imagined it would someday become both a smoothly calibrated industry and a surrogate religion for millions of people; that its rituals would be performed by warrior-capitalists more recognizable to the public than kings and senators.

Nor could they possibly imagine that any of its original Tom Sawyers could survive the transformation without surrendering the gulping glee they brought to every collision, the smudge-faced impishness they spread on every field.

One did.

He retired Tuesday, undefeated.

Jim Marshall was professional football's eternal boy. Every day for more than 20 years he brought to the arena more than muscle, glands, and combat. He brought the wind and the sun. They nurtured and propelled him. He never looked on the places where he romped and tackled as stadiums or coliseums. They were playgrounds. For Jim Marshall, a day without football was a day without color or soul.

That he played the game with extraordinary skill and energy was something he owed to his physical gifts and his competitive zeals.

That he played it for so long, that he was alive to play it at all, was something he owed to the unapologetic child in him.

It made life a daily wonder and adventure. It flung him into a dizzying search for identities and excitements. He leaped out of airplanes and hunted for sunken treasures. He pondered mysteries. He took yoga positions one day and somersaults off the high board the next. He plowed down ski slopes scarcely built for the gangway charges of defensive ends, and when he pitched himself into a helpless heap at the bottom, he roared and demanded more challenging runs.

Even poor black kids could create their fictional universes, where they would perform deeds of valor, explore the wilderness, feel the wind. If the world would let him, he told himself, he would feel those sensations some day.

He felt more.

He also felt the world's ridicule and its cynicism.

There was never any question about his athletic endowments. He was swift and intuitive. In high school and at Ohio State, he did things rarely expected from or programmed for people who played defense. He scored touchdowns. He won games by himself. He went to Canada to play for money, very little of which he retained, but somewhere between there and Cleveland and Minnesota in his formative years as a professional, life became a kind of astrological wipeout. Wherever he went and whatever he did seemed hounded by some sour or downright malicious jinni.

He nearly died of sleeping sickness at 21, shortly before he joined the Minnesota Vikings. He accidentally shot himself with a revolver. He was one of the only professional football players of the decade who was hospitalized for a week for wrongly swallowing a grape. And on a cloudy day in San Francisco in 1964, he plucked a fumble and raced triumphant 66 yards into the end zone—his own.

So he became a cartoon. For a couple of years when you said *Jim Marshall*, people smiled. It was a comforting, superior smile in an inoffensive way, because it was a delight for people to know that there was at least one professional football player capable of numbskull acts and goofy predicaments.

It was inoffensive to everybody but Jim Marshall.

He cried in the San Francisco locker room a few minutes after his outlandish wrong-way run, because he understood the long memory of the football fans and their thin margin for forgiveness.

But he was a kid, for all that.

15

And when the sun came up the next day despite his worst suspicions, he laughed a little himself, although he retained the hurt for years.

I called him the day after his blunder, appealed to him for the second time to join me in a dialogue at a gathering of football fans in a downtown hotel. He tried to talk me out of it, but he came.

They gave him a standing ovation—not before he walked in, but when he walked out, because he stood there for five minutes, returning their grins, confessing it was a lunkhead thing, and explaining that he couldn't understand how a man of his undoubted genius could run 66 yards in a wrong direction.

A man of superficial dignity would not have shown up, would not have responded to the snickers with some of his own.

Marshall's dignity goes deeper. It could survive that, and it could survive that wild daily slapstick hysteria of the locker room where he dwelled for so long, the rich and unrestrained vulgarity of it, the ego deflations in it. It could survive defeats in the Super Bowl, his casual budgeting practices that put him in occasional trouble with creditors, and the exuberence of his child-appetites. It could even survive the stances of solemnity that Jim Marshall felt he had to adopt now and then in his later years with the Vikings.

But the internal Jim Marshall was never tilted by what pro football became or the legend's toga they draped on him. He's still the adolescent in the rutabaga field.

And that as much as anything explains the moisture that trickled down the granite features of his head coach Tuesday afternoon when Bud Grant and Jim Marshall announced the approaching end of their long partnership.

A piece of both of their lives is going. The youth, the spiritual indomitability of Jim Marshall from Grant's; the coach-to-player trust and veneration from Marshall's.

There are others to trust, of course.

But Grant recognized in Jim Marshall what other coaches, other players, the fans, might not have. There was not only athletic virtuosity there, but depth and commitment.

He built his football team on Jim Marshall, and three or four others like him.

And Marshall never gave him reason to regret it. He played in sunshine and storm, with fevers and fractures. His environment was the locker room and the stadium-playground. It renewed him every year, tantalized him, and, on Sunday afternoons, it electrified him.

We will be brothers forever, in a way. On one important night of our lives, we walked together in the snow, against a blizzard. He was in part of the group ahead of us, walking with Paul Dickson, a teammate; with a 15-year-old boy, another man, and the one woman in our snowmobile caravan in the mountains, Marilyn Waples.

All of us almost died. One good man did. Marshall was scared part of the time, hallucinating other times. He was honest enough not to affect phony heroics, but when the time demanded, he and Paul Dickson clasped the tiny woman between them, let her borrow the warmth of their bodies, let her cry on their cheeks.

And when we were reunited, he looked at the rising sun, and said life was good and great, just as it had always been for Jim Marshall.

But it will be a little less great at the stadium after Sunday.

Tommy's Two Minutes Were Prime Time

SEPTEMBER 21, 1981

HE CAME TO work with a scowl, a two-day growth of beard, and a string of profanity on his lips. In another scenario, he might have been a dockwalloper or gunfighter.

Wait a minute. Most waterfront brawlers and hired guns don't play quarterback in the National Football League if they want to hold on to their heads or reputations.

But the man from Houston shuns the penthouse etiquette of the quarterback's lodge. A football game is a street fight. Some quarterbacks are bashful about getting their capes dirty. This one comes with mud on his face and blood on his jaw, and yes, the Detroit Lions tried to remove his head in the fourth quarter at Metropolitan Stadium Sunday.

But he was still standing at the finish, on his one good leg, and the scoreboard was flashing 26–24 for the Minnesota Vikings. The clock showed somewhere around 3 p.m., but that was an illusion. The time was really high noon.

Tommy Kramer's time.

It has other descriptions: the two-minute drill, cardiac gulch. Your preference. Whatever you call it, the man you want playing quarterback when it happens is Tommy Kramer.

"He's got the character for it, one of those tough old Texas quarterbacks," said tough old Texan Doug English in the orchestrated bewilderment of the Detroit Lions' locker room. It was orchestrated because the Lions are usually discovered in this attitude when they come to Metropolitan Stadium.

They play football in Minnesota with all the assurance of a man walking beneath a falling safe. Sometimes they play remarkably well, as they did for most of the sun-washed afternoon Sunday, but almost always they blow it.

Sometimes this process requires a great deal of ingenuity by the Lions, but Sunday what it required most was Tommy Kramer; and nothing defines Tommy Kramer's special stamp and indispensability to the Vikings as the last two minutes — which is a world unto itself in pro football, baffling to the public because nobody who plays it or coaches it has ever adequately explained it.

How do you explain a time when curses on the bench mingle with communion? When the team that is leading gropes in sullen withdrawal, looking condemned, when the team that is trailing seems invincible, when all of the actors seem gripped by some astrological force of inevitability and déjà vu?

The communion was Rick Danmeier's. He is a man of belief. When the scoreboard clock is blinking down to the last digits, Rick Danmeier's mind moves methodically through the checklist of the professional kicker's preparations, but a piece of it is also locked in meditation.

You can call it prayer.

Why not? Danmeier does. He is not an innocent and he knows about some of the cynicism he attracts when he credits his "relationship with God."

Where was God, somebody wants to know, when you missed the chip shot in Chicago? God helps field goal kickers who have a 15-mile-an-hour tailwind and a steady Adam's apple. Danmeier has heard them all.

Still, communion on the sidelines.

The man from Houston, on the other hand, undoubtedly has beliefs of a fashion but he also has a very hard tongue and a bleeding jaw, and the fighter's gut. Which is why — just before the two-minute offense — he gets docked 15 yards for blasting an official with every four-letter word he remembers from Houston and a few from the Bloomington strip because nobody called the Lions for interfering with Sammy White when (the Vikings swear) they almost stripped him in midfield.

At this stage it was almost hopeless, is that correct? The Vikings have to punt with fourth and a half mile to go and there are only three minutes left and Kramer is faintly groggy, tired, getting intercepted now and throwing into the ground.

It is not correct because they do not play the last two minutes by the same rules or levels of sanity.

Why, Ahmad Rashad, tell us why.

"It wasn't just that the Lions were dropping back a little trying to avoid getting hurt deep," said the restored virtuoso, his two-game oblivion suddenly ended by the appearance of Tommy Kramer.

"It's a lot more. It's the urgency of it. That actually takes over. Adrenaline, sure. You know this is now or never. You come together. When you have success, you build on it. The other team sees it. They start doubting themselves. They're retreating and they see you getting closer. They can't stop you. We had that here with Fran Tarkenton.

"Tommy saw it, but he has his own nature. He is pure competitor. He lifts us because we've done it exactly this way before. He's also one smart guy."

You can't go 82 yards in 1:56 on instinct. You can't do it on adrenaline alone, or with the catching of Teddy Brown and Joe Senser. You need more, in fact, than the blast-all-of-your-eyes performance of the Viking offensive line, the Yarys, Rileys, Swilleys, et al., playing with the fraternal zealotry of the besieged. They got a bad rap from the crowds and the commentators Monday night. They got blamed for all of the sacks by the Oakland defense, but mostly they played a sound football game then. And Sunday they were downright fierce.

But that doesn't explain all of it.

Something more than the mood changed in the last two minutes. Something had to trigger the traditional late-game panic of the Lions and the sudden euphoria of a football team like the Vikings that had been blighted for four straight series by Bubba Baker, English, Bill Gay's attempted demolition of Kramer, and the Lions' secondary vets.

Kramer is never so much Tommy Kramer as he is when he can free-lance, to bring his run-and-gun instincts, his arm, and his underestimated smarts to a broken football field.

The Viking tacticians broke it up by shifting to three wide receivers in the last two minutes, maneuvering the Lions into coverages that spread the defenses and almost invariably put one receiver—a Brown or Senser or even a Sammy White—one on one against a defender.

But none of it meant diddly unless the quarterback was able to see it on every play, to isolate his receiver, to translate intuitively on the line of scrimmage.

And Kramer did it on every play.

He did it with a speed and clarity that turned the 82-yard drive into a laboratory exercise, and by the time they passed midfield, the Lions were seeing ghosts again. Déjà vu. They're doing it to us again. The prevent mentality works more than the public realizes. The pros can show you statistics proving that most of the time, when you make an offense go 80 yards with short throws underneath, eventually something or somebody will break down. The quarterback will be sacked. The flanker will drop the ball. Time will smother the offense. The official will drop a flag.

It never happened, and the Lions caved. Maybe you can handle Rashad or even Kramer, but you can't beat the zodiac. And when the Vikings reached the 26, exactly where they stood against Tampa Bay, almost down to the exact tick of the clock, Kramer saw the defensive rotation.

Senser had to be one on one against the linebacker, and was. There would be no interception by Neil Colzie here. A Steve Dils might have been unlucky or found himself pressured by a defensive shift. Kramer has been there longer. The ball went to Senser, and bought seven yards, and time. Danmeier told Grant a minute before: If we get to their 28, I can kick it. Grant nodded. Harry P. Grant may believe, too, but he believes in the additional virtues of yardage.

They got to the 3, where almost no providential help is needed. Danmeier kicked it through. The Lions knew it before anybody, four downs before.

Les Steckel's Trial-by-Crocodile

JULY 24, 1984

No ONE IN the Minnesota Vikings training camp has volunteered yet to submit himself to the bite of the tsetse fly or a tankful of piranha in the interests of medical science. But if either is proposed as a serious option to the conditioning program now being waged by the head leatherneck, Coach Les Steckel, you should look for a stampede to the infirmary by purple-headed warriors dedicated to preserving part of humanity — in this case, themselves.

The Minnesota Vikings may be the only team in pro football whose starting team in September will be nominated for the Medal of Honor. There is already pressure in Mankato to identify all team candidates on the roster by height, weight, college, blood type, and next of kin.

Les is the coach who has brought an exciting new concept into professional football: Show me a team that agonizes and I'll show you a team that maximizes. He may be right. Viking losses after three days of Steckel's camp have fallen within the limits most combat officers consider acceptable. The former Pro-Bowler Dave Casper, describing himself as the father of two chidren, appealed to the Vikings' higher familial instincts. He asked to be removed from the roster as an act of simple amnesty.

Such requests are usually alien in pro football. Granting such requests is even more alien. But the Vikings complied and put Casper on the waiver list, probably concluding that it was a tossup between sending him to the piranha tank or to the Detroit Lions.

Otherwise, a couple of the lesser ones quit and two or three passed out. A few were revived with oxygen and one with the promise of water. Defensive lineman Mark Mullaney pulled a leg muscle, and two others, Doug Martin and Brad Van Pelt—both richer than most of the Vikings and therefore smarter—refused to show up.

It's obviously too early to assess the wisdom of Les Steckel's attempt to convert red-blooded American jocks with Cadillacs and dependents into kamikaze cadets. It could work. Les Steckel says, "Don't tell me the sergeant's been shot—take that hill."

I expect Krazy George to use a version of that thrilling summons to arouse the crowd at the first Vikings home game. Mike Lynn will distribute 62,000 miniature purple and white swords to the customers and they will put a picture of Lynn and his horse on the scoreboard, impersonating Teddy Roosevelt at San Juan.

"All together now," George will roar, "TAKE THAT HILL." Swords will flash in unison in the stale butter splendor of the Metrodome lighting, and 62,000 customers will leap to their feet, imploring the Vikings to scale that hill.

Don't ask me, "What hill?" How do I know? I'm not sure Mankato is the most realistic place to retrain the Vikings anyhow. I would relocate the Vikings' two-a-days in Colorado and put them on Pikes Peak. If they can't do that, they ought to shift the training site to Rochester, Minnesota, where the Mayo Clinic is available.

Nobody should doubt Steckel's warm instincts. Beneath those fiercely creased dress blues throbs a heart of devout tenderness. Steckel would be the first to respond to the wails of a linebacker's wife and children when they insist that Daddy isn't the same anymore with two charlie horses from doing leg presses and shell shock from remembering the blissful years of Bud Grant.

I think Steckel would listen to these voices. For that reason, I think he will reconsider Phase II of his training program, urged on him by his more exuberant Marine sidekicks from Quantico and Montezuma. You have observed that the Vikings are now being required to climb 20-foot ropes, charge through brick walls, and pump 500 pounds of iron for the next four weeks. Steckel's pals then want to move him one step beyond, where the Vikings would go one-on-one against live crocodiles from the Minnesota Zoo and swim underwater from Gray's Bay in Lake Minnetonka to Minnehaha Falls.

These exercises would be restricted to men in the so-called skilled positions. Linemen would undergo more realistic training by crawling on their bellies the length of the Lake Street bridge under live tracer ammunition.

As I suggested, Steckel is a man with compassion. If the Vikings take that hill, I don't think he'll put in Phase II. If they don't, my advice is to stay away from the Lake Street bridge.

Karl and Baby Chris: It's a Wild Dialogue
NOVEMBER 14, 1979

CHRIS AND KARL Kassulke peered at each other in attitudes of mutual amazement.

To a bystander, Karl Kassulke expressed the flat conviction that no other American male five months old could be so beautiful and modestly intelligent.

"I have obviously fathered a wonder child," he said candidly, confirming his preliminary findings.

His gnarled and corrugated nose, sculpted by collisions with a hundred tight ends and a few goal posts, nuzzled close to Chris' chin. His smile quickly acquired the general contours of Carlsbad Caverns and it appeared headed for larger, more concussive things. The Kassulke bellow, one of the most extraordinary vocal instruments known to man, began its pre-eruption tremors.

He stopped.

"Mama," he said on reconsideration, "I better be careful or the kid will get a big head. Maybe I should try restraint."

Mama didn't argue. Marshmallows in a bonfire would be more competitive than restraint vs. Karl Kassulke. But it looked like the start of another hour-long dialogue between her husband and son, and it was always the feature show in the house.

Chris seem hypnotized by the soul-wracking emissions of the large, rubbery face in front of him.

The kid just stared from his infant seat, motionless in his blue jumpsuit. He might have said "what hath God wrought here," but what he did say was "whar." He also burped, and more.

It was the formal launch of another probing conversation between Karl and Chris Kassulke.

"They go on and on," Sue Kassulke said. "I don't know what they tell each other."

There were some things, her husband said, that had to be left strictly man-to-man.

The firstborn of Karl and Sue Kassulke is healthy, mannered, and calm.

Should that be a surprise? Should it be a surprise that there is a firstborn at all?

Only if the imagery of wheelchairs and invalidism is so ingrained in the beholder that he or she ignores the regenerative powers of the human body and the harder-to-define currents of undefeatable mirth and hope that flow through this battered man, once so boisterous, still so gentle.

But the kid lying content and suitably adored in the middle of the dining room table is not the only small miracle of the house above the mapled ravine in Eagan.

You remember Karl Kassulke, football player. A motorcycle crash crippled him. The word is ugly, but using one more generous won't change his condition. People who admire him now didn't know him before the crash. There was a huge amount of Karl Kassulke to like before the crash. He was a man with a pumpkin heart for people in trouble, a quick hand for a round of beer, guts that never stopped as a competitor. But there was a part of him that got lost in the subsequent narratives.

He tried to devour each day with his clanging guffaws and his full-bore gustos. Some people felt good being in control of their lives. Karl envied that whenever he felt a flash of guilt, but most often the orderly life bored him. He had an antidote. Chug-a-lugs and good times; shaking the chandeliers; stomping around with his buddies on winter basketball tours. Feeling the horsepower under his buns in the summer. He was a pal to the world, but he was reckless emotionally, and he understood that, but there wasn't much he could do about it because if he surrendered that he surrendered his soul.

He blew his first marriage refusing to make that surrender. She was a substantial woman, the mother of his two sons, studying to become a medical doctor. She loved him for a long time, his barging impulses, his noisy tenderness, all the rest, but in the end she could not handle the unquenchable jockism that ruled his life, and some of hers.

So he lost her, and then he crashed on a highway outside of town one day. Within a year he lost his family, his football, his legs, the roaring good times.

The undefeatability in him got him through the agony. He was so good at it, with his self-deflating clowning and rampages, that he didn't appear to be suffering much at all. The thousands who came in contact with him loved him for all the other parts of Karl Kassulke that deserved it.

But he was drifting and lonely and dreadfully afraid of being buried under the pity of fans and friends.

His nurse suddenly made him feel normal again. She hazed him and punctured him, laughed at his barnyard jokes, cried sometimes at his deliberately unheroic efforts to reclaim a life for himself. Her first sensations of curiosity and admiration deepened, and they found themselves depending on each other, trusting.

Her parents were from northern Minnesota, Italian. He called himself a kraut from Milwaukee. With her romanticism and his hard-headed knowledge of the real facts of life, he said, they ought to be able to found a dynasty.

A son or daughter would help, he conceded.

Christopher Karl Kassulke was born by Caesarean section, a little more than six pounds at birth. Because of a temporarily low blood sugar level, he stiffened up a couple of days after he was born and his eyes rolled back. The mother was terrified, but the doctors said they could handle it.

He hasn't had a bad day since.

And the father?

He wheels through his ramped house among the maples and oaks, conducting a tour. The place is beiges and browns, immaculate, the de rigueur trophy room downstairs, paintings of the athlete Kassulke always resembling Omar Sharif ("Painters are susceptible to bribes, did you know that?"), a sun deck lifting above the ravine. He opens the windows and wheels onto the porch.

"Isn't it something?" he said. "Everybody needs his own little

27

world some place. This is mine."

He spends time there watching, talking to squirrels, being grateful, sometimes praying.

A year ago Sue and Karl Kassulke accepted Jesus Christ.

Should that be a problem for some who don't like to get God mixed in with their jocks and their undefeatables?

"It was a nice house but just a house until Chris came," Karl Kassulke said. "Now we want to have another, and another." He looked at his dark-haired wife, whom he congratulated for the fifth time in 30 minutes for getting more beautiful every day.

She concurred with his plans for a family.

That gave it the force of law.

Without campaigning for it or trying to recast him, she has brought peace into the life of the bellowing jock who lost everything six years ago — and found something he summarized unintentionally when a friend called to say he might be getting married in a few months.

"If you find as much happiness as I have," Karl Kassulke said, "you'll have enough to give away."

Which he does. An hour with Karl Kassulke, and Sue, dissolves oil and prices and rush-hour traffic.

He is on the Human Rights Commission now, looking for a permanent 8-to-5 job, perhaps teaching, possibly something else. His football pension keeps them solvent, and he doesn't need millions. He is quieter, but his laughing honk still shakes the plaster and there is not much time for reverie in the house of Karl and Sue Kassulke. "The only thing that bothers the kid," he said, "is dead silence."

He is not likely to get a foothold in this house.

Years of Fear End for a Giant Named Carl Eller

SEPTEMBER 29, 1981

HIS VOICE RUMBLED from his massive body with a resonant solemnity that seemed to rise out of the rocks of ages. It has always had that scriptural quality.

But there were alterations in the rest of Carl Eller.

His eyes were clear and his calm seemed genuine. He was broke, but to a friend who greeted him in a downtown Minneapolis restaurant Monday, he looked like a million dollars in his reserved business suit and his unhurried sociability.

He said it simply.

"I'm not scared any more."

For 15 years he was one of the most powerful of all men in a game where might and size are the currency of the trade. Quarterbacks said he was so terrifying in his best years that he would blot out the sun. To thousands at Metropolitan Stadium and millions in the television audiences he was the symbol of a part of professional football that made it so magnetic to them — its recurring theater of giants-in-collision.

But even when he was being paid $125,000 a year and playing in the Super Bowls, Carl Eller was scared.

It was never enough to keep him ahead of the money he was spending on drugs, nor enough to dig him out of the social abyss where he was sinking, to pry him loose from some of the crooks with whom he traded, or to dissolve the fear that someday the wardens of pro football were going to learn the truth and throw him out.

"In my last three or four years of pro football," he said Monday, "I spent $100,000 a year on drugs. I think for all the time I was in pro football I went through between a half million and three-quarters of a million dollars in cash to get them. It wasn't enough to buy back the friends I lost. Except for my teammates the only people I associated with the last few years were people I partied with, the ones I got the stuff from. Some of them were underworld people. They'd get jailed and they mentioned my name. I never trusted anybody enough to deal drugs myself, so I never got arrested. But it was just a matter of time. When I hit bottom I had gone through something like $3 million in net worth and I was bankrupt and owed the government big money in taxes. If I hadn't listened and gone into treatment, I would either be peddling drugs or in jail. Or I might have been dead."

He makes an effort not to sound wise for recognizing the truth, or heroic for making his sickness public.

"I didn't want to see it," he said. "I didn't want to end the fun, or what I thought was fun. My whole life away from football was escape and denial, indulging myself, anything but living the way normal people live."

Professional football people are not normal by at least one definition. Their work and lives are under scrutiny by millions. In most other ways, they mirror the virtues and sins of the public around them. There are good fathers and neighborhood joes among them, substantial citizens, bounders, and in-betweens. But their celebrity confers privileges and extracts a price. The freebies and propositions come easy. But when trouble comes, the world is going to learn about it, and with it the humiliations.

And when the trouble is booze and drugs, at least a part of the public wants to know: "Did you play in that shape?"

A man with more than an academic interest in that is Bud Grant, coach of the Minnesota Vikings and one who developed an authentic friendship with Eller.

"A football coach can't be a cop," he said. "He does have control over the place of his jurisdiction, which is the locker room. From the beginning we made sure there weren't going to be any amphetamines, or pep pills or whatever you call them, available to people on the Vikings the way they were in other places. I can't tell you anything with any real validity about how extensive drug use is in pro football. I'd say alcohol is a bigger problem, just as it is in society. We had one player who acknowledged drinking a quart of Jack Daniels a day. One of the things we insisted on almost from the start was that the old system of going out the Saturday night before a game was over with, and if you couldn't spend a quiet Saturday night in a hotel thinking about football and not getting tanked up, you weren't going to play for the Vikings.

"Moose and I talked several times. He'd come in to a practice and I'd say, 'Moose, you look kind of rough. I don't know what you're doing on your own but I think you ought to look at that.' I think as the years have gone by everybody understands a little more about the nature of chemical addiction, the sickness part of it, and we've tried to be human about helping players who need it. But everybody who plays for the Vikings understands that if they do anything illegal in connection with drugs, such as being found in possession or whatever, they can't play any more for this team.

"I don't know if Carl's lifestyle affected how he played toward the end. A coach might have suspicions, but how does he know? I do know that I'm thankful he's healthy again. He's got some great qualities as a human being."

The story Carl Eller tells now in his appearances at colleges and halfway houses is not intended to litanize his troubles as a standard horror story of the famous athlete gone wrong. Eller wants people, especially youth, to grasp what he did in the St. Mary's Treatment Center, the disease quality of chemical dependency and the availability of help to those willing to recognize it; but he also wants to focus on the special snares any athlete might be walking into the moment a drink becomes something more than a beverage.

"A ballplayer lives in a protected society," he said. "Basically he's protected from the time he first starts doing things better than others in athletics. From then on, reality gets turned upside down. He never really has to face some of the problems other people face. Everything is done for him. He has coaches and general managers and equipment managers and agents.

"So he goes on a pedestal, and he gets full of himself. I felt unique. It was great feeling that way. People wanted to have you around, and it was a kick doing that. I didn't want that feeling to go away.

31

And if it did, I found something to keep it there. I drank some when I was at the University of Minnesota and I went to marijuana from there and then to cocaine, and in the off season I partied so much the days just ran together and I couldn't separate one from the other. After games there were drug parties, and I went for a couple days after that, but I was smart enough to know you had to taper off with a game coming up. Sometimes I took pills before games. I needed some energy because I didn't have enough rest. I don't think they had much effect one way or the other. I don't really think my using affected how I played until much later, when playing didn't matter to me like it used to. I was preoccupied with how my businesses were going and I suppose I was preoccupied with my habit. When things would go bad I'd vow to quit and I actually believed I could do it by myself, but I know now that was crazy. The thing led to divorce and I did wrong things by my family, and it got so that some of the new friends I made, mostly women, couldn't stand me after awhile."

When he needed money he'd go to the Vikings and ask for advances, as a number of players did. The club is the ultimate godmother for an athlete in a world in which godmothers take different forms: doting fans, suppliers, trainers, agents, equipment managers, et al. It works only when the athlete is important enough to require the club's special attentions. In a fashion, reluctantly, maybe without knowing, motivated by its own urgencies to win as well as the institution's occasional loyalty to a veteran player, it becomes what the dependency authorities call an enabler. It nourishes the ailing player's habit by replenishing his source, and it may close its eyes to what it knows to be the truth.

"But I was afraid of getting kicked out of football admitting I couldn't control the drugs and alcohol," Eller said. "I don't know if I was even willing to admit I couldn't control them. I was screwed up for sure, and eventually it cost me my liquor store and my plans for a restaurant and only when there was no place to go was I willing to listen to a woman I have a relationship with. She said the only thing that was going to save me was treatment. I was afraid of it. I was afraid of admitting what I was. But it was something almost miraculous because I found people who didn't give a damn that I was a famous athlete, because they had the same problem I had, and they wanted me to know."

Today he works in a downtown office as a job recruiter for Viking Personnel, an employment agency unrelated to the football team. The NFL believes he has a message its players—and management—should hear. He is broke, healthy, jogging and clear in the morning, and content. "It's amazing," he said, "how your values can turn around."

The Truth about Dutch
Was Better Than the Myth

MAY 3, 1983

YES, HE WAS a reconstituted Captain Bligh, defiantly prowling his turf in cleats instead of buckled shoes. And yes, he once threatened to heave a delinquent linebacker through the door, which unnerved the linebacker severely because the door was 32,000 feet above northern Ohio at the time.

When professional football folk talked about Norm Van Brocklin they rarely dabbled in the mythology that grew up around him from Los Angeles to Philadelphia and from Minnesota to Georgia, where he died Monday at 57. The truth about him was so much better, irresistible if you like your football creatures to come at you stark and unvarnished, in the raw of their egos, their gifts, and their passions.

He was vivid and tyrannical, heroic at times and vindictive at others. As a football coach he had a virtuoso's mind and a dockwalloper's tongue. He bullied the collections of orphaned drifters and novices into competitive squalling football teams that usually played beyond their skimpy talents. They had to, because they constantly played on the edge of an emotional cliff. They lived on turmoil and the awe and half-comic, half-real terror their coach generated.

He was a human being who gave to friends, harbored grudges, brought adopted children into his family, and accepted his ostracism from coaching without a public whimper the last few years, in times of illness and probably resentment.

Both as a player who reached the highest levels of greatness and as a coach doomed by his private demons, the Dutchman divided the world into two distinct classes: the Real Ones, who belonged

34

in the pro football lodge as he defined it, and the Phonies. He was not always, or often, generous in whom he stuffed into this unloved category — general managers, some coaches who looked cultivated, some players who sounded independent, some newspaper people, fans who tried to butt their way in.

He died of a heart attack, very much one of the Real Ones to the end.

"You would come in and sit on Van Brocklin's first playbook session," said one of his players, Paul Flatley, "and get the feeling that this man knows so much football that you could never possibly learn it. It wasn't just what he did with the Xs and Os but the way . . . well, what the hell, whoever heard of a guy practically declaring war when he showed how to execute a simple dive play?"

For Van Brocklin, football was both war and fraternity, first as a quarterback and then as a coach of the Minnesota Vikings from 1961 to 1967, and later in Atlanta. He brought to it a range of appetites and instincts that dictated the moods of his teams. He was intellectual and profane, a man of alternating ferocity and mischief. When he talked off the wall he colored his speech with an irony or scorn that lifted him to the edge of pure literature. He once told a newspaper editor who had pleaded with the Vikings to move their training camp closer to the centers of publicity: "What the hell do these 36 stiffs need with publicity? What we need is cover and concealment."

It's a fact that when he was braced by a reporter years ago and asked how he would solve the problem of soccer-type kickers infesting pro football, Van Brocklin snarled: "Tighten the immigration laws."

It's also a fact that when he was asked to explain his swollen right fist (incurred when he swung at a Dallas newspaperman and missed after a dinner party) Van Brocklin said he was the victim of an unprovoked attack by a post.

Nobody I've met in athletics or elsewhere raged as beautifully or as originally as Dutch. Those who played for him and lived through his training camps shared a camaraderie that could only be appreciated by survivors of the Spanish Inquisition. Incensed by a curfew violation by one of his veteran cornerbacks, Van Brocklin got into his car at 1:30 a.m. and reconnoitered the parking lots. He found the felon in the back seat of a car, grabbed him by the collar, and pried him out of the arms of his startled inamorata.

I lived with him daily for six years during the football season. They were unforgettable. It was continuing chaos and hysterics. Covering the French Revolution might have been close, but Van Brocklin was a lot funnier than Robespierre.

You could sift your way through his furies and his roughhouse joys to find a guy with razor wit who lived codes of loyalty and lived generously. But whatever burned inside of him, the competitiveness and suspicions and storms, never stayed inside of him very long.

He stuck his head through the beaded curtains to challenge me to a fistfight in a hotel lobby in Detroit at midnight, on grounds that I had been seen talking to the then–general manager of the Vikings. In Van Brocklin's mind the guy was an alien character. We settled it by going to an all-night steak house, where for three hours the Dutchman lectured on the ingratitude and stupidity of quarterbacks who scramble out of the pocket. All this time he kept pumping the machine with quarters to hear Ray Charles sing "I Can't Stop Loving You."

"How can you call Tarkenton stupid with his kind of offensive line?" I said.

"I told him again last week," Van Brocklin said, carefully trying to avoid strangling a bottle of beer, "that third and 18 is no time to get creative."

His most sustaining quality as an athlete and coach was an unbreakable belief in himself and what he did. As a coach he thought he could and should whip them all as if everybody played with the same deck of talent. We'll never know the true verdict on Van Brocklin the coach because the furies that propelled him as player and coach, and to some extent as a human being, eventually drove him out of coaching.

He was capable of tenderness, when reminiscing with old-guard players or when a family would ask for a football for a sick kid. He would bring the squad together and produce an autographed ball in five minutes. He offered money to old pros who were broke or drunk. He gave his roof and love to kids from halfway around the world, and when he finally left football he did it his way — snorting his defiance, declining to compromise. He came from a time when the coach was autocrat. The players could be roustabouts and they might have hangovers on Sunday but they sucked it up and played.

Much of that went with the wind at about the time he discovered there was no place left for a Norm Van Brocklin in coaching.

But he was real, he was an original, and he was a man.

The Vikings' Weeping Millionaires

FEBRUARY 8, 1986

FOR PURE CORDIALITY, the crocodile pool at the zoo is now a model of trust and understanding when you compare it with the board room of the Minnesota Vikings.

If you accept no more than half of the warring partners' testimony, you have to believe these people were perfectly capable of giving each other wrong directions to the men's room.

Open the door and get hit by a falling mop.

Before examining their novel behavior any deeper, please remind yourself that all of the principals in this dung-throwing exercise are millionaires by most conventional definitions.

The next time a windmilling motivator in the go-for-broke seminars exhorts you to rush out and experience the unlimited joys of wealth and power, consider these transcending rewards of power in the Viking board room:

Here is John Skoglund, who owns one-third of one of the most successful franchises in professional football. That is power, correct? That is an estate in life entitling Skoglund to the trappings of veneration in the board room and the heady feel of the great ship moving when he touches a lever. Isn't that what the seminars promise, John?

It is.

So where is John standing when the great ship begins stirring?

He isn't. He's sitting on the poop deck. If Skoglund's testimony is correct, Max Winter let him on for the ride but wouldn't let him near the gearbox. As a matter of fact, Skoglund pictures himself as one of the ship's cocaptains who was never allowed to see the compass.

Power.

Here is Jack Steele, who also speaks for one-third of the stock. Jack is portrayed as a man with so much influence on the Viking board that he is consulted only when somebody wants to buy his stock and make him corporately disappear.

Clout.

Here is Winter, who is representing himself as the victim of a conniving troika on the board, headed by Mike Lynn. Lynn is Max's protégé. He was brought in after Max presided over the removal of Jim Finks, who made the Vikings a championship franchise. Mike was imported partly to portray Max as the benevolent Mr. Chips of pro football, filled with love and concern for ticket buyers and the orphan's friend. Max's present legal dilemma: Will he sell his stock to the alleged connivers or to his friends? Either way, he makes $25 million but right now, he says, he feels devastated and wiped out.

Here is Lynn, who came into the organization half a step ahead of the process servers and is now worth a million dollars a year. For years, he and Winter took turns telling the world how much wisdom, loyalty, and fondness for stray dogs resided in the other. They are now trading accusations of trying to railroad each other. Lynn has emerged as the most powerful man in the organization, but he is miserable because he has a sense of being unloved, untrusted, and unrepresented by stock.

Fulfillment.

Only the clairvoyants can tell you how all of this is going to end, but my suggestion is to hang on to your job and the limited destiny of paying bills and bringing in groceries.

On the other hand, you could become powerful, rich, influential, catered to and adored by loyal partners.

But don't ask them the way to the men's room.

Lou Holtz's Short Term As a Messiah

NOVEMBER 28, 1985

IF YOU'RE INCLINED to grind on Lou Holtz, look at it another way: Who was the last person you know who turned down a chance to escape Minnesota winter and earn consecration in the same week?

I offered this thesis to a luncheon group gathered Wednesday to examine the depth of its abandonment in the wake of Holtz's decision to leave Minnesota for Notre Dame. I was brought in as a kind of grief counselor. Before the session was finished, they were looking for a rope. Trying to bring the warm breath of conciliation to the meeting, I nearly got strangled. In the span of 45 minutes I made 19 enemies and 11 probables, an impressive performance considering that there were 30 people in the room.

I'll tell you how these people acted. They acted squelched, sandbagged, and marooned. It wasn't necessarily directed at Holtz or even those who hired him. Maybe it had something to do with life on the glacier and being doused by the frost of reality again after two years in the greenhouse. Holtz was the man who brought the ferns and philodendrons. Tens of thousands of people in Minnesota had chewed their hearts out for years at the sight of hysteria on TV in Oklahoma, Ohio, Michigan, and Nebraska. And then for two years Holtz turned the igloo into Camelot. Pandemonium in the stadium, gold and maroon on your chest, and esteem in the soul.

When the bigshot announcers talked about Minnesota, they spoke with respect again, and Holtz did it. He took ordinary players and made them feel important and competitive. He juggled slogans and formations, hustled and wowed the crowds. Nobody was ever quite sure whether he had a built a mirage or a football team, and he was crafty enough to let you feel comfortable either way. But half the time they won and often they played well. And while this was going on Holtz created something very close to exuberance in the Minnesota public, which scientists insist is almost impossible to do under the known laws of chemistry.

But he pulled the drawbridge Wednesday and Camelot sagged into the pale green sludge.

It didn't make much sense to tell the little platoon of luncheon mourners that they didn't have a logical right to feel sold out or exploited. You can feel whatever strikes you, and being logical has nothing to do with it. So I didn't tell them they had no right to feel misused. I simply said the man was almost dragged up here into the drifts and he insisted he would come only if his contract allowed him to switch to Notre Dame, should that be decreed by God and the incumbent's win–loss record at Notre Dame. And his future employers at the University of Minnesota said this:

We are in chaos and nobody wants to coach us. Our team is so bad we may have to use the Salvation Army to sell tickets. You are the best CPR man in football coaching, and our football team last year was so far gone it failed the mirror test. We will pay you, we will create muscle-building emporiums for you, and we will even turn Goldie Gopher into a ferocious creature of the wilderness. Notre Dame can offer the Golden Dome and the Mother Mary, but we've got Harvey Mackay and we consider that a push. We will gamble that in two years you are not going to run off and make us look silly. The reason we're willing to do that is not because we're brave but because we're desperate.

If Holtz had simply dawdled in place for two years at Minnesota, waiting for a summons from South Bend, I would have gone for the rope myself. But he blew sparks wherever he went, galvanized the public, building belief and what was almost certainly going to be a winning football team. So he left after two years. He also left new buildings, some new resolve, and no scorched earth. He had warned he might go, and his employers agreed to the ground rules. He is an obsessive fortune hunter, a mercurial and high-salaried vagabond. He is also an opportunist and goal-setter. Notre Dame was his goal from the beginning. He was honest (and smart) enough to put it in the contract. And you can't logically lynch

Notre Dame for being as observant and as desperate as Minnesota was.

Having agreed this all more or less made sense, the luncheon crowd had to find some target for its distemper, and it settled on the man who brought the news.

Somebody said the university should have made Holtz's escape clause public two years ago, but what do you think were the chances of hiring him if it had been?

"It was the media that built up Holtz and all the hysteria," somebody yelled.

If you were in the media and ignored Lou Holtz you would also ignore the Titanic and film the migration of blowfish.

I don't think there's any enduring lesson for us in Holtz's departure. He is a phenomenon, fun, a good football coach, and an irresistible peddler. His leaving is no catastrophe and should orphan nobody, psychologically or otherwise. We will talk about him until the search committee starts leaking some new names, after which it will be time again for the unleashing of Harvey Mackay.

Harvey, we can't offer the new guy Cargill and the first 75 miles of the Lake Superior North Shore. The university is holding that for Lou Holtz, in case he can't find an option quarterback to run the Notre Dame offense. They gave him almost everything else.

Tell Us about Hockey in the Dark Ages, John Mariucci

MAY 15, 1981

MAYBE THE GODFATHER ought to make a speech to the North Stars, telling them they are living in historic times this week and the ghosts of the Depression days rat pack in Eveleth, Minnesota, expect them to do something historic.

The Godfather is not numerically identified in the printed program of the Stanley Cup hockey championships. It has been more than three decades since he lacerated left wingers but only four years since he threw a bolo punch on the players' bench in Austria—at the age of 61—at one of his own players, one Lou Nanne, who now signs his expense checks.

Intimates and thousands of Iron Range settlers will recognize the Godfather as John Mariucci, who is grandly listed in the North Stars' dossiers as assistant to the general manager. Don't be slickered by bureaucratic titles. Mariucci this week is a walking bridge, the man who connects Minnesota hockey in its ore-dusted origins with the silver plate of the 1981 Stanley Cup.

In Mariucci's home town there is a national hall of fame where they keep the symbolic candles burning to honor American hockey players. The regiments of guests who file through each year invariably ask about Mariucci in the same tones in which visitors to the Tower of London might ask about Sir Walter Raleigh and Oliver Cromwell. The eons seem that distant.

"Wait a minute," Mariucci objected. "Sir Walter Raleigh got beheaded. I never got close to that except some nights when we played in Boston."

Maybe the North Stars have acquired coin and applause so

quickly they haven't found time to understand the legacy of the Godfather and Minnesota hockey in the iron pits.

Tell us now, John:

"It was something, but I don't know if you'd call it inspiring. In the Depression everybody in Eveleth was poor, and if you were a kid the only way you could get in to see the Eveleth Rangers play, that was the town hockey team, was either dig your way in or sneak in while the cops and the Communists were beating on each other.

"The Communists were trying to get a foothold on the Range, with the conditions so bad, and they put out these big banners saying people ought to be let in the games free because the team was supported by the city. They demanded free tickets and told people to join them when they tried to crash the gates.

"They did try to break through the gates. When they did, a bunch of us came in behind them. We didn't know a Communist from an ore car, but it was a way to get in to see Frank DeLeo, Vince and Joe Papike, Joe Jagunich, and all those other studs play hockey. The cops were waiting for the Communists. While they were belting each other, we just ran in. How were they going to belt us? Would you knock your little brother's head with a night stick?

"If that didn't work, we dug our way into the Hippodrome by building a tunnel. It was just like tunneling out of a prisoner-of-war camp."

When you played hockey as a kid 40 or 50 years ago in northern Minnesota, no Little League quartermaster came with helmets, mouthpieces, gladiator gloves, shin guards, and masks. You didn't register for the league and the only traveling you did was to walk across the street from the rink to the church to get warm in the boiler room between periods.

Mariucci's hockey upbringings were heavily graced by horse apples. "We used them for pucks," he says. "You didn't have to freeze them. That was sort of their natural state because it got to be 30 below zero up there. We played until they broke, and then we sent a guy after more horse apples behind the sausage store. Either that or we cut the heel off an old shoe and rounded it off. We used magazines for shin guards and when we played on the streets we made goals out of snow chunks. We never had officials, but we didn't need many rules because it was pretty easy to figure out that the idea was to get the puck in the goal, and how you did it didn't matter all that much."

The inquirer noted that in his home town on the Range kids often used *National Geographic* for shin guards.

"You guys must have been on some kind of government dole even then," he said. "Nobody in Eveleth could afford the *National Geographic*. We used five-cent magazines. *Liberty* was a big favorite. So was *Colliers*, which was longer than most magazines and came down to your ankles."

The Godfather is 65, an honest-to-God patriarch now. The grooves and chicken tracks created by scores of surgical stitches have merged agreeably with the more traditional needlework of time, and the old warrior presents a striking face to the world: a roughened dignity, canny, whimsical, somehow undefeatable.

He was so much the waterfront jock that the high school basketball coach refused to give him a uniform. "I really had some ability in basketball," he said. "I couldn't make a hook shot or stuff the ball, but I was a terror on layups. The coach must have figured I was an insurance risk, and he thought the Eveleth high school basketball team could face the enemy without Mariucci. That made it tough because my mother was scared to death I was going to get hurt playing hockey and she wouldn't buy me a pair of skates. My uncle Pete bought them for me, and I played hockey ever after."

He also acquired a steamy disdain for basketball ever after — or rather he pretended to because it sold well to audiences — and somewhere in his coaching years at the University of Minnesota he authored the line that his disciples of two generations shamelessly cribbed: "Watching basketball is like watching two old men fish."

The hockey they watched in Eveleth even before the Depression was some of the best in the world, played by Canadians imported into northern Minnesota before the National Hockey League became the accepted forum for professional hockey. The Iron Range kids learned it from them, and that became the beginning of Minnesota hockey. Mariucci was one of the apostles, a gruff and no-retreat defenseman employed by the Chicago Blackhawks primarily to keep their young forwards out of traction. Only a half dozen Americans made it safely past the Canadian doorkeepers in those years—Mariucci, goalies Mike Karakas, Frankie Brimsek, and Sammy LoPresti, Cully Dahlstrom and Doc Romnes from the Twin Cities. And in his years as the Minnesota coach Mariucci struggled to keep some manageable limit on the young Canadian pros being recruited by rival American colleges. He did it not so much because Mariucci had loftier principles but because he was trying to win with less experienced and younger Americans.

But the roster of the North Stars today is laced with American names like Broten, Christoff, Roberts, Carlson, Sargent, Polich, Younghans, and Jackson, and the Minnesota professional hockey team today, obviously well and thoroughly stocked with Canadians, does not have to apologize for calling itself Minnesota.

"Wouldn't it be historic, John, for the North Stars to win the Stanley Cup the first time?"

"Yeah. It would also be profitable."

If you grew up on the Range in the Depression, that is not an afterthought. But why did you scuffle with Lou Nanne when he came off the ice that day the American world team played in Austria?

"Did you ever see the old man and his kid go at it in northern Minnesota?"

"Yeah."

"All it was," he said, "was another form of love."

A Place That Deserved and Cherished
Johnny Blood

NOVEMBER 27, 1978

THE PORT PLAZA INN in Green Bay, Wisconsin, surrounds its lobby gawkers with walnut walls 30 feet high, capable of resisting lurching wee-hours guests and the advance of the 20th century with equal fortitude. The Port Plaza is a congenial antique, partial to older tempos and more boisterous nomads. It used to be called the Northland Hotel, which rings with the kind of primeval bluntness that a name as hopelessly fastidious as Port Plaza could never approach.

Johnny Blood must have screeched in indignation when they changed the name.

Blood is one of those historic engravings that belong in a hotel like the Northland. He was never engraved in the Northland, which is not the same as saying he was never plastered there. And while, thankfully, he does not yet qualify for the status of a ghost, John is one of those timeless souls you expect to see striding through the walnut panels on his way to wherever good fellows convene today in Green Bay.

Johnny Blood was the rogue halfback, born John McNally of substantial parentage, with access to money and the heritage of a classic education. By preference, he became a bum. He drifted unimpeded, although sometimes vigorously sought, from St. John's in Collegeville, Minnesota, to the Twin Cities, to the potato fields of semipro football. Without seriously offering his candidacy, he became a pro football immortal. He belonged, both because of his splendid gifts and because of his tendency to visit eighth-floor hotel rooms by means of window sills.

These and even more hazardous feats, almost invariably involv-

47

ing blondes but sometimes brunettes, assured him reverential audiences in his later year of reunion in the suites and ballrooms of the Northland Hotel.

I stood in one of those very ballrooms yesterday and recalled, not without a damp eyelash, Blood's summit performance as a restored legend the night before a Packer championship game in the 1960s.

John spent most of the night, and possibly all of it, in a dark blue business suit and red carnation that accentuated his patrician white hair. Even in his 60s he had the features of a movie star and dramatic qualities that were probably superior. Unprovoked, John would deliver half-hour recitations in English literature, more obscure as the evening flowed on. I arrived well after the dinner and the speeches, which meant John had already been through the first six or seven waves of potential listeners, and was now selecting targets of opportunity.

As he spotted me threading through the congestion on my way to the canapes table, John made a move that bespoke years of open-field artistry and unlabored gynmastics. That move allowed him to close in on the target by systematically cutting off all escape routes. My last such route was the kitchen door, which was bolted, as Blood undoubtedly knew.

Not far from John was a uniformed Green Bay policeman, who was always furnished to the Northland free of charge as a kind of personal escort and counselor to Johnny Blood whenever there was a reunion.

The reason for this was that John was very flexible in how he reacted at reunions. It was usually a toss-up whether John would recite Hamlet's soliloquy or punch out the assistant manager.

In view of these doubts, the cop's presence was considered a useful compromise between martial law and a midnight riot.

"Hello, John," I said. "No, I don't want to hear 'The Lay of the Last Minstrel.' I don't want to hear Kipling's 'If,' either. It reminds me of the wasted opportunities of my youth."

"Tonight I have chosen from John Donne," he said. Blood closed his eyes, and spoke throatily, profoundly. "No man is an islande, entire of itselfe," he said. "Every man is a piece of the continent, a part of the maine."

A 1928 defensive tackle, on his way to the men's room, caromed accidentally off John's shoulder and disappeared in a potted plant. Blood continued undistracted. "If a clode be washed away by the sea, Europe is the lesse, as well as if a promontory were. . . ."

He clutched me by the tie. "Don't you just throb with the brotherhood," he said.

"I'm throbbing, I'm throbbing," I confirmed.

To do less meant a hurried flight into the potted plant to join the tackle.

They Didn't Need Lilies to Bury the Met
SEPTEMBER 30, 1981

ELEGIES IT DOESN'T NEED. Songs around the hibachi cookers it does. It's all right to get limp and lumpy remembering Killebrew's home run against the Yankees; but the highlight film of the Met should have been shot from the bratwurst stand on the second deck, not home plate.

Somebody should have brought a video tape of the totally juiced customer from Iowa circling the bases in the middle of the seventh inning and sliding grandly into third ahead of an imaginary throw from left field. The constabulary hauled him out of the arena to the jeers of 20,000 people who thought he got there ahead of the ball.

"That'll be a hundred bucks," the judge said later.

"What for?" wailed the undesignated base runner. "It was a perfect hook slide. The third baseman missed me by two feet."

There was a homely kind of democracy about it that made this ballyard-by-the-prairie the fan's house more than a show window for the jocks. They claimed that architects actually designed it, but I think the plans were donated by the guy who built steelworkers' meeting halls, the ones without a whole lot of chic and comfort but plenty of room in the back for the cash bar.

It was the only big-league baseball park in the country where the management had to bring in extra security on opening day in 1968 because kids were jumping into the park from snow piles plowed behind the fences.

In other parks they hired expensive chickens and pantomime artists to entertain the audience when the action subsided. In later years at the Met they tried a chicken. But it went unnoticed because nobody could distinguish it from the other oddly dressed creatures who showed up in the stands.

No, the really creative entertainment at the Met was in the parking lots. The parking lots at the Met may have been Minnesota's most significant contribution to the performing arts in the 20th century.

Historians believe the mass tailgate party was a legacy of the Minnesota frontier, when homesteaders circled their wagons for mutual protection against both the irritated Chippewas and the sand lizards. Most of them were Swedes and Norwegians. Being practical, they decided to eat communally, and thus did the smorgasbord tradition migrate to America. It made its last stand in the parking lots at the Met.

So today in honor of the last baseball game at the Met, yes, clear your throat in memory of Allison sliding through 20 yards of swamp to rob the Dodgers of extra bases in the World Series.

But how can you forget Ching Johnson's even more heroic tailgate party in the Baltimore lot in 1971, when Ching invited 400 of his most intimate friends for lunch in a semitrailer?

All of them showed up, but not all of them left, at least not conscious.

Among the casualties were four musicians, who were installed in the corner of the semi and were plied with free drinks on the completion of each set. By the time the game started the musicians were beyond revival, and Ching stepped into the breach by leading fight songs through a gas-can funnel converted into a megaphone. With this instrument as an aid, he led survivors across the uncharted asphalt wastes into the sanctuary of the Stadium Club, where most of them watched the game on closed-circuit television.

That was part of the loony magic of Met Stadium, you understand. Sometimes the ball game wasn't all that critical in an appreciation of the broader ambiance at the Met. On Camper Weekend, people would drive hundreds of miles and moor their roadhouses somewhere outside of center field. There they would spend the next two days in some serious picnicking, listening to the cheers 50 yards away and watching on TV.

Should it have been so surprising then that a bartender from

Duff's and his adored got married in the Kansas City lot before the kickoff of a Viking–Green Bay game in 1970? The table setting was magnificent, laid with sterling and flower vases, punch bowls, and gourmet food rushed to the stadium by limousine.

A judge united the couple while admiring friends stood beaming in their snowmobile suits and face masks. It was the only wedding of the season where the newlyweds spent their honeymoon in a Winnebago at halftime.

Don't tear it down for a while, boys. Let it sit so we can appreciate it. And then let us all raise a long bratwurst in salute to the Met.

Finding the Faraway Place:
Adventure and Adventurers

An Explosion in the Heavens Stuns Us
JANUARY 29, 1986

THE UNDERSIDE OF adventure is risk.

Telemetry and mission controls cannot reduce that unchangeable truth, although for years we convinced ourselves they could. Because the space flights have been so successful, because the upbeat theater they created on television put us in a continuing never-never land of happy endings and smiling, modest heroes, the thought of risk and catastrophe rarely intruded on the show.

It may explain why the country's grief is so profound, approaching depression.

It was one more romp in space, this time with an effervescent novice on board, a schoolteacher whose presence in her flight suit seemed to be telling all who dream: "It's OK to dream."

So far had the space flight technology progressed. The launch, the rocketry, the space plane were safe enough to put ordinary people into the heavens and the unknown. They could travel in space with professionals who had the right stuff, joining them in an orbiting social.

And then the fireball.

It was crushing, lethal, and final. It broke an illusion.

Space flight has been a kind of national toyland for years, where the adventure we were witnessing was played out free of harm to ourselves or hostility to others. A trip to the moon menaced no one. It was competitive, yes. The Soviets were out there. But there was something about the innocence of space that stirred both sides to thoughts of cooperation, and led them there.

Was there any more powerful symbol of what the divided people of the earth were capable of becoming than the sight of American

55

and Soviet astronauts living and working in the same spaceship, bound to each other by their shared technology and sense of wonder?

The price tags of space exploration were controversial, and so was the country's proposed militarization of it. But that was heavy budget stuff, the material for the Sunday morning oracles to chew on in the network panel shows.

Space flights were festival, or something very close to it. They entered into the American consciousness as something highly suspenseful, and a new wellspring for a national pride and identity. We flew in the capsules with John Glenn and walked on the moon with Neil Armstrong. As one space vehicle after another flew the course on the television screen, year after year, the space flights became a kind of recurring parade in their effect on the public. They were fun to watch, they had a predictable ending, and nobody got hurt.

Tuesday, in the skies above Florida, the festival shattered and fell into the ocean in a thousand pieces, while millions wept for the buoyant spirits on board who fell with it.

It was shocking because we had come to rely on the competence of American spacemanship, a reliance that bred an aura of perfection. It had to be right and perfect, or the computers wouldn't let the rocket go. It was on the money and looking great; and then the fireball.

The finest tribute to what the country's space people have accomplished in 25 years is that it created this very sense of trust and reliance. That will be examined. But people will go aloft again from Cape Canaveral.

You can argue that we will fly in space because it is part of our defensive preparedness. But that is not the real reason, is it? Human beings will explore in space because since the sunrise of time they have been searching to find what is beyond them.

Sometimes it brings them marvels. And sometimes they fail. These we mourn with special grief today because their dreams were ours.

Breath of Life for an Exhausted Mountaineer

JULY 16–18, 1979

HIS EYES DECLARED *all the symptoms of acute high-altitude sickness. They were glazed and lethargic, barely reactive to word and movement.*

He tried to sit up in his sleeping bag but sank back onto the tent floor, defeated by exhaustion and by the Andean night wind that contorted the tent's fiberglass poles and deflated its walls.

The wind needed no resort to the sound effects of terror, no shrieking or orchestral tantrums. It was constant and inescapable. This was its dominion, at 19,000 feet in the frozen cascades and glacier fields of the Cordillera Blanca in the Peruvian Andes. Those who intruded accepted that as a condition of their brief and tenuous habitation. It was nonnegotiable.

In spite of the wind, you could hear Rod Wilson gagging and snuffling.

A few minutes before, he awoke the native porter, Fausto, and me. He did it by sitting up and nudging me with his foot, and by speaking in a voice that seemed drained of all animation and yet possessing a toneless, bizarre dignity and a thread of apology.

Rod Wilson said he was dying.

He said there was water in his lungs; he could hear himself gurgling when he tried to breathe. He didn't know where he was and he felt himself drifting. He said he had to tell us.

I put a flashlight on Rod's face and pulled the stethoscope out of our first aid pouch. To get acquainted with our bodies' norms, we had listened to each other's heartbeats and breathing rhythms a half dozen times—Rod, Doug Kelley, and I—first in the Monterrey Hotel room in Huaraz at 9,500 feet and at the overnight camps thereafter on the route to Nevado Huascaran, a mountain whose summit rises 22,200 feet above the sea.

A critical hazard on a mountain so high is pulmonary edema, a condition

brought on by inadequate acclimatization to thin atmosphere, and character-
ized in part by gurgling in the lungs when the victim breathes.

Rod's face was gray, puffed, and expressionless. It revealed neither fright
nor pain. I put the stethoscope under his lungs and on his back. I don't know
how the medical people define gurgling in the lungs. I heard a crackling when
Rod breathed. I had no training to judge its severity. I did know he was dis-
oriented and, from the events of the day, dehydrated and ground out. Rod's
own frail diagnosis of his condition seemed accurate. Listless and hallucina-
tory, he looked like a man about to die. There was a medicine capsule in my
hand, and a hypodermic needle. I broke off the top of the capsule with a pair
of pliers and extracted the medicine with the syringe.

Rod rolled over face down, and I emptied the needle in his bottom. He
didn't cringe, flinch, or groan. He said, "Thanks, doc," and lost consciousness.

And then Fausto Milla strapped on his crampons and crawled out of the
tent to begin a 5,000-foot descent through the night wind and glacial
crevasses for an oxygen bottle at the base camp a millennium away.

Have you seen the Andes?

Where the Rockies peak out, the Andes' everlasting snow and ice
are just beginning. They ride in the sky above the jungle and above
the sea in their startling architecture, an Alpamayo that flings its
summit to the sun like a white diamond, a Copa with its symmetry
of connected peaks laced together with ice ridges that give it the
look of some celestial suspension bridge.

And Huascaran. The highest in Peru, although hardly the pretti-
est. Actually a double mountain separated by a high saddle at
19,000 feet called La Garganta, the gate to its ascent either on the
north side or the true summit to the south, Huascaran Sur. It has
the classic contours of the conical mountain, but it is too immense
to be loved. Climbing Huascaran, unless one encounters a storm or
loses the route, does not demand gymnastic technique. In some
places it is a slog and a grunt, although in others it offers the airiest
kind of pleasure to the mountaineer under control. And yet it is not
especially forgiving.

Doug, Rod, Fausto, a young porter named Jacinto, and I clam-
bered up the glacier's lateral morain from Camp One, strapped on
our crampons, and walked onto the ice, carrying packs.

It was a supernatural place.

We walked among great blue grottos and amphitheaters, icicles 50 feet long, crevasses 300 feet deep. The Andean sun blazed them into a concerto of turquoise, amethyst, and cobalt. The Pategonia pile we wore already was steaming, so we removed that and scaled down to two sets of underwear and moisture resistant Gore-Tex® pants and jackets.

The sun burned through the glacial cream but we were moving higher and higher, leaping the crevasses and listening to the avalanches rolling down Huascaran North, and I could not help remembering George Patton: "God forgive, I love it so."

And in time we would love Fausto Milla.

He called us *amigos*.

His scrambled, breakneck Spanish and highland patois could not accommodate the names of Doug, Rod, and Jim, and his English was an outright surrender. His copper face was a reconciliation of the races of man, reflecting the broken visions and struggles of the centuries, the elfin innocences and the leathered wariness. Yet for all that he was bouncy and sociable. His ancestries sprang from the islands of the mid-Pacific, the Indian clans that flowed from them, the Spanish gold-diggers who conquered them, and the undefined nations that gave his features a timeless universality.

He was listed in the expedition registries of the Andes as a guide-porter, but this was shamelessly inadequate. He was also part burro and part roadrunner. He had the undefeatable tinkerer's soul of a garage mechanic down to his last cotter pin in the house. He smiled with the simple radiance of the rising sun and he was the lodge morale man in the tent, quizzing his clients about their love lives and their gastronomic prejudices. But on his home terrain, the glaciers of the Cordillera Blanca, he was despotic and rude. If you hired Fausto Milla to escort you through the crevasses, perish something as offensive as an original thought.

Moreover, he carried a ton.

There was practically nothing in the smorgasbord of camping and mountaineering gear that could not be borne, voluntarily and eagerly, on Fausto Milla's back. He was 32 and could not have weighed more than 135 pounds, but there were days when he carried close to a hundred. If you proposed to relieve him of a few of those, Fausto Milla scowled and dismissed the suggestion as the addled notion of a tenderfoot. As a climber he was sure and brave, but dangerously primitive in his rope management techniques and his conceptions of ax work.

Beyond all, he was an *amigo*, a friend, almost always optimistic but, at the critical times, direct. He wanted to reach the summit, but it was still a day's work if he didn't. It all depended, he said, on *tiempo*, the weather.

"*Tiempo mal mañana*," he would say each evening, "*aqui*."

If the weather is bad tomorrow, if it is too cloudy in the La Garganta high saddle or an Andean hurricane is blowing on the route to Nevado Huascaran, we stay in the tent.

"*Tiempo bueno mañana, arriba*."

If it's good, we climb.

"*Tiempo mal dos, tres dias, abajo*." A virtuoso performance with the fingers accompanied this announcement.

If it's bad for two or three days, we go down.

The equation was compact and impossible to misunderstand.

But there was one other part in it that had nothing to do with the *tiempo*.

Doug Kelley was *mal*, which is to say he was queasy and inert.

In his natural ambience, Kelley is a sportive, chattering man-about-the-world, filled with the confident lawyer's wit and irreverence and the ex–Green Beret's pride in his musculature and stamina. He is also one of the best climbers in the northern United States, a sophisticate in the use of all the Yosemite rock-climber's jangling hardware.

None of that opens doors in the Andean stratosphere. The reaction of the body to its thin air, especially with limited acclimatization, is unpredictable.

An Adirondack backpacker might go as high as the jets.

A muscle beacher might fall into a stupor 7,000 feet below him.

Doug was laboring at 16,000 feet, grabbing for air, his insides already knotted from an unsuccessful bout with breakfast at Camp One's 14,600 feet.

He upbraided himself and searched for explanations.

By the time we reached Camp Two high on the glacier at 17,000 feet—exactly a mile beneath Huascaran's south summit—he was dragging.

He struggled against the nausea and torpor sucking him down, tried first to overpower it and then outtalk it.

For the three days we were weathered in at Camp Two, Kelley scarcely took solid nourishment. He pretended. He was sly. He would grab a couple of spoonfuls and then walk around the tent unsteadily, dumping the rest of the contents of his canteen when he thought nobody was observing.

His *compadres* observed.

He would wake up in the morning announcing he had experienced a miraculous rehabilitation. But he almost never left the tent, and his face began swelling under the eyes. His lips were thick and crusted and he looked consummately miserable and sick.

Doug struggled into his climbing clothes on Saturday, made an obligatory but futile try at breakfast, and then sat on his pack, distant from the others.

"Take what you need from my gear," he said finally. "I'm going down. I'm too weak to climb, and there's no use holding you up."

He did not sound nor look very heroic, but a climber will understand the fundamental sacrifice. He might have invoked, indirectly or silently, some musketeer's code requiring all of us to go down and await his recovery. Big expeditions would never entertain that indulgence, but there were only three of us on Huascaran, and we had nurtured the climb for months.

We thanked him with respect and concern, and he wobbled off down the glacier with Jacinto, much of his equilibrium gone.

Above Camp Two vaulted the technical crux of the climb, a 450-foot icefall where the glacier broke over a series of rock cliffs. Wilson and I roped with Fausto and began chopping a route up the wall with our axes and crampons. Halfway up it occurred to me that Wilson's bad leg must make this exercise painfully awkward. He had wrenched his knee six weeks before, jumping out of a canoe, and it was still stiff.

I asked him about it on the icefall, and got the same tape-recorded answer he had been giving us for weeks.

"Good," he said.

"That's some summation for a lawyer," I said.

"It was the best I could do on short notice," he said.

We cleared the icefall, waded hip-deep in soft, ascending snow for an hour, and then encountered the Garganta's predictable gales a half hour before reaching Camp Three.

The winds had accelerated to something close to 60 miles an hour by the time we reached the campsite at 19,000 feet, still at least one day and 3,200 feet below the summit. Pitching Kelley's dome tent under these conditions compared in raw aggravation with installing an overcoat on a three-armed man. When you got part of the fabric under control, a loose end would billow and flap and threaten to launch all three of us into the stratosphere.

By 6 p.m. we had eaten the chef's specialty (mine), freeze-dried beef Stroganoff from the shelves of Midwest Mountaineering, and were snuggly fortified against the wind.

While the nylon crashed and the fiberglass poles twisted and doubled, I lay in my bag, taking an inventory.

The night before a high climb is a time for that. It should avoid melodrama but still acknowledge that this is an alien place for man, of the unknown and of hazard that could never be completely controlled. So that there was some remote chance of this being a last night on Earth, and therefore a time for summing up. I gave thanks for the good that had come to me, and hoped that whatever good I had done overscaled the injuries I had inflicted, and the neglect. I thought of those close to me, summoned their faces and the best of our times, and I experienced both love and regret, but when I finished I was content.

The wind subsided by morning. It was going to be a gaudy winter's day in the Andes and it was going to be hot despite the four-mile altitude.

Wilson said he was eager and ready, and established this beyond all dispute by throwing up his breakfast.

We were going for the summit, lofting above us, silver and metallic, in arpeggios of ice cliffs. But we weren't going very fast. After one hour we were heaving for air with almost every stride, Wilson and I, fighting the 20,000–foot altitude. In two hours we had to resort to grubby goals: Twenty-five strides, and then breathe for a minute. Maybe two, or three. Wilson, trudging behind me, was tiring. His leg, partly. His malaise from early morning, partly. But Fausto Milla, in his Cordillera wisdom, had decided on the additives needed to get us to the top: a heavy supper the night before. Eat everything in sight. We tried. What about water? The gringos weren't raised in the Cordillera or the Incans' adobe. They needed at least four quarts of liquid a day to keep going.

And Fausto Milla had packed a one-quart plastic canteen of water, for three people, for a 3,200-foot ascent, and descent, on a hot winter's day four miles above the sea in the Andes Mountains.

Some climbers get sustenance out of snow. Wilson does not. At 21,000 feet he asked for lip balm. I pulled a tube of Lip Ivo out of my pocket and, absently studying it, discovered for the first time that the raspberry-flavored ointment we had been smearing on our lips was manufactured in Minneapolis. Alms from Hiawatha. The high sun ignited the snowfields and flung the glare and thermal power into our goggled faces. Fausto and I swabbed another layer of zinc oxide, and Wilson drenched himself in some high-powered sun screen. The track was firm, but endless. How high is the sky?

We resumed.

Now we were down to 20 strides and recuperation. When Wilson sucked in all the air he could, he called "yo," and we moved again. Fausto Milla seemed annoyed and impatient, as though we might be needlessly goldbricking, and he tugged at the rope. I yanked it the other way and cursed. I walked up to him and jabbed a finger into his chest. "We're gringos," I said, "going as fast as we can. If we can't breathe, we can't walk." Fausto grinned sympathetically. I apologized. The little man was still an *amigo*.

At 4:05 p.m. we mounted the little snow dais decorated with orange flags left by an Austrian team and stood on the summit of Nevado Huascaran, 22,200 feet above the sea. We hugged Fausto Milla and said, "*Grácias*."

Some gringos were crazy and some were obsessed, Fausto said in Spanish, and he wasn't sure where we belonged.

"These," I said, "are not obsessed. They are just tired."

Summit attitudes on a big mountain usually do not make good theater. No one I know falls to his knees to worship the view, although the view may be extraordinary, as it was here at the zenith of the Cordillera Blanca on a day when the sun bejeweled a whole congregation of gigantic peaks. The architecture was numbing. It assembled white pyramids, obelisks, massive domes, and elegant massifs spun together by ridges of glistening blue ice.

Mostly you feel relief and gratitude.

I told Rod Wilson he deserved the summit more than anyone I knew. He nodded in appreciation but seemed momentarily to disagree. Dehydrated and ailing, he decided not to risk the exertion of a reply. What he was doing with his remaining mental acuities was figuring out ways he could prolong the delays downward. It is a wily art founded on sheer survival instinct. It might or might not matter that the others on the rope are aware of the techniques. Let them breathe on their own time.

Fausto was preceding us on the rope at the most dangerous time of any strenuous climb, the downward drag when the elations and anticipations have receded and the drudgery and fatigue-fed complacencies take over. He was showing the way, but he should have been doing it from the last position on the rope, not the first, the better to belay or secure in case of a slip.

We reached a high-angled ice sheet that required front-pointing with the teeth of the crampons and simultaneous leverage with the ice ax. Fausto was 25 feet below me and well to the left. The rope was looped tight around his imbedded ax, but he was in no position to exert immediate tension on the rope in the event of a fall.

The front points of my crampons gave way and I started to slide.

I dug the pick of the ax into the slope, but kept sliding, 25 feet, until the ax stopped the unwilling glissade.

Fausto and I glared at each other.

"*Cristos*," I said.

Fausto grinned. "I had it," he was saying, "all the way."

All the way to where?

So now Rod, limping and fatigued, began his descent, his rope looped around my ax. Five feet down the slope, he lost control, and then his ax.

There could be no tension on the rope to arrest his skid for at least

35 or 40 feet. He streaked down the ice, struck an overhang and shot onto a lower slope with an 800-foot runout.

As he did I drove my shoulders into the ax and buried it to the pick.

The rope came taut, and held.

And his ax came down in Rod's lap.

We called once, and got no response. Again.

Rod lifted an arm. I cramponed down to check him out. To reach him I had to make a long step over a snowbridge.

A snowbridge over what, it occurred to me?

Over a crevasse. It was four feet wide and it was walled in incredible blue and it must have reached halfway to Peking.

In tumbling down the overhang, Rod had missed falling into one of the deepest crevasses on the mountain.

He dusted off and kept plodding downward. A hundred strides, then gulp air. Swab on some lotion, anywhere. The face, the wrists, only do it very fastidiously to buy more time.

He never complained. But it was taking forever. By nightfall we were still nearly an hour above the Garganta's plateau and Camp Three just below it. Fausto had lost all of his impatience and was generous and thoughtful at the sound of Rod's wheezes. We got off the slope and were now walking the plateau toward camp, toward a conflagration of stars, toward the Southern Cross.

There wasn't a whisper of wind, almost uncanny for this hour and this geography, where the usual powerful wind might have finished Rod.

We had neighbors. A low-slung little tent and two larger ones. We got Rod into the tent and removed his crampons and boots. Fausto started the Optimus inside the tent, which is not enthusiastically recommended by tent makers or tent dwellers, but the conditions were not normal.

Rod took two sips of soup and turned down everything else. He was asleep in two minutes. At 11, with the wind rising, he awoke us, ashen and gagging, and said he thought he was dying from pulmonary edema.

Fausto got ready to descend 5,000 feet to Camp One for the oxygen tank we stored there, at Doug Kelley's suggestion. In the adjacent tent was another native porter and his client, a television photographer from Cincinnati. Fausto persuaded the porter to descend with him. While he did, I rummaged around the rest of the tiny village, looking for help. In the low-lying tent were an experienced Swiss climber and his girlfriend, equipped with more pertinent medical stores than we had. The Swiss volunteered medicine he said was useful for malaria victims and might do something for Rod's blood and circulation.

Fausto was just leaving when I made the injection.

"You have to hurry," I said. "I know it is not easy going down from the Garganta at night, but he may die unless the oxygen is here by afternoon."

Fausto and the other porter began their descent shortly after 11 p.m., in strong winds and full moon. It was at least three hours to Camp Two at normal pace and another two to Camp One. Allowing 15 minutes to a half hour there, plus seven to eight more hours for the return ascent, I calculated Fausto could not return with the oxygen until at least 1 or 2 in the afternoon.

Rod drank some hot chocolate at 7 a.m. but in movement and speech he was fogged and disoriented, a zombie who did not want to impose. He spoke tonelessly to people who weren't there and talked about the impending try for the summit, vowing he was strong enough to make it. By now he must have lost at least 20 pounds.

I had scooped out a fresh batch of ice and snow to boil on the Optimus shortly before 10 a.m. when somebody twanged, "Hey gringo."

Fausto Milla materialized with the crate of oxygen.

Imagine.

Down perpendicular ice walls in the middle of the night past Camp Two, threading crevasses unroped on the two-mile-wide glacier. More than 5,000 feet vertically to Camp One, and then retrace.

He had done it all in less than half a day, three and four hours ahead of what I thought was a reasonable timetable.

I unhooked the crate and handed Rod the nosepiece.

Pure oxygen flowed into his lungs for 30 minutes.

"Is *bueno* (good)?" Fausto asked Rod Wilson. He was fraternal, worried, an amigo.

"*Bueno*," Wilson said.

He took oxygen at intervals for the next two hours, and then we roped up with two relief porters from Camp One for the descent of the ice fall.

His pulse was close to normal by the time we reached Camp Two, and at Camp One the next day, he was eating again. We conscripted a horse for Rod on the descent to Musho, and learned there that the proprietor of the little cafe on the dusty main street was Fausto Milla himself.

His cook came with hot soup and rolls, with an entrée of rice and creole sauce and sauteed chicken. There were meats in the soup that were sweet but palatable, and I didn't have the nerve to ask ther origin but I know they weren't beef, pork, or veal, or anything close.

"*El condor pasá, Fausto*," I said with some vague philosophical urge.

"*Si*," he said gravely.

I went outside, extracted my ice ax from the pack, and handed it to Fausto. Rod did the same with his glacier glasses. The Peruvian's brown eyes expanded and shone. Behind him was a little Indian girl with her bright costume and shawl and funny square hat, for whom I had plucked a flower on our way into Musho.

She had a flower for me.

And it occurred to me that one little native girl's smile can melt much snow and ice, and sometimes the best and most enduring discoveries do not require an ascent of 22,000 feet.

Could a Rattler Puncture a Bike Tire?

Casper, Wyoming

A MILE ABOVE sea level and 800 miles from home, we are riding the Wyoming Plateau and jousting now with rattlesnakes, tumbleweed, and oil pumps.

There is nothing in the footnotes of the bicycle manual advising you how to deal with terrain features like these. Maybe we should be grateful. The sauce of traveling is its surprises, and you can't pedal the American West by bicycle with any serious claim to boredom, unless you find rattlers tedious.

He was loafing on a road shoulder somewhere west of the Sand Hills in Nebraska. I thought he was a strip of shredded tire until I saw the stripes, and at this point I executed a piece of acrobatics that defies the design engineering of the Mariushi bicycle. The rattler must have been impressed because he swished into the field grass.

Can you imagine trying to collect a warranty, claiming your front tire was punctured by a rattlesnake?

The motorist entering the West rarely entertains thoughts like that, which is one of the bonuses of witnessing it from a bicycle seat. We are 250 miles and four days from the Teton Mountains, aching some, but feeling a rising excitement and also a kind of vulnerability that is suspenseful itself in the presence of such mighty forces. The sights and sounds of the West, the immensity and the marvel of it and the random fright it generates seem more acutely personal.

From a car you are a spectator. By bicycle you are part of the action, riding with the wind, immersed in the stillness.

You also have to dodge the odd clump of bumptious tumbleweed. I thought I had it outmaneuvered as it bounced across the highway east of Casper. But my daughter Amy was giggling behind me.

"You better stop your bicycle," she said. "The tumbleweed is all snagged up in your spokes."

No damage. How could anything as mischievous as a tumbleweed harm a stranger, here where no one speaks discouraging words.

Well, almost no one. A joy of biking through the big country is the chance to monitor the voice of America. Here's a bitching session in the Snack Shop at Crawford, Nebraska. An old farmer with 58 harvests behind him: "Three inches of rain all summer," he said. "To hell with it." But he brought in the first load of wheat—something about 12 percent moisture—and it led off the news on the Chadron radio station. His pal at the table was grousing about cars. "Why the hell did they ever stop making the Model A? It had iron on it. It gave you 22 miles a gallon. You could use bacon rind for bearings and it lasted forever. You back into a curb wrong with a new car and they cancel your insurance."

America talking. But the wanderer notices something missing. For years the blocking dummies for this kind of talk were the bureaucrats in Washington. Out here, in the summer of 1981, they don't bitch about the federal government—at least not today.

Mountains now. Ridge piled on ridge, stretching toward the culminating summits of the Wind Rivers, and the Grand Tetons that are still beyond sight. We are riding the alkaline steppes of the great plateau. Baked and treeless, but not quite a desert. Cattle and horses and sagebrush. You can't bicycle across country very long without getting adept at fantasy. Today the winds are benign on the 104-mile leg from the antelope hunters' rendezvous at Lusk to Casper. Imagine you are riding the purple sage, a cowboy chasing a stray, a ghost rider chasing his sins. Zane Grey or Frankie Laine. So why not sing. I do. "Goodbye, old paint, I'm leavin' today." The white-faced cow glares at me and moos.

I accept the rebuke without a grudge. Cows have rights, too. Amy giggles again. "It's the Chadron radio station with a commercial for the Chamberlain Mortuary. They are putting on the hymn of the day." And thus, while a chorus of 55 fills the western sky with "Holy, Holy, Holy," we snort up a 1,000-foot hill that lifts us onto the plateau.

We must be a sight. I have that feeling as relays of semitrailers give us two amiable bonks on their air horns. And then I remember Amy has slimmed down to her swimsuit top. The ultimate salute is a light blast from a passing freight train.

Never minimize the fraternity of the road.

On second thought, we are a sight. Towels and shirts never dry after the night's sudsing. So we hang them out on the bicycles' rear racks and have covered the better part of the West resembling a rolling Laundromat.

The first oil field appears east of Casper, declared by the mechanical mynah birds silently pumping the earth for its treasure thousands of feet below. And suddenly the New West accosts the visitor with refineries and storage tanks, Texaco and Continental conversion plants, honky-tonk music and billions in wealth.

Zane Grey, rest in peace. It's progress, unavoidable. Tumultuous. But there is no argument today from me. Just go away for a while, refineries. We enter Casper and get depressed because one private campground looks like a junkyard and another is halfway to San Francisco. A policewoman says there is a nice Lutheran minister and his wife named Holm who might be from Minneapolis. Steve and Marilyn Holm tell us there is pizza in the oven and a stretch of lawn in back of their house. He attended Northwestern Seminary and she graduated from Augsburg. We talked for hours. They are delighted and howl over the "Holy, Holy, Holy" story.

But back on the road to the Tetons this morning. The shoulder is a scavenger's playground. We slalom through the flotsam of the rolling public. You can construct a whole scenario from what you see. Here's a roll of stereo tape, two empty Diet Pepsi cans, and what seems to be a used condom.

No harm there. None of that can puncture tires.

At the End of the Earth, Twenty-four Hours of Darkness

JANUARY 14, 1984

Spitsbergen, Norway

THE EYES AND ears tell the startled visitor this place must be another planet, existing beyond the rules of reality that govern the rest of the world.

But the Norwegians, who have more practical minds than the rest of us, shun that notion. They call Spitsbergen the island of the cold shores. And yet walk this morning into the blackness of midday, and ask yourself where else on earth are there sights like these:

• Five regal reindeer are bounding over a snowfield near the playground of a kindergarten 700 miles from the North Pole.

• Outside the windows, small cyclones of spindrift snow blot out the moon and the spectral slopes above the northernmost town on earth.

• Two stubby forms trudge up the hill nearby. They look like penguins. When the wind dies and the snowdust settles, it can be seen that they are carrying milk buckets. In a moment they materialize out of the frozen *morketiden* — the time of darkness — and reveal the standard armament of the Spitsbergen kindergartner, cherry cheeks and enormous blue eyes.

A few hundred yards away hundreds of men, Norwegian miners, burrow more than a thousand feet beneath the earth, extracting coal from the permafrost.

Another 25 miles away hundreds of other miners, Russians, do the same in their own frigid enclave, two colonies of workmen from rival cultures functioning in a bizarre coexistence nearly a thousand miles above the Arctic Circle.

In the ice-filled fjord that forms their common coastline, a polar bear may be clambering up from a lead of open water, grubbing for food.

A few miles inland, in a little variety store indistinguishable from thousands like it in small-town U.S.A., there is a sale on stereo cassettes featuring Michael Jackson and Ludwig van Beethoven.

Consider the improbable end-of-the-earth dominions of Svalbard, Spitsbergen, and Longyearbyen.

First, wipe the spindrift out of your eyes. Look straight overhead for what may be the oddest sight of all. There are the end stars on the scoop of the Big Dipper, and five times the distance between them is the pale luminosity of Polaris, the North Star. It is not in the northern skies tonight. It is straight up. To compound the unreality, this is not tonight. This is today.

Up here it is black night for 112 days. Up here it is so far north the aurora borealis plays to the south of where we stand gaping.

Yet, if you discount the wind chill generated by those sporadic gusts from the fjords, it was warmer Friday in Longyearbyen, a few hundred miles from the North Pole, than it was in Minneapolis.

If that makes you feel deprived, be consoled in this: There were fewer polar bear warnings emanating from the ice of Lake Calhoun than there were from the ice of the Spitsbergen sounds.

The Norwegian pragmatists were probably wrong. This may be another planet, after all.

So what are the Russians doing here in the middle of it?

Three hundred years after the Vikings found it—undoubtedly on their way to Alexandria, Minnesota—the Dutch explorer Barents rediscovered Spitsbergen in 1596. It didn't take the ancients long to massacre all of the big whales and practically all of the walruses. The world was about ready to abandon it to the icebergs and the polar bears when somebody found coal on Spitsbergen, the biggest island of the Svalbard archipelago.

If you have any doubts about how our lives and times eventually are interwoven, dabble with the name of J. M. Longyear. Longyear's mining and exploration family has roots in Minneapolis and northern Michigan. It was on the cutting edge of the opening of

Minnesota's Iron Range, and in 1906 Longyear began mining coal in Spitsbergen.

By the time he sold out 10 years later the principal settlement bore his name, and eventually it swelled to the present population of 1,300. Nobody much cared who ran these frozen boulders until then, but in the 1920s an international treaty gave sovereignty to Norway.

The same treaty gave any other signatory nation the right to develop the islands commercially. The Soviets dug a coal mine shortly thereafter and have been operating it, at a place called Barentsburg, for years. They have almost twice the people in their coal mine that the Norwegians do in theirs. But the Norwegians generously accept those odds as part of the civilized man's burden.

"It rather evens things out," sighed one of the old-line Norwegian administrators, Henrik Varming of the state-owned mining company. "No more than fair. They have more people to produce about as much coal as we do."

The Norwegians are nothing if not generous with their competitors.

There never has been much hostility. The two communities come together now and then in a kind of strained sociability that takes the form of ski races, chess tournaments, and even an occasional songfest.

But nowhere do you find a documented intermarriage. "The Russians," Varming explained, "find our language difficult, our food even more difficult, and our customs almost impossible."

They do manage to keep a prudent eye on each other. There is no militarization of the island. But Norway belongs to NATO, and Russia is the Soviet Union, and because of the islands' strategic if not immediate military importance, the Norwegians 10 years ago decided to upgrade their presence here.

For hundreds of years Spitsbergen was a trappers' and whalers' preserve, a place for the Yukon Erics of the world. Today hundreds of Norwegian women live on Spitsbergen. Some of them are here as wives, but many are here to cash in on the low tax rates, the adventure, and the highly favorable male-female ratio.

The residents used to live in barracks, but today you find neat flats civilized by television, weekly food deliveries from the commissaries, snowmobiles, and—just a few miles from glaciers a thousand feet thick—at-your-door taxi service.

But they still don't let you leave town unless you pack artillery for the polar bears.

Do Polar Bears Knock before Entering?

JANUARY 16, 1984

Spitsbergen, Norway

YOU COULD HEAR him between the gusts, rummaging outside our cabin door. He was pawing and clumping, and he wanted in.

He was what Arctic dwellers call an ice bear, and the rest of the world calls a polar bear. No matter how you identified him, he was snuffling at the pine-board entrance to the remote hut where we were trying to outlast an Arctic snowstorm.

Let me be frank.

Apart from wanting to experience God's wild nature in its most naked honesty and force, I cannot give you a valid reason why Kjell Bergh and I were sitting at this crude candle-lit dining table Saturday night in our wools and Sorrel boots, dragging on hot coffee and listening to the baying wind. It came hurtling straight off the North Pole ice cap a few hundred miles away, and maybe that is reason enough.

Our escorts, Austrian-born Elfie Varming and her 17-year-old daughter, Elisabeth, had left three hours earlier, herding their snowmobiles into the spinning snow and the polar darkness. They joined us for julekage, jam, and coffee before they strapped into their snowsuits. This was the family hut on Spitsbergen, miles into the interior of the most desolate land on earth.

Never mind that they owned a comfortable home in the coal-mining town of Longyearbyen on the frozen seacoast. There is no place in the world north of Longyearbyen, but coveys of the residents make their ritualistic escape "to the cabin" in the 24-hour-blackness of winter or the midnight sun of summer.

"What is a Scandinavian without his cabin?" Henrik Varming, the family elder, asked. "There is some compulsion to privacy, even here in the most private and impossible place on earth."

He handed me an ancient but functioning Smith and Wesson revolver. The law in Norwegian-owned Spitsbergen does not bar you from venturing into the glacial wilderness outside of town without a gun; common sense demands one.

The heaviest concentration of migratory polar bears lies on the islands to the northeast of here. But the animal is often sighted by the Longyearbyen residents. The mining community maintains a warning siren that tells the people when a bear has been seen. The siren means take cover. Because this is a place of self-sufficient and untheatric Norwegians, most of the village sagas about polar bears are shaggy pieces of whimsy that kid the idea of a sudden encounter with the hairy beasts.

But they're here, and they're killers. And you should never forget it. Not long ago one was spotted just a few yards from the village kindergarten—which is now fenced with reinforced wiring 10 feet high.

Fed and refreshed at the cabin, Elfie and Elisabeth motored off into the storm about 8 o'clock. It was one of those nights you conjure up when the candles are dying and somebody decides to recite Robert Service or Jack London. It was an honest-to-God Arctic gale out there last night. From the cabin windows we could see the surf of windblown snow ravaging the parked snowmobiles in the drifts, burying them. The planking of the hut creaked and heaved, but the little building was durable and cozy in the warmth of the kerosene heater.

Bergh and I talked for hours. He is a worldly and amusing creature but deeply sensitized, and we hit it off amiably. At midnight I cranked in the little transistor radio, and we divided our time for a few minutes between Norsk folk music from Oslo, Soviet newscasts from Murmansk, and, I swear it, a disc jockey from Pittsburgh.

What can I tell you? It was the rarest kind of night, the kind you want to engrave in your mind and insides as something both slightly mad and unforgettable.

The scratching and crunching started about 1 o'clock Sunday morning.

"It could be the outer door," Bergh said. "Sometimes cabin doors make sounds like than in the wind."

"It could be the door," I said from the depths of my sleeping bag, "but it probably isn't."

"No," Bergh said, "it probably isn't."

The moaning of the wind rose and fell as the hours ticked off. Its eerie arpeggios triggered sympathetic groans from the cabin's outer door, but sometimes when the air was still, brushing and grinding sounds unrelated to the wind crept through the tiny living room where we slept.

Something living was outside, and it was probably white and large.

Bergh developed a sudden taste for American pop standards, vintage 1925, on the cabin tape deck. It was the first time I have heard "Ramona" in the middle of a blizzard.

We lit a candle and examined the Smith and Wesson. Glumly we regarded it as less than devastating to any hostile ice bear. I burrowed into my backpack and found something even less comforting, a hunting knife my old pal Jerry Gruggan of Minneapolis had found for me in some Hong Kong bazaar. We laid the revolver and the knife on the table and blew the candle. At about 3:45 a.m. I was stirred by the most ancient of all summonses, and announced to Bergh that I would have to step outside or disgrace the family name.

"You can't be serious," he said.

"It's a true fact," I said.

Solemnly I made my preparations, strapping on the World War I aviator's cap and snowsuit Henrik Varming had lent. I opened the cabin's kitchen door, carefully nosed through the little vestibule pantry beyond, and then prodded open the outer door with the barrel of the Smith and Wesson, in the fashion of Matt Dillon entering a rustlers' bunkhouse.

The blowing snow hit me in the face. Holding the revolver with my left hand, I went about my mission in the howling snowstorm outside the cabin door. It occurred to me that any polar bear witnessing this scene should more logically be plowed into hysterics than into thoughts of homicide.

But as I was closing the door behind me I glanced at the snow-bank sculpted by the wind between the cabin and the great sweep of tundra.

There was a large depression in the snow. It looked more than six feet long, and it looked fresh.

When I got in I lit two more candles and Bergh turned up the volume on "Ramona." By the time we silenced the cassette three hours later, we knew the lyrics backward.

Near the Summit, a Time to Invoke Ghosts
AUGUST 28, 1985

Grindelwald, Switzerland

WE WERE 15 MINUTES from the summit of the Eiger and about 100 feet below it when the long snow crest of the Mittellegi Ridge narrowed and iced.

The snow on the north side was hard and resisted step-kicking. The snow on the south side of the ridge was more compliant. It was also seductive. It was an insurance seller's nightmare because sections of it were supported by nothing stronger than 5,000 feet of air. The climber calls it exactly what the architect calls it, a cornice.

We stayed right, or north, with no debate. The firmness of the summit ridge snow gave us an option. We could keep going in boots and thread our way along the crest, or we could strap on crampons, the metal soles with 2-inch teeth. Werner Burgener tossed a look of appraisal over his shoulder. We were going smoothly and swiftly. Crampons would give us a few more degrees of safety. But putting them on within sight of the summit, looking down the long shadowy throat of the Eiger's north face, aroused no sparks of enchantment from the young guide.

"We will be there in a few minutes." It was less a pledge than a directive. The only one of the day. Hurriedly we strode over the thin track toward the top. Our axes were available to control a slip. But the art gallery guide in Werner could not allow this occasion to pass without sharing some history.

"You'll notice that large stake just below the ridge on the south side," he said. "It's what they used to rescue some Italian and German climbers who were trapped on the north face. They couldn't move. They were just below the exit cracks that we are climbing above right now."

Once more, the invocation of ghosts. This fascination with the obituaries of Alpinism is not considered bad form in the climbing lodge. It's especially true on the Eiger, where the first attempts seemed to be closer to theatrical suicide than legitimate climbs.

Yet I found myself hooked on Werner's recital. Walking the slippery ridge, I mentally thumbed through the catalog of the Eiger north face, its bathos, blood, and triumph: the Hinterstoisser Traverse, the Spider Icefield, people twisting in the ropes beyond help, the names of Hermann Buhl, Gaston Rabuffat, Lionel Terray, Ricardo Cassin, and all the other climbing superstars—some of whom died on relatively easy walk-ups after surviving the Eiger north face.

This was another route, a first-rate climb, but not one intended as an avenue to Valhalla. We mounted the last icy rise and stood together on the summit at just over 13,000 feet.

In the emotions it generates, reaching the peak of a large mountain usually measures the years the climber has been plying this odd game rather than his personality. Noisy hugging sessions are acceptable. So are kissing, waving of arms, and impulsive thanksgiving to God and the rope manufacturer. Whatever feels right is OK. Professionals on the mountain produce a courtly smile, offer a hand, and say some equivalent of "well done."

Werner is not loaded down with the conventions of his trade. His big grin covered half the lunar surfce. He extended his right hand and clamped his other on the back of my neck. "It's a great climb," he said. "We have cause to celebrate."

We yodeled eight bars together and then split some cheese and sausage. What I usually feel on a mountain summit is a mixture of relief and contentment. This one deserved a holler. So we hollered a little and then looked down the west ridge.

"It looks like a nice climb down on rock until we get to the snowfield," I said. "It must be a good long run on snow down to the Eiger Glacier Station."

"It is, but we shouldn't go that way," he said.

"Why not?"

"I want to show you the best mountain tour in Switzerland. It will take us to the Jungfraujoch. Magnificent."

"How many more hours?"

"Only four."

With the summit of Eiger out of the way, this guy was saying we could now do some serious climbing. I spluttered something in English, which mercifully he didn't understand.

Old Faithful Performs for a
Gaping Audience of One

FEBRUARY 15, 1986

Yellowstone Park, Wyoming

IT IS THE only concert I've ever seen that began with a scream in the night.

If you look on the midwinter eruption of a geyser as the performance of a fragile but compulsive ballerina, never was there a more bizarre concert hall than the amphitheater of Old Faithful.

The audience is one, and the temperature is 29 below zero. The sky is incendiary with stars. One of them, the North Star, hangs directly above the geyser's crater, as though taped there by a stage director. The brittle air settles in the nostrils and eyelashes. Unless you are wearing polar equipment, you could freeze to death waiting for the coy ballerina and her veils.

So why wait?

Because there is no other sight on earth as startling as this most celebrated of all fountains flinging its boiling streamers into the cold night air while the onlooker gapes in solitary witness.

In the summer it plays to hordes, a number I joined for my first viewing 30 years ago. I was thrilled, and made the sight of Old Faithful a mark of renewal as the years advanced. With other snow creatures, I began coming in winter, when Yellowstone presents a magical scene of paradox that stretches the mind—fire and ice, herds of bison grazing in steaming meadows surrounded by snowfields.

Platoons of skiers and snowmobilers now flock daily to Yellowstone in winter. But, while its wilderness ski trails give me an unarguable excuse to come here in February, the spectacle of Old

Faithful exploding above the snow remains the idealization of Yellowstone in all its whim and might.

So I crunched to the observers' rim and listened for the sounds of the geyser's subterranean preludes, rumbling and gurgling; and then silence while thin vapors floated above the crater, announcing the imminent arrival of the star.

The ballerina is a tease. I walked half a mile to keep the blood flowing. Somewhere close in the forest a dying animal screamed. There was a killing, one animal dying to nourish another even as the witness strolled nearby seeking a different kind of nourishment. The same nature thus bred violence and spectacle, and it reminded the intruder that he is never far from one jungle or another.

A meteor flashed in the western sky, speeding above the snags of steam thrown up by the thermal basin. Another whizzed across the sky a few minutes later. What was this? Call it a fair exchange for a numb nose—an unscheduled light show in the sky to heighten the surrealism of a night in the geyser basin.

A minute before Old Faithful erupted, the Castle Geyser a half mile away rustled and blew. As though piqued by the intrusion, Old Faithful vaulted its sinewy white jets a hundred feet in the air, obliterating the North Star. As the boiling plume drifted upward, it offered a final amazement: The geyser's steam cloud seemed to fill the bowl of the Big Dipper, dangling by its handle in the northern sky.

Almost without further sound, the fountain receded for another hour, yielding to the muffled pounding of the Firehold River a mile away.

If nighttime stagecraft and thermal occult don't tingle your skin, wait until morning and you can ski eight miles to Fairy Falls, past the prehistoric pageant of bull elk and bison pawing in an oasis in the steam. The geyser clouds have created a local drizzle of snow, which cools the face. You whisper thanks, because despite the sub-zero temperatures, the sun provokes torrents of sweat.

The trail jogs a mile further through the lodgepole pines and then reveals a waterfall of exquisite lace, spilling 200 feet and creating along the route of its fall ice pendants of turquoise and robin's egg blue.

It is not a bad way to end a walk that began with death in the night.

An Abominable Snowman Gives Him a Shower
MAY 5, 1986

THE SHOWERHEAD IN my bathroom worked as advertised Saturday morning, delivering fine rhapsodic streams of clean water on my deserving head. I watched regretfully as the once-resourceful silt of three weeks' trekking in the Himalayas coagulated in small pools on the floor of the tub. From there it dribbled with dignity into the oblivion of the city waterworks.

I say regret because in the last shower I took in the Himalayas, the good honest dirt had a fighting chance.

Nowhere on Earth is there a shower like the one they engineer for 10 rupees in the village of Pheriche on the road to Mt. Everest. Pheriche has no electricity, streets, or notable sanitation. Practically all its residents are mobile and weigh an average of 1,500 pounds, which is the going displacement for yaks at 14,000 feet on the Himalayan tundra.

The herdsmen of Nepal are poor, but let nobody accuse them of lacking enterprising zeal. Fifty feet from my tent I spotted a rude little building across the trail from the one outpost of commerce in Pheriche, the town hotel and soup-and-rice-beer shop. There, drop-in Everest climbers and trekkers sit around a dirt floor in stubborn camaraderie, fighting off suffocation from surfs of black smoke blowing out of the chimneyless hearth. The little building nearby had the general size and contours of an outhouse, which would have made it an architectural imposter, because there are no such amenities in Himalayan trekking.

Yet nailed on the peak of the little building was a sign announcing "hot shower." Enthralled, I vanished into the black smoke to inquire at the hotel hearth. The custodian of the shower was a young man with the typical round eager face of the Sherpa natives who now make walking-around money hustling the dusty pilgrims.

Ten rupees is the equivalent of 60 cents. The young proprietor called himself Pasang and gestured confidently at the little wood building. "Shower is good," he said. "Ready in 10 minutes. If no good, money back." It was the Himalayan equivalent of the *Good Housekeeping* seal. No American traveler could resist it. I told Pasang if he could produce a hot running shower in the middle of the yak herds I would pay triple the listed freight.

In 10 minutes Pasang rattled my tent and declared the shower ready. Nobody who treks in the Himalayas expects a marble floor Jacuzzi. What they do is dump a pailful of hot water into a pipe or funnel and tell the customer, "Enjoy."

The engineering of the hot shower at Pheriche was more sophisticated. It had a little sprinkler system screwed into the pipe, making it capable of unleashing a spray. It works on a signal system. While the pail holder stands on a ladder poised over the pipes, the customer inside bangs on the tin wall to signify his readiness. I was halfway undressed when the downpour started. Maybe I hit the wall with my elbow, although it could have been something else. Pasang read it as the ready signal.

I was still in my boots when the water came.

Feverishly I flung off the rest of the clothes, but in the process unlatched the door. I now found myself confronted by two young Sherpa women who were curious about what the commotion was and looked inside. Both giggled uncontrollably. This made me oddly grateful for bringing a new art form to Pheriche. I closed the door and returned to the nozzles.

When it was over I had to lift one foot so I could towel without getting the foot dirty. In this vulnerable position I lost my footing and banged my head against the metal wall. Pasang heard it and promptly delivered a second pail of hot water. Groggy but game, I got off my knees and felt something in my left hand. It was a piece

85

of the clothesline. In trying to keep my balance when I fell against the wall, I had accidentally pulled down the clothesline and dumped all my fresh clothes on the dirty floor.

I gave Pasang 30 rupees and said he could put my personal endorsement in the Tundra Tribune.

From Bourbon Street to Nome, 9,000 Miles in a Canoe

NOVEMBER 16, 1977

HE TRUDGED THE gravel road into Nome, Alaska, like some north-woods Johnny Appleseed, bearing the scents and burrs of thousands of solitary miles.

Residents gaped, an attitude accorded few visitors to Nome. It is a place scoured by the arctic wind, a rude little enclave of humanity between the tundra and the polar sea. Not many visitors impress Nome.

People come to Nome—some of them reluctantly—by plane or by boat. They don't normally canoe 9,000 miles from New Orleans to get there, or walk the last 250 miles over cliffs, ocean-bay ice, tundra, and three feet of snow.

"We thought you were dead," a bearded house painter told Jerry Pushcar at the bar of a town saloon where the 27-year-old wanderer from Biwabik, Minnesota, was toasted with the Nome version of the champagne special: a double boilermaker—two shots of brandy and a beer.

A month ago, an Alaska newspaper published a report that Pushcar was feared lost at sea in the hours before the winter freeze locked the waters of Norton Sound.

The report, Pushcar acknowledged, was not far from the truth.

On the last full day of his three-year transcontinental canoe journey from the Gulf Coast to the Bering Sea, he went for an enforced swim among the ice floes, wearing only his wool underwear.

"I pulled in to shore with night coming on and was getting some firewood when I looked up and saw the canoe floating out to sea.

I stripped down and swam after it. God, it was cold. I was numb in 30 seconds. The canoe was out about 25 or 30 yards, close enough so I could get to it before going stiff.

"When I got back, I was shivering so hard I couldn't light a match. I had a little chemical fire-starter, which worked. If it didn't, I think I'd still be back there. I kept thinking about that crazy poem we read in school, about this guy who had a mortal fear of freezing to death on the marge of Lake LeBarge, or something like that. I kept that fire going all day the next day.

"For six days, the wind blew a gale on this little cape where I was stranded. I couldn't put the canoe into the water to try to finish the last 200 miles or so to Nome. On the seventh day, the sun came blasting out of the sky and it was just a beautiful, calm Alaska morning. I walked down to the shore, looked out on the ocean, and just hauled that canoe back into the bushes and started hiking. There was ice as far as I could see, and there were some seagulls frozen into it."

Pushcar long ago denied harboring any heroic qualities. He calls himself stubborn and inquisitive, akin to the woods "and maybe a little kinky about wanting to know how far is far." His objective in January of 1975 was to make Nome, Alaska, in three years. With the sea frozen and his canoe immobilized, there was still 250 miles of swamp, tundra, and 3,000-foot hills between the inquisitive man and his destination.

"I don't know what choice I had, when you come to think of it," he said. "That uninhabited cape on the frozen ocean was a helluva place to spend the winter unless you happen to be a walrus."

For three weeks, he walked in snowstorms and rain, wearing blue jeans, Canadian Sorrel boots, a wool shirt, and an old nylon-and-down jacket he found in an abandoned camp. He lived on rabbits he snared, fish he caught, and the donations of villagers in the three hamlets he passed between Shaktolic on the sea and Nome.

Three times he had to chase off scrounging bears in his little camps. He got sick with hypothermia, a potentially fatal condition caused by rapid loss of body heat. The wind chill dropped to 60 below zero one day, but he made it through the nights using a caribou hide for ground cover and a plastic tarp for a blanket. Resting one evening after a hard day's walk, he was about to prepare for bed when he found it impossible to remove his boots. "After all that sweating," he said, "my socks were frozen to the boot liners, and the liners were frozen to the boots."

He thawed them the next day, by walking.

After three weeks on the tundra, Pushcar walked into Nome late Saturday, a prepackaged celebrity. Interviewers from the local radio station accompanied him into town. Two men he had met earlier invited him to share their lodgings, "which was a break because before I picked up some money my family sent from Minnesota I was broke, and I checked out the apartments. There was a nice little two-bedroom number going for $800 a month. Hotel rooms are $50.

"But it's really a balanced town socially. There are seven saloons and seven churches. I think there's some kind of ordinance which keeps them even. I didn't see a whole lot of modern plumbing. In most of the public places, they used what they call honey buckets. It's a really friendly place, though. I want to spend the winter up here, maybe doing some trapping in the Alaska mountains. You could call it a sort of vacation. I spent two or three nights in the bars here, and that gets a little old. Civilization creeps up on me fast. I'm really a guy for the woods."

Townspeople who befriended him found Pushcar amiable but something less than a chatterer. It takes him a while to catalog and define his experience of the last three years, which must certainly occupy a unique place in the chronicles of solitary travel in the wilderness. He is a restrained if droll fellow conversationally, still touched by a low-key wonderment of the wildwood as few people have experienced it.

"At the start, it was really a case of wanting to know if I could do it," he said. "It was something I set for myself, not to show anybody else I had hair on my chest. I really love canoeing alone. Doing it the way I did, three years up the Mississippi, Lake Superior, the Pigeon River, Lake Winnipeg, Great Slave Lake, the Mackenzie and Yukon Rivers, wintering twice in the woods, well you can't do all that without learning something about yourself and about the earth.

"Sometimes, though, I could get to hate the canoe. I had to haul it up 50 miles of rapids through the Richardson Mountains in Canada on the Rat River. With all the fiberglass repairs, and the water that stayed between the layers, the damned thing ended up weighing 125 pounds. But you couldn't really hate the canoe when you were riding free down one of the big Alaska rivers and watching moose graze on the river banks and those mountains rising way off with snow on the summits.

"Sometimes the loneliness would get to you. But I tried to be constructive. Whenever it was really heavy, I began doing some mental architecture. I would build my dream cabin in the woods right from the foundation up. Fireplaces in every room, with logs two feet long for firewood."

Hundreds of people from the Mississippi levies to the mining towns of Alaska have encountered the once-bearded canoeist. ("I shaved before coming to Nome. It was getting kind of crawly"). They left him their names and address, thanking him for his stories, and telling him how much they envied him.

"I don't think they would have envied the time I nearly got crushed between a barge and the lock gates near Lake Pepin, or the time the wild dogs almost chewed me up in Arkansas, or that mother eagle north of Winnipeg," he said.

"I saw this eagle's nest high in a tree and scrambled up to take a picture. I'm a freak about pictures. I didn't molest the baby eagle. I wouldn't harm something like that for the world. I don't think you could have convinced the mother eagle, though. I heard this terrific screech and turned just in time to avoid this huge swooping bird. It nearly took my head off. I disappeared fast."

His memories, though, won't pay the rent. "I want to do some carpentering here for a while and then probably head back to Minnesota. I don't know how. Maybe by canoe."

The thought of feminine company after all those years in the brush is not entirely alien to the roaming bachelor. "The ladies," he said, "seem abundant in Nome. I almost had a romance the second winter near Lake Athabasca. There was this trapper's daughter, Mollie, the one who brought me two pounds of moose meat to get acquainted. After a couple of weeks I left my cabin and moved down to the trapper's village to get better acquainted. I'd like to write, but I don't think they pick up the mail for that place more than a couple of times a year. It's not the best arrangement for a steady romance."

Give Her Matching Jumper Cables:
Minnesota and Minnesotans

Minnesota Is No Place for the Oversexed
FEBRUARY 4, 1977

A BOSTON NEWSPAPER columnist mourns the decline of sex in New England as a casualty of the coldest winter of the century. Her melancholy is marbled with malice. It is not enough that she must grieve for the frozen glands of Massachusetts. She must also slander the state of the erotic art and the quality of passion in Minnesota.

She writes from the pits of despondency, with a despair and bitterness that must arouse the tenderness in all of us no matter the woman's erratic logic. Her account, evidently autobiographical, bespeaks a woman deprived, untended, and unsteady. Marital relations all over the North, she contends, are cooling. She argues the truly sensuous person needs warmth and titillation, a condition she says is strangled by the sight of the love partner in ski mask, boots, wool mittens, and flannels.

"People are suddenly remembering," she broods, "that *The Joy of Sex* was not written in Minnesota."

No, but it may well have been inspired here, I am told by University of Minnesota psychologists whose judgments I have found to be restrained and trustworthy.

The Joy of Sex, after all, is not so much a book as a consensus. Portions of it, the psychologists tell me, bear the unmistakable stamp of traditional Scandinavian love-making technique which is as old as the Kensington Runestone and may very well have been introduced to America at Alexandria, Minnesota, long before Columbus. Which is simply to say *The Joy of Sex* did not have to be authored in Minnesota. It was already part of the folklore.

This aside, the lady from Boston surely should be reminded of the hypothesis advanced by one of the University of Minnesota psychologists—and never challenged in the academic community or elsewhere—that snow shoveling in moderation tends to stimulate people erotically.

And yet we find ourselves portrayed in New England as stiff-hinged penguins who go courting with icicles hanging from our nostrils and street sludge in our shoes.

I was reflecting on these delinquencies in American journalism when my telephone call to the Munsingwear company was returned. I called Munsingwear as a favor to another eastern colleague who wanted to know what the winter was doing for underwear sales. Munsingwear is the local underwear house. It sells nationally, of course, but also must consider Minnesota needs and taste in such garments.

"The East," declared Bob Brazil, one of the product executives at Munsingwear, "is flooding us for orders for long johns. We sent an emergency shipment to Pittsburgh a couple of days ago."

"And Minnesota?" I said. "I suppose Minnesotans, being nurtured in thermal clothing, have bought up all your supplies of long-john woolies."

"We don't sell wool underwear anymore," he said. "They're expensive and it's probably a myth that Minnesotans prefer it. We're selling long johns all right, but the big thing from Munsingwear of Minnesota is bikini briefs for men. It's gangbusters, man. All we have to do is put them out on the counter and they're gone. You can't believe it. Mesh, see-throughs, the works."

"Right here?" I asked, startled. "In Minnesota?"

"In Minnesota more than anyplace else. Gangbusters."

"Whatever happened to the little golf shirts? Didn't you used to retain one of the big professional golfers as your corporate symbol?"

"Who needs Jack Nicklaus or Johnny Miller?" he said. "We'd rather have Alice Cooper."

"What happened," I asked, "to boxer shorts?"

"You mean the balloon seat?"

"Whatever."

"Yeah, you can still get them. But the big thing in Minnesota in men's underwear, stimulated by wives, our research tells us, is the bikinis for men in stars and stripes and hearts and all kinds of geometric designs. That's how Minnesota has responded to the winter."

Boston, I'm told, has put in another order for long-john woolies.

Never Mix Sarma with Restraint at Rudy's

JANUARY 5, 1978

MINNESOTA IS THE only state I have ever experienced where the governor fixes you a doggy bag before walking you to the door of his house.

As a host, Rudy Perpich gives parties that would never play in Georgetown, because nobody on the Potomac would have understood Lou Kosovich, an Iron Range Jackie Leonard whose syntax is a sort of smouldering compromise between Yugoslavian and Italian.

Kosovich entertained at Perpich's ethnic dinner party in the governor's mansion last night. So did Ray White, a third-generation Finnish minstrel from Hibbing who tries heroically to grapple with the Croatian language, with which bewildered invaders have been fighting a losing battle for thousands of years.

Perpich is a Croatian. This, I must tell you for the hundredth time, is a nationality and not a visitor from outer space.

Like scores of nationalities, Croatians are very chauvinistic about the food they cook. The governor's continuing devotion to dishes like sarma and candied mrlin (the Croatians believe neither in mixed marriages with Serbs nor in the letter "e") has attracted the professional stares of a number of people in my trade. Accordingly, Perpich and his wife gave a dinner last night so that all outstanding libels and suspicions directed against Croatian food could be dissolved.

Let me first observe the formalities of the menu. It began with wild rice soup and moved in measured stages through buttered crackers, pear or kruska salad, sarma (an amalgam of ham, pork, and beef wrapped in cabbage), casserole roasted krumpir (potato), candied mrlin (carrots), kruv and putar (small bread crusts seasoned and buttered), walnut potica (a layered pastry), apple strudel, cottage cheese strudel, and coffee.

Most Croatians I know on the Iron Range regard this ocean-going inventory as little more than an appetizer.

By the time Perpich's guests were two-thirds of the way through, there were calls for the litter bearer.

But not, I must add quickly, because of the quality. The sarma, for example, was personally prepared by Lola Perpich, the governor's wife. Seconds were offered by her husband, functioning as the house's number 3 waiter.

Perpich was mobbed. I can speak authoritatively on sarma. It is like listening to flute music. It can be a celestial experience or it can be a penance. Mrs. Perpich's sarma floated and sighed. It was tender and merciful. It was magnificent sarma, and I will be the first to admit ordering two in my doggy bag.

Less prudent guests afterwards accepted what was described as a temperate glass of slivovitz. Words can be corrupted in any language. No amount of corruption, however, could justify a description of slivovitz as "temperate." It is like inhaling a moderate amount of chloroform or taking a pleasant stroll through a viper pit. Slivovitz is Yugoslavian plum brandy. It is said to be a liqueur, but it actually embodies the mixed characteristics of No. 2 lighter fluid and battery acid.

Kosovich was relentless. He is a clothing store operator in Hibbing who greets all new acquaintances with a dazzling smile and an evaluation of his inseam. "Hello," he said to me. "My name is Looka Kosovich. I put you down as a 29½."

I told him I have been called worse.

White sang and plucked the guitar amiably for 15 minutes, after which Kosovich came on with the latest cultural developments on the Iron Range.

"The competition for status, especially among the Italians," he said, "is getting fierce on the Range. I was listening in on a conversation the other day. I got a friend, Liugi. He said his son, just two years out of law school, is drawing down $100,000 a year out east.

" 'Liugi, thassa nawthing,' my friend Sergio told him, 'you gotta boy who make $100,000. My boy, Alfredo, heesa doctor. He go through the finest schools in the west. Heesa now make $200,000, Liugi. What you think of that?'

"Giuseppi, the third man," Kosovich related, "told them he was very impressed but would have to tell them about his oldest boy, Mario, who never went to college.

" 'Mario, heesa mechanic in Chicago,' he said, 'and heesa make-a $250,000.'

"Naturally, the others gasped: 'How you have a mechanic make-a $250,000?'

" 'Easy. Heesa fix things.'

" 'What he fix for $250,000?'

" 'Heesa fix football, basketball, horse racing. . . .' "

Everything but sarma.

Dayton's Can Fill Your Every Fantasy— but Not Your Buttonholes

JANUARY 31, 1979

HUNDREDS OF THOUSANDS of Minnesotans have grown, withered, and gone to their proper deserts with an unbreakable faith in three institutions: the church, the potluck supper,and Dayton's department stores.

Before there was ever Social Security or Medicare, there was Dayton's. It was there before shopping centers and credit cards. It has outlasted the League of Nations and the British empire. Multitudes of people have walked through the city hall's portals quaking for their fate and prepared to distrust their ears, but nobody every walked into Dayton's with any dread or doubt. If you couldn't find it at Dayton's, either it didn't exist or it was illegal.

Except for the sheltered first years of my life on the Iron Range, when I applied this same intuitive trust to Zupancich Bros. Grocery Store and Sausage Counter in Ely, I have accepted Dayton's paternal presence as a condition of life, along with everybody else.

I never telephoned or checked the ads. It didn't matter if I wanted a houseboat or a size 4 spoon for a canteen kit. Dayton's had it. I never questioned how or why it achieved this role in my life, but I haven't thought much about the origin of the sky lately, either. And so it seemed as natural as walking in slush to find myself hustling around the first floor of Dayton's yesterday, 10 minutes before closing, asking the directions to buttons.

We have agreed here before that America is no longer capable of producing garments with buttons that stay on. You can buy a $300 overcoat in November and face almost certain attack from pneumonia or frostbite by January because you have been stripped of all essential buttons. The clothing industry blames the violent tendencies of the American people, such as turning to drop a grocery bag in the back seat of the car or stooping to put on rubbers. It urges that we adopt calmer lives in deference to our buttons. I personally have pledged to pursue this goal. But my problem yesterday was the overcoat I was wearing. It lacked a middle button. My spare lacked a first and third button and the brown suit I wanted to wear last night lacked one large button on the front and one small button on the cuff—in other words, a relatively normal state for my wardrobe in January.

A woman in wallets directed me to the notions counter in the basement. Crowded for time but otherwise content, I charged down the corridor toward the stairway, beneath formations of overhead banners declaring another supergoliath white sale, past the fudge counter, down the steps and into notions.

"Buttons," I said brightly. "I'd like to see your buttons."

A lady with correctly groomed gray hair and a manner of solemn competence gave me the news.

"There are no buttons here."

"You are saying you have no buttons in notions."

"Yes."

"Then where can I find them?"

"We don't sell buttons."

"I'm sorry, madame, I misunderstood you. For a moment, I thought you were telling me Dayton's doesn't sell buttons."

The lady was not argumentative. She was not annoyed. She was not impatient. She was simply very clear.

"We don't sell buttons anymore."

My mind spun wildly in the face of this stunning proclamation.

"But Dayton's has ALWAYS sold buttons," I pleaded. "I remember distinctly there were little ladies standing over boxes and bins of buttons. You could get orange buttons and buttons with seven eyes. You could get leather ones and zinc ones. Never have I walked into Dayton's without my every need being satisfied and a few new ones being identified. I can buy a round-the-world trip in Dayton's. I can buy — or I could if didn't have to buy gas — fur coats, diamond rings, and mobile homes from Dayton's. This store has spawned billions of dollars in trade. It has made shopping centers as indispensable as water and tax advice. It has built Target stores from one end of the country to the other. You can be guilty of every misdemeanor in the book when you go into court, but if you have an active credit card at Dayton's they'll release you on your own recognizance. And you are telling me that I can't buy a button in Dayton's?"

The lady sighed. I think she was about to suggest a television with a six-foot screen on the seventh floor.

She did not. She suggested Amluxen's.

Which was closed.

Maybe you better check that little old sky today to see if it's still there.

Pasties Need More Dignity, Not Ketchup

APRIL 30, 1980

BECAUSE HIS HOMETOWN of Eveleth is outside the mainstream of communications and cultural exchange on the Iron Range, I will forgive radio's Steve Cannon for his distorted recital last night of the evolution of Cornish pasties in Minnesota.

I do not believe Cannon intentionally twisted the historical truth. He is, after all, the child of his upbringings. When Cannon went to school in Eveleth on the Mesabi Range, the guileless young scholars were never told that somewhere to the northeast was Another Iron Range, where artistic grace and social gentleness flourished, where people actually banked in banks instead of tomato cans, and where elections were held without pollwatchers recruited from the 47th Division Riot Squad.

Sociologists will instantly recognize this lovely Arcadia as the Vermilion Range, where, by a kink of coincidence, I was born and grew up.

Its existence was strenuously hidden from the youth of the Mesabi Range in order to prevent a wholesale migration to Ely and Tower-Soudan, which would have thrown all of the truant officers out of work on the Mesabi and also badly damaged the bar business.

The first known appearance of the Cornish pasty in Minnesota was at a Methodist Church Ladies Aid sale in Ely, where it was viewed with wonder and a certain amount of alarm by the Yugoslav and Italian Catholics arrayed across the street. This is documented in papers on file in the old English consulate in Section 30, part of the Ely exurbia of the early 1900s. I bring this to your attention on the chance that some of you may be unfamiliar with the institution of the Cornish pasty—a centerpiece of the southward advance of civilization from the Vermilion—or that you may have been seduced by Cannon's airy claims of last night.

Cannon contends the Cornish pasty was introduced by the Cornish mining families directly into the Mesabi Rnge from northern Michigan and Canada. The claim is highly odorous because the cooking stove was largely unknown on the Mesabi Range until shortly before World War II. I say this in no way to discredit the inhabitants of the Mesabi Iron Range, but merely to show the hardships and limited view of the world in which the natives of Eveleth, Hibbing, Virginia, Biwabik, Coleraine, Keewatin, and the rest of the open pit hamlets grew up.

Recognizing this, we encouraged special buses and tourist visits from the Mesabi so that the children, at least, might be broadened and somewhat tempered. The most successful of these attractions was the annual Saturday Night Kazoo Concert at the Ely Community Center, where hundreds of the artistically hungry from Eveleth and Virginia would be entertained.

My friend Cannon invited his listener to sample the Cornish pasty even at this late date, and in this I heartily join. But only under the deepest duress should you accept Cannon's suggestion to swab the pasties in a "a few dabs of ketchup."

Would you spread mustard on a filet mignon at Charlie's?

Would you mix Fresca with caviar?

I will tell you about Cornish pasties.

It took the Finns and Yugoslavs, the Italians, Bulgarians, and Greeks, the Swedes, Norwegians, and Lithuanians at least two generations to overcome their early suspicions of English cooking. This is tolerable, considering the reputation of English cooking.

But once accepted, the Cornish pasty quickly became the ecumenical jewel of Vermilion Range cookery and the pot luck galas.

They bulged the miners' dinner pails and filled the house painters' brown bags. In our house, Thursday nights were the big pasty meals. We had sausage Monday through Wednesday, and generously dappled through the weekend, but you went to hell if you had meat on Friday, so it had to be Thursday.

My mother used to buy the beef at Kovach's Fairway Foods or

Lozar's Table Supply, and from the round steak she cut cubes that she laid into the pie dough. To these she added potatoes, rutabagas, onions, salt, pepper, some butter, and a swatch of parsley.

The grownups in Ely used to drink Muscatel with their pasties. I do not vouch for the vintage or even the safety of this particular wine, but they survived it almost unanimously.

But ketchup?

Only the lowest brows took ketchup with their Cornish pasties. A far more acceptable sauce was horseradish.

It's what separated the cultures of the Vermilion and the Iron Range, Cannon.

There are a lot of ways by which you define refinement.

The Day Harvey Mackay Outtalked
Johnny Carson

JULY 29, 1980

To EXTRACT THE true essence of the scene on the tennis courts at the Hotel du Cap on the French Riviera the other day, you have to be able to comprehend Harvey Mackay.

Harvey is not a complicated man. He is rich, but not offensively so. He is an extroverted pitchman who is impossible to wear down or outtalk. He has hustled his envelope business into one of the most successful operations of its kind in the province, a status that has allowed Harvey to unleash his creative energies as a civic evangelist. In this role, he has embraced — occasionally to the despair of his intended beneficiaries — the domed stadium, the University of Minnesota basketball team, and a whole collage of cultural projects and visions.

He cannot be ignored or evaded. He is as relentless as Niagara and almost as tough to silence. But because he is bright and likeable and does his schoolwork, his quarries find themselves psychologically paralyzed, making escape difficult. You need a symphony hall, recruit Harvey. He has the numbers, the Dun and Bradstreet ratings, and all the vulnerable fat cats. He also has their golfing handicaps. It is not always hard to turn him down the first time, but about the 25th or 30th, the defenses begin to quiver. One of Harvey's uncommon gifts is the ability to convince the potential donor that nobody he has met commands the bedrock intelligence, the sensitivity and the nimble perception of the big picture as the very person he is talking to, the potential donor.

Capitulation, thereafter, is inevitable. Harvey emerges as your friendly, neighborhood tycoon, a jock with a Dale Carnegie panache. He is the guy who will bring the bats and balls and bratwurst for the block slow-pitch game, and then buy uniforms and pack them in his company's envelopes with a picture of his family on the cover.

How can you resist Harvey Mackay?

The porters at the Hotel du Cap didn't try. Harvey tips well. This in itself is no trivial achievement at the Hotel du Cap, an 18th-century chateau that is patronized by royalty and millionaires. They don't print the prices on the menu at the du Cap, nor are the room rates listed. Somebody in a tux hands you the bill when you leave. It is the only money transaction of the visit, but it is impressive.

Into this atmosphere of Mediterranean chic walked Harvey Mackay, his wife, and three kids.

In front of the seascape, Harvey spotted a tennis court and immediately changed into his sporting garments. "The best time," the pro said, "is about 5 p.m. You should be able to get into a game then."

Harvey materialized at precisely 5 p.m. A man in white shorts and shirt walked up to him. "Hello," he said. "We have three and could use a fourth. Would you mind joining us?"

Harvey advanced on the court at a restrained gallop. With his heartiest camaraderie, he introduced himself. "Hello," he told the first. "I'm Harvey Mackay from Minneapolis." The man said hello, mentioned Boston. "Hello, I'm Harvey Mackay from Minneapolis," he announced vigorously to the second. The man said hello and mentioned New York. Harvey turned to the third with gusto still undiminished, and identified himself as Harvey Mackay of Minneapolis.

"Hello," the third said, "I'm Johnny Carson."

Harvey's teeth unlocked to form a picturesque ravine.

"Migawd, Johnny," he said on recovery, "I'm sorry. I didn't recognize you right away."

Carson though that was perfectly fine and explained that people who spend most of their time watching the ice thaw can't be expected to save a lot of time for television.

Harvey paired up with the guy from Boston against Carson and his attorney.

"He plays a good game," Harvey tells us, "but we won the first set. He was funny most of the time, but somewhere in the second Carson laid into an easy lob and hammered a ball right into my crotch. He said on the Riviera, nobody takes prisoners. It got to be 8–8 and I stopped the game. I told Carson that if he and his partner won the set I was personally going to see to it that he got a lifetime supply of Mackay Co. envelopes with his named embossed.

"He came to the net very solemnly, put his racquet over his heart, looked up at the blue Riviera sky and said 'Harvey, that's something I've wanted all my life.'

"Well, in spite of that incentive, Carson and his partner lost. He was great after the match but when we left, my 17-year-old, David, grabbed my arm as we were heading back to the hotel and said, 'Dad, for goodness sake, stop trying to trade one-liners with the funniest guy in the world.' "

Harvey, being Harvey, thought he got at least a draw. "But I really want to send him something," he confided. "So I'm printing up 50,000 of the world's smallest envelopes, 1 inch by 1 inch, and sending them to Carson with the suggestion that he should mail them to his friends and fill them with everything he knows about power tennis."

On the other hand, Carson may try to fill them with all of the one-liners worth recording from a match with his old pal Harvey.

Justice Overtakes Miles Lord

JULY 20, 1981

MILES LORD ARRIVED at a friend's wedding reception last year and voluntarily identified himself to the groom's 10-year-old stepson as "the most famous judge in Minnesota."

His Grace is nothing if not a man of candor and service, and the boy was totally impressed to be in the presence of such high eminence.

He was also somewhat surprised because, bluntly speaking, His Grace did not talk like most judges talk on the daytime serials. He opened with a fish story and closed with ten minutes on the godawful condition of his big toe.

Juries in His Grace's courtroom have been subjected to confidences of equal poignancy. And for this and a dozen other reasons, the friends of justice should rejoice today in the choice by 42,000 American trial lawyers of Miles W. Lord of Chanhassen, Minnesota, as the outstanding federal trial judge in the republic.

Any political disagreements among us should melt before the plain good sense of this act of homage by the judge's neighbors, countrymen, and sizeable platoon of critics.

Never mind that His Grace is an unreconstructed Democrat, an unshackled spirit with a cozy style in court, and a source of bafflement to some of his starchier colleagues.

Consider Miles W. Lord one of the state's natural resources.

For a while he was even an endangered species. His overseers on the court of appeals ran him off the big Reserve Mining case five years ago because they claimed he was prosecuting the mining companies instead of judging them. Miles smouldered about that because—while he didn't deny it—he contended privately a judge ought to be able to do both.

And then a year ago, one of the more gossipy of the legal house-sheets described Miles W. Lord as one of the 11 worst federal judges in America on grounds that he was unpredictable in his legal stances, unjudicial in his style, and combative in his rulings.

All of which may have been true.

But it was a lousy rap notwithstanding because of the slim sample the publication used for its findings. Moreover it did seem shallow and vindictive in view of Miles W. Lord's undisputed impact on the legal community in a half-dozen blockbuster cases.

So the judge suffered this embarrassment and vowed vengeance, if any was available, or exoneration, if his friends could manage it.

His friends carried the battle to the trial lawyers, and today His Grace stands redeemed.

They are never going to nominate Miles Lord to the U.S. Supreme Court, and they are probably not going to demand a textbook from him on the techniques of judicial demeanor.

Nobody who confides the state of his kidneys as part of his charge to the jury is going to acquire such canonization.

Miles W. Lord decided long ago there are limited virtues to solemnity in a courtroom.

But once in a while a voice should be heard from the bench, willing to use some clear barnyard language to undress some of the humbug and profit-making dawdling that passes for the legal process.

Sometimes he has been boisterous and sometimes he has been wrong. But there were some very critical things that had to be said in the Lake Superior pollution case, and in the big pharmaceutical case, and in the continuing struggle to preserve some of the public treasure against the urgencies of profit.

Lord has said them wearing the black robes of an accusatory justice.

All right, sometimes he has said them improperly and a lot of times he has said them intemperately.

And he may have deserved some of the rebukes from his overseers, but today he has by and large made his peace with them, and the republic is still intact.

There are some issues involving the anonymous little guy's battles against the legal–corporate cartel that were just too big to ignore, he argued, and just too delicious for a judge who can't avoid a good brawl.

I telephoned congratulations.

His Grace is in the aftermath of a prolonged family reunion that brought 350 Lords in various forms to Minnesota.

"The one guy in the family tree I have the most trouble explaining," he said, "is this one who thought it was awful for the colonists to do what they did to King George. The guy was over here at the time of the Revolution. So he migrated to Canada. He was some kind of Whig or Royalist. At least that's what they called them at the time. Actually, what he was was a Republican. And it's something you just have to live with."

Whereupon the best federal trial judge in America finished cleaning a mess of bass in the basement.

The Silence of a Forest
Pays Tribute to Sig Olson
JANUARY 14, 1982

A FEW HOURS before he died, Sigurd Olson teased a friend whose sociable chatter on the telephone was keeping him indoors. "I want to get out in the snow on these new snowshoes the kids got for me," he said. "Elizabeth [his wife of 60 years] is all bundled up ready to go."

The old man and his lady strolled the evergreen forest behind their home in Ely, romping and trudging in the snow as they had hundreds of times, feeling the sting of the northern winter but clothed in the easy intimacy of one more day in the woods together.

Not far from his house Sig Olson, 82, collapsed of a heart attack. He died shortly afterward in a hospital in Ely. Funeral arrangements are pending at Kerntz Funeral Home in Ely.

The silence of the forest was a requiem for a man who for more than half a century poured his eloquence, nerve, and endurance into the struggle to preserve the earth's dwindling wilderness.

He was the flint and the soul of the conservation movement in America, both warrior and missionary. He was revered by millions who read his works and were lifted by the sensations they evoked of humanity united with the earth and nurtured—if for only a few hours out of the year—by its mystery and sublimity. And they were aroused by his summons to save that fragile treasure.

But he was denounced by thousands of others, some of them townspeople with whom he had lived for decades. To many of these he was an elitist, a pine-needle apostle with selfish notions about keeping the lakes and woods of the Boundary Waters canoe country for a few loon-watchers and ski freaks.

He understood their suspicions and even their contempt. For

113

them the north woods was not a museum or a retreat. It was the place where they lived, fished, hunted, and played. It was also a place where some of them profited from the loveliness and bounty of the woods and water, as he himself had years before as a guide and outfitter.

But there was enough for all, he insisted. There were thousands of lakes where motorboats could run, accessible by roads, millions of acres where people could frolic on their snow machines.

But there was no other canoe country quite like the Boundary Waters left on earth. It was not an absolute wilderness, but it was one of those rare places in the world where people could come and feel once more in their marrow the currents of physical and spiritual renewal with the nature that gave them life.

"Deep down in his subconscious," Sig Olson wrote, "a part of [man's] pool of racial memories is an abiding sense of oneness with life he cannot deny. Within him is a hunger and craving for wildness and nature, which he cannot quite understand. He must feel the ground under his feet, use muscles as they were meant to be used, know the warmth and light of wood fires in primitive shelters away from storms. He must feel old rhythms, the cyclic change of seasons, see the miracles of growth, and sense the issues of life and death. He is, in spite of himself, still a creature of forests and open meadows, of rivers, lakes and seashores. He needs to look at sunsets and sunrises and the coming of a full moon. Although he is conquering space and producing life, ancient needs and longings are still part of him, and in his urbanized civilization he still listens to the song of the wilderness."

This, he said, was the gift of the hidden forest. He experienced it for the first time as a young man, the son of a Chicago minister, canoeing the waterways of northern Wisconsin, the arrowhead country of Minnesota, and Canada. He became a biologist, later the dean of the community college in Ely, then a full-time advocate and lobbyist for the wilderness ethic, and finally author-statesman of the conservation movement.

He was no wooly visionary. He looked at the wildwood both with the naturalist's precision and curiosity for detail and with the poet's lyricism. They were combined values that gave his writing an unassailable conviction. He belonged with Thoreau and John Muir in bringing to masses of people the power and the marvel of the natural world. And perhaps more than any, he lighted the fires of yearning of people who wanted to feel the calm exhilaration he did, and dramatized its vulnerability.

His thesis was straightforward: People who want to develop the wilderness, to log it or mine it or mechanize its waters, have no trouble forging some urgency with their arguments. It's good for the economy, it creates jobs, it's in the national interest, or it's somebody's right.

Somebody always has a justification for his profit or for his convenience. But if those arguments had prevailed in the 1920s, the dam builders would have devasted the Boundary Waters; in the 1930s, the road builders would have opened it to honky-tonks. Olson and his allies in the environmental movement fought off those, and the airplanes in the 1940s. Their antagonists were resort operators and thousands of northern Minnesota residents who saw them as arrogant patricians who were enlisting the government to create a private Shangri-La.

The battle reached a new peak of acrimony in the late 1970s before Congress passed legislation that will have the effect of protecting 75 percent of the total lake surface in the Boundary Waters from motorization.

His critics hanged Sig Olson in effigy again during one of the hearings in Ely, just three years after the community had given him a testimonial dinner honoring his lifetime as a voice for conservation and a man of international acclaim.

He never looked on them as villainous people. They had their own particular fight, as he did. He resisted personality battles or attitudes of martyrdom. He was poetic but he wasn't naive. He had the politician's savvy in dealing with struggle, and he knew that name-calling and recrimination didn't win many wars. Moreover, it wasn't his style. Although he never temporized about the wilderness, he wasn't a brawler. His language was thoughtful and restrained and he made a striking appearance with his silver hair and tanned good looks.

He was as comfortable in the classroom as he was in the hearing room in Washington, but the places that defined his life and his cause were his cabin in the woods near a place he called Listening Point, and the little shack where he produced an extraordinary literature that told of walks among the birches, vigils beside a backwater stream, reveries on the trail. He was absorbed by the chemistry of man-and-nature, that idea that we carry in our blood and our genes the awe and dependencies that evolved from primitive man when there was *only* wilderness. He wrote about it in *Listening Point, The Singing Wilderness, The Lonely Land, Open Horizons*, and *Hidden Forest*. He talked about our interdependencies, our need for simplicity and a time for wonder, now more than ever with the world spinning faster and sounding its tumult.

"Through a vein of rose quartz at its tip can be read the geological history of the planet," he wrote, "from an old pine stump the ecological succession of the plant kingdom, from an Indian legend the story of the dreams of all mankind."

If there was any part of him that was a dreamer, it was the part that believed the miracle of these discoveries should be available to all. And they could be available only if there was still something we call the wilderness, a place of repose and personal restoration, whether in the Boundary Waters of northern Minnesota or the mountain sweeps of the Wind Rivers in Wyoming.

He underwent a cancer operation three years ago and, although he experienced facial tics and a gradual physical decline in later years, he was still strong enough to snowshoe on a winter's day the last year of his life. He lived to see himself become an international celebrity, to have schools named after him and magazines dedicated to him. He appreciated, but he was never overwhelmed. When Sig Olson got the impression that he was something really significant, a friend said, he would hike to his Listening Point and look into the waters and listen to the insects and hear the sounds of the forest. And then he knew again what and who he was.

But he *was* significant to millions, and in a way that will give his idea and his ethic a special kind of immortality.

The Ely Steam Bath Could Be Minnesota's Niagara

JUNE 13, 1983

NIMBLE MINDS IN St. Paul are calculating ways to spend $6 million to bring vacationing safaris in touch with the thrills of life in Minnesota.

Rough drafts are beginning to surface cataloging the state's splendors for gawking visitors. These range from the outpatient and records departments at the Mayo Clinic — a walking tour for hospital comptrollers who want to unwind temperately — to standing broad jump contests and life vests for athletic tourists who want to leap across the Mississippi at its source.

Nowhere have I seen the name of the Ely Steam Bath on any list of powerful lures to put vacation gold in Minnesota. The oversight should be corrected. Properly promoted, the Ely Steam Bath could compete with the glamorous spas of Bavaria and the south of France, a resource to which clamoring pilgrims would throng, electrified by the thin filament of hope that there may be a Fountain of Youth after all.

Let me give it to you straight. There are no elixirs in the Ely Steam Bath on the Iron Range. You are not going to breathe eucalyptus fumes and imagine yourself walking young and innocent through an Arcadian rainforest. What you get for $2 in the Ely Steam Bath is what you see and feel.

I'm talking steam.

This is not Minneapolis Athletic Club steam or Decathlon Club steam, where whorls of warm and sociable fog envelop the squatter like toothless cheesecloth. This is steam with a direct lineal tie to the Bessemer open-hearth blast furnaces.

If you want your pores opened and your systems decently

cleansed, take steam in the clubs in Minneapolis. It is a nice, tran-
quilizing interlude that does not force you to notify next of kin.
You can walk out into the lobby 15 minutes later, unassisted and
coherent. But if you want to get your systems reamed, synthesized,
and hung out for recycling, head north.

Arrange in advance for relatives or male nurses to hold you erect
when you make your reentry into fresh air. The shock can produce
effects best understood by deep-sea divers who don't make it to the
decompression tank. But once this barrier is safely crossed, marvelous sensations are available to people who have experienced the
Ely Steam Bath.

If I wanted to induce tourists to stampede northern Minnesota,
I would offer the service of Sailor Maki as the head guide and all-
around swami of the Ely Steam Bath's Fountain of Youth. Sailor
is somewhere around 60 now. In World War II he served on a
minesweeper, fighting the Japanese and anybody else who was in
the mood. Years ago his midriff was hard as armor plate, but he is
retired from his little business in Ely now and the Sailor spends a
lot more time in the galley than the engine room. But he still looks
a little roguish in his Melvyn Douglas mustache, and he has lost
none of his absorption capacity or exuberance for steam.

The Ely Steam Bath is no cocktail-hour sauna cut out from *Better
Homes and Gardens*. This is a guts-and-eyeballs steamroom. The
building is a 60-year-old battlewagon with bruised and cracked tile
for a floor and old tile terraces for sitting shelves, fronted by a
chamber of hot rocks with a water pipe hanging over them.

When the rest of our companions left Saturday afternoon, Sailor
plopped himself under the valve controlling the water pipe 15 feet
away. This was the classic reunion of the local old lion with returning native. The unwritten rules required them to measure each
other without letting on. Good manners are important to the steam
bath aficionado. Feelings should be spared, but not at the expense
of an end-to-end purging of the systems.

"Got a wedding party coming up tonight," he said. "I want to get
good and cleaned out so I feel fresh and ready."

The Sailor valved 20 seconds of water onto the scalded rocks.
Great white surfs of defoliating steam charged across the room. For

awhile the Sailor was invisible. I thought I handled it moderately well, holding down the gagging sounds so they were almost inaudible.

Sailor Maki now swung generously into a monologue about his last shore leave in Hawaii, interrupting every five mintues or so to pipe more water into the cauldron. The technique for the bystander here is to keep scrunching lower and lower into the rubber pail of cold water that customers bring into the steam bath to avoid ignition.

I go back to the Ely Steam Bath at least twice a year, which means Sailor wasn't getting any greenhorn. To prove it I took along two water pails, one for each leg. With his shore leave finished, Sailor confided for 10 minutes how he was being grossly overworked by his wife, risking physical breakdown every time he left the kitchen. By the time he switched to the senior golf tournament, we had shared 25 minutes of steam heat. For something comparable, imagine sitting on the cone of Old Faithful for three eruptions.

We left the room together, but Sailor was still babbling about the wedding party. I was closer to the solid ingot stage. Still, that receded. And when I walked into the late afternoon air, amazing things were taking place in my body. I experienced a kind of floating good will toward the world. Buildings look leapable. People said I looked young. A can of diet pop crunched in my hand, which was unusual because it was unopened.

If you need any more convincing, bear in mind the proprietor, Rick Ahola, hasn't changed his prices for 10 years. So here is a Fountain of Youth that defies inflation. I'm saying this should bring more tourists than 20 eelpout contests.

Consider the Benefits of Lousy Weather

NOVEMBER 24, 1983

SIXTEEN RADIO ANNOUNCERS advised me not to drive north Wednesday and nine said if I drove south I faced doom or disappearance for up to six weeks. Several varieties of oblivion were predicted to the east and west. One meteorologist warned that if grandma lived over the river or any farther than Columbia Heights, she should be left to the canned peas and soap operas on Thanksgiving Day. Another told how to use a subsurface breathing pipe in the probable event that 5,000 tons of snow avalanched from the IDS.

I speak with no irritation. Snowstorms are to radio stations what grocery ads are to newspapers. They are a perfect welding of the profit motive and our organic needs. We are conditioned to check the food pages to maintain our carbohydrate levels without going bankrupt. We are conditioned to listen to the weather to learn how miserable we ought to feel, which is an indispensable part of the information age. Knowing this, historians now wonder how Father Hennepin ever made it to St. Anthony Falls without a radar report from Winona.

But I appeal now for justice. The snow isn't that bad and deserves more than mass hibernation and panic. I believe there is credible evidence to show that snowstorms actually insulate Minnesota from general depression, emotionally and financially. Please consider these redeeming gifts of a foot of blowing snow:

• Lousy weather boosts employment in Minnesota.

The first snow brings immediate admonitions from teams of announcers to everyone within earshot, warning us to stay home if we want to avoid hypothermia, pneumonia, and vapor lock. Because we are an instinctively compliant people, almost all citizens accept this advice and stay indoors until April. Huge stores of junk food and pop are consumed. The retail economy booms. Because of the nutritional imbalance, digestive disorders plague families and the hospitals recover from their slump.

Consider also the virtues of street salt. Street salt follows a snowstorm as gangrene follows an open wound. This can be a hidden benefit. Street salt means green slush, and green slush means ruined footwear. This, in turn, produces a run on the shoe counters and averts Chapter 11 in stores all over town. Employment is further fueled by frictions that ignite when people are cooped up for months at a time. Fierce domestic troubles develop, and hundreds of psychologists are kept off the welfare rolls.

• Easy martyrdom is assured.

It takes the Catholic Church hundreds of years to verify the martyrdom of some of its saints. The first blowing snow of the season does it for thousands of Minnesotans overnight. Trying to understand the city's snow emergency regulations is a quick road to martyrdom. Another one is trying to rescue your impounded car when nobody less than an atomic scientist could figure out the emergency numbers. Getting two estimates for your maimed grille and front bumper is another. Also, if you do not become an instant martyr trying to avoid jail by feeding a meter buried under six feet of snow, there is no hope for you and you probably deserve hell.

• Snowstorms are a boon to lovemaking.

This is verifiable. A university psychiatrist long ago conducted tests demonstrating that snow shoveling, moderately performed, stimulates people erotically. This later was updated to include first broomball playing, then cross-country skiing (blue wax only), and now ice fishing. That is correct. I received a call yesterday from a Chris, a woman who is native to California and arrived here three years ago only because her husband is rich and has to work in Minnesota to stay in that condition. The second reason they live in Minnesota, she said, is her husband's unflinching mania for ice fishing. She calls Minnesota winter the pits, but tells me her love life has never been better. The moral is, ladies, if you want a productive sex life buy your husband an ice auger, a broom, and a snow shovel, and burn your tickets to Cancun.

• Never knock green slush (2).

There is an unappreciated spin-off from the arrival of green slush after each snowstorm. The salt, as you know, is sifted into the snowpack to speed the melting process. Its effects on pants cuffs and overcoats are ghastly. They provoke hundreds of thousands of dollars worth of cleaning repairs, but they do spare thousands of dry cleaning attendants from the caves of loneliness. I think this may be the highest benefit of all. Ministering to mobs of slush victims gives dry cleaning attendants a kind of missionary aura that lifts them above the tedium of exploring for ketchup stains. It also relieves them from the one universal syndrome that afflicts the rest of us in winter: Guessing when the dome is going to come down.

By the way, what day do *you* have in the pool?

The Economy Rates for Six Geese A-laying

DECEMBER 11, 1983

I HAVE A message of hope today for all despairing true loves who had resigned themselves never to get the fully wrapped, end-to-end harvest of the 12 Days of Christmas, starting with the partridge in a pear tree.

After two days of rough-and-tumble negotiations, during which I bargained ruthlessly with the Como Park Zoo (three French hens and six laying geese), the musicians union, and a half dozen other agencies, I can offer you: The Affordable 12 Days of Christmas.

It is a triumph for restraint in holiday shopping and it should stir pride in the new financial conservatism in Minnesota, because I have carved more than $7,000 off the costs being thrown about by a professor from that hatchery of reckless extravagance to the east, Wisconsin. You can now get the complete package, including a live Parker pear tree, for $2,445.25.

I want you to be impressed.

That price is so low it may be ready for Target and K-Mart. Let me give you some perspective. Since moderns first starting putting a price tag on the haul promised by the energetic suitor in the old English ballad, the numbers have scared everybody but Howard Hughes and Curt Carlson.

Here's Professor John Skinner of the University of Wisconsin, for example, with his latest quotation of $10,314.92, a figure that could be loved only by the head buyer at the Pentagon. To arrive there, the professor doled out several thousand dollars to put 12 guys named Lord through a six-month gynmastic course so he could deliver 12 lords a-leaping.

I have pared that item down to skin and loose hair, and for this you can thank that last dispenser of jackpine justice, the Honorable Miles Lord, judge of the federal court. I called His Eminence, asking him what he would now charge to produce 12 Lords a-leaping. These would be drawn from his immediate relatives, and in-laws if the family tree started to thin out. Reasonable transportation expenses would be allowed, I said.

"You can write off the transportation costs," the judge replied frugally. "There's Maxine and myself, four kids, all in the Twin Cities, my brother and his family in Prescott, Wisconsin, and a couple of dangling in-laws. Put them all in our dining room, tell Maxine to yell that the food is ready, and you'll have 12 Lords leaping. If I check the grocery ads I can hold that down to $80."

No gymnastic Lords with their thousand-dollar somersaults need apply. This is white-sale stuff, beginning with the partridge.

"I don't want any high-pedigree, raised-in-France partridges," I told John Fletcher of the Como Zoo. "We're talking love here, so it has to be tasteful, but be reasonable or I'll go up to the St. Cloud zoo."

"You can get a passable chukker partridge for 15 bucks," Fletcher said. "From our suppliers I think I could get you a pair of turtle doves for $30 and three French hens for $35. I never heard of a calling bird."

Actually, it's a colly bird. Blackbirds, when you come right down to it. Four colly birds.

"You could hold it down to $5 apiece, $20. A fair price for a laying goose would be $7.50, which comes to $45 for six. Seven swans a-swimming are going to bury you. Swans are expensive. Your only shot at economy is to give the true love some cygnets. Young ones. She ought to like those. She can watch them mature day by day to their full plumage."

I told Fletcher he could ring me up right now and we would go with the cygnets.

"That ought to be around $125 apiece or $875. But we don't have any gold rings around here."

LaBelle's discount house, however, did have five gold rings.

Can we be confidential? I do understand you want the intimate best for true loves. The tremors of romance always set my eyes fluttering. But Goodman's and the others are peddling barrels of carats. Those are the ones on the commercials showing geysers of passion and adoration leaping into the eyes of women who get their rings by firelight.

All you basically need, though, is five gold rings. LaBelle's in Richfield said we could have five 3-millimeter wedding bands for $29.90 apiece. You don't have to be a hot dog about rings, do you? I told the lady that 3-millimeter gold were completely acceptable, and so was the total bill for $149.50.

Plus tax, she said.

All right, all right.

Bongards Creamery offered eight maids a-milking for $7 an hour or $56, which I have to admit I recorded in the ledger. I then got a call from Bob Moran of the Dairy Workers union. He said that figured because Bongards is not unionized and his people would get $14.05 an hour for milking, plus big insurance and other benefits.

I listened to both of these figures noncommittally and promised to offer optional maids a-milking when the suitor got to the eighth day. Nine drummers drumming and 10 pipers piping, however, presented anguish.

There was danger of budget slippage here. Good musicians don't come cheap, and I wasn't going to put any teenie-weenie band in front of this true love. The agent at the Twin Cities musicians union agreed to give me the rock-bottom rate. "For two hours of Class B jobbing with first-class musicians you'll have to pay $36 an hour, plus the standard 25 percent of that for the leader. I'm saying $855 for two hours of drumming and bagpiping."

If the true love's ears held out, it sounded fair. Since we already had the leaping Lords nailed down, this left 11 ladies dancing still unaccounted for.

Dean Constantine, the Greek P. T. Barnum, hounded me all afternoon. "I can give you the greatest ballroom dancers," he said, "doing the most exotic dances for one hour for $100 apiece." I told

Constantine it was $25 apiece for an hour's worth of polkas or I would go to Arthur Murray.

He folded. When you include the Parker pear tree from Dundee Garden Center, we have a package for just under $2,500. If I were a true love, there is no way I would want to escape to Wisconsin.

What This Place Needs
Is Some Marketable Stress

APRIL 3, 1984

WE'RE GOING TO have to do something drastic to make Minnesota more competitive with the stress leaders of America. Figures announced last weekend showed Minnesota ranked 43rd in the nation in the amount and quality of its stress. That means life in Minnesota is more orderly and civil than almost any other place, judged by such indicators as a stable population plus the low percentage of school dropouts, illegitimate births, divorces, and labor strikes.

This is bad. It is a major hurdle to overcome in the current campaign to make Minnesota behave like everybody else. Ordinarily you might vent a cheer and orgnaize a small neighborhood snake dance on news that Minnesota ranks so far down the list in the amount of tension in the citizens' life.

That is an obsolete attitude. Admiring the conditions of life in Minnesota means you are a potential subversive and an outcast from the mainstream, because the doctrine today is to feel lousy about Minnesota. This is because the business climate in Minnesota is so vile and benighted only escapees from Chinese-cookie factories and ice-auger salesmen should consider coming to Minnesota.

The real role models for Minnesota today are the Nevadas, the Georgias, and the Mississippis. This is because Nevada, which ranks number 1 in stress, also leads the country in gambling, and we already have embarked on a gallant effort to catch up. Mississippi has been ranked 50th in so many categories over the years it has almost retired the jersey. Still, it is a place where taxes are relatively low, so it is always compared favorably with Minnesota. As a stressful place to live in, moreover, it is right up there among the heavy hitters in eighth place.

The message is obvious: We need to promote big league stress. To get it, we have to develop strategies. I think serious consideration should be given to these:

1. Deport all Minnesota Scandinavians to the Nevada desert.

This is a hard price to pay for moving up on the stress ladder, and it would sadden me terribly because of the many friends and loved ones I have who are Scandinavian or almost pass as Scandinavian. I should explain why it is a creative solution to the problem of engineering more tension. The historic Scandinavian calm and wisdom has contributed immensely to orderliness and the absence of top-of-the-line social stress in Minnesota.

This used to be viewed as one of the great windfalls of living here. But the technologues have now convinced us those old chestnuts about stability and social responsibility go hand-in-hand with bad business climates. What Minnesota needs, therefore, is dynamism and constructive turmoil.

Good-bye, Swedes.

It's going to be a culture shock out there in the dunes. I would approach it positively. Retraining is available and blue wax is rarely needed. The Lava Beds of northwestern Nevada, flanking the Black Rock Desert, offer excellent settlement opportunities. Norwegians, always careful to maintain their own marvelous identity, might consider the area called Alkali Flat, just southwest of the Earthquake Fault Area. By instinct, most Norwegians are alien to stress. I guarantee they will acquire it living southwest of Earthquake Fault. It is one way to integrate with the local customs quickly.

2. More guns for the Twin Cities.

A movement is under way in the legislature to force the Twin Cities to come under the same gun legislation now in force elsewhere in the state. Although many law enforcement officers oppose it and maintain that even the marginally stronger gun laws that exist in the Twin Cities have helped reduce crime, they are being told that uniformity is important. This may not make the communities safer, but it is almost certain to cause a little more stress. This will help give us momentum in pursuit of Nevada.

3. Encourage the immigration of gamblers to Minnesota.

This strategy meets one of the main criteria in the successful pursuit of stress. Stress usually flourishes when a lot of new people come into a territory. They have to learn the habits and laws of the natives. The importation of horse-racing experts into Minnesota is a start. Next year we will bring in experts to teach us how to play lottery. Results may be disappointing at first. But when the delegation from Santa Anita gets its first exposure to a November blizzard, that is stress. If the hospitals and courts can handle it, we may finally be on our way to the Super Bowl of stress.

He Was Hammy, Gutsy, and a Pain—
and Often Right

MAY 21, 1985

Two of the town's legal dynamos were locked in the usual pretrial impasse in a civil case over exorbitant amounts of money their clients were demanding from each other.

Both got a telephone call to attend a court-arranged meeting in a downtown hotel. A short time after they sat down, somebody knocked on the door. It was the bell captain bearing a six-pack of beer. With it came a message: The door was going to be locked. They could make the beer last as long as they wanted, but the door wouldn't be unlocked until they reached a settlement.

The beer and the ultimatum both arrived with the compliments of the Honorable Miles Lord, judge of U.S. District Court.

According to the account, they settled.

Nobody has denied the account.

Miles's resignation is being viewed by some of his friends as an act of kindness to his family, which is certainly one of his intents. What it is at bottom, though, is an act of charity to the physicians who are charged with controlling the ulcers of all the appeals judges who have tried to cope with His Eminence the past 20 years.

To his more sedate superiors, the judge has been a handful and a pain in their robed posteriors. His sins as a federal judge have been impressive. He has been noisy, prosecutorial, self-serving, and morally right—in a way that has continually rattled the ancient timbers of federal court tradition.

The stylists will forgive me for not referring to the judge by his last name. Almost no one who deals with him, whether captivated or offended by him, calls him anything but Miles.

It's something more than simple familiarity with a public figure.

It means the judge's saucy personality and courtroom style have made him so inimitable that he has become part of the social landscape. For better or worse, and sometimes both, he has become an irreplaceable resource.

I say "worse" only because of the havoc the judge has spread with such relish on the historic role of the court in our society. For good and cogent reasons, judges shouldn't be combative and partisan and use the bench as a stage for personal vendettas and social monologues.

This one has. The fact that he has and can still leave the federal bench under his own propulsion says much for his durability, his friends, and his luck. It also says much for the system's safeguards against easy removal of a federal judge.

But it speaks even more forcefully about the focus Miles Lord put on human and social issues that came before his court (or that he maneuvered into his court) and on the economic powerhouses he assaulted. He had the right handle on most of them or he would have been flattened before now.

He's leaving mostly because his family understands even more clearly than the judge that the political times have outrun his kind of boisterous populism and humanism on the federal bench.

Circuit court judges in St. Louis have been hearing charges again, brought by conservative lawyers who insist that his courtroom and public oratory have brought discredit to the federal bench. There's no telling who inspired these latest charges. But considering the range of the judge's conservative critics in and out of the federal court system, it's fascinating to speculate.

Because Miles has always been hammy as well as gutsy, he couldn't resist an appearance on TV's "60 Minutes," and in it he did some silly posturing about other judges and arrogant corporations.

He was probably accurate, but his technique was lousy. So if this latest inquisition didn't nail him, another one would. Miles might have reformed temporarily and adopted the garments of straight-arrow solemnity. But he couldn't be Miles Lord and spend much time in any courtroom without dropping that hopeless masquerade.

I think society is better today because he so elected himself. His rulings and his courtroom speeches indicted economic Goliaths whose power and respectability allowed them to injure, kill, or defraud innocent people in the interest of profit.

He acted to preserve wilderness and clean air from exploiters. He did it imperfectly, and he didn't exactly shrink from taking a bow here and there. But he spoke with nerve and necessity, and he was a good and memorable judge for that.

Dave Moore Recedes, in Style

FEBRUARY 16, 1985

ONE OF THE not-so-subtle hazards that a public person like Dave Moore faces in making a major change in life — one that will make him less a part of ours — is the temptation of his audiences to start talking about him in the past tense.

It may give him a slippery feeling. He is 60, healthy, and lucid, a good condition for any television anchorman to be in. Nobody with those credentials deserves an obituary. Giving up the 10 p.m. news doesn't mean he is ready for chimes and it doesn't mean he's retiring. But it does mean he is receding, which in turn causes a sense of loss approaching actual grief among thousands who have given him their trust and friendship without having met him.

It is the rarest kind of honor for a person in the communications craft. As a viewer I join in extending the same trust and loyalty; and as a colleague and acquaintance of Dave Moore I have seen nothing in his words and actions privately that would make me feel differently.

Television anchors are not typical people. Their faces and personalities become familial. Yet while their audiences reach into the millions, the very nature of their vehicle, the sound camera, gives them a face-to-face intimacy with each one of those millions. Television is now such an overwhelming component in our lives that people like Moore — some of them deservedly and some not — come to us in the mixed garments of town crier, counselor, and superstar.

But the popularity of this particular town crier has bridged three decades and even more generations. This should be more than gratifying for people who like Dave Moore. It should be instructive. Being a superachiever, even in the most competitive arenas,

133

doesn't demand a nonstop commitment to the arts of jungle warfare.

Moore is so far removed from that element that I don't think he could realistically umpire a kids' softball game. Each time he called a kid out at the plate he would have to interrupt the game for a five-minute monologue explaining the possibility that he might be wrong. Unaccustomed to such relentless humility, the kids would mutiny after five innings, leaving Moore to call in the meterologist and retreat in dismay.

That is a side of his personality that obviously cannot announce itself on every newscast, because the anchor should be authoritative. How? Well, start with grasp of the news. From there, sureness of delivery, and then a presence that bespeaks professionalism without treading too far into detachment. He or she should be comfortable and entertaining, depending on the rhythm and content of the show. The irreducible bottom line is credibility.

Pause to grade Dave Moore in those categories.

The scores you give him explain why he has been anchoring the channel 4 10 p.m. news since 1957. But there was another moment a few days ago that explains it just as convincingly. The station proposed that now might be the best time to bow out of his night show. He reacted by saying that he had been thinking about it himself, but that he just didn't know how. It was a moment without pretension or wounded dignity.

Nobody could thrust himself into the living rooms of hundreds of thousands without nurturing an ego or without courting approval. But when Dave Moore gives you the impression that he is always startled to find himself the object of veneration, it is not really an act. And I think it is that quality, as much as his easy professionalism and his mugging reactions to the godawful weather forecast, that have buoyed him against the sometimes zany trendiness of his business. His other sustenance was the mature management of his station. It's a management able to look at the lengthening lines on the faces of its older employees with something more civilized than the horror that grips most TV managers when confronted with age.

Someplace in one of the golden-rule books there's a maxim about people receiving from life about what they deserve, assuming fair opportunity. Much of that depends on the good will we invest in our daily lives. To make it you may also want talent and energy, but if we are talking about receiving contentment AS WELL as honor, the feel for people around you must come first. And so it has with Dave Moore.

The North Shore's Gnomes Give a Concert

FEBRUARY 1, 1986

I DON'T KNOW whether you realize that invisible gnomes inhabit part of the Lake Superior North Shore.

I believe I can document this.

Something tuneful and mischievous tinkled outside my cottage window on the North Shore in the darkness before sunrise a few days ago. Musicians might have called it counterpoint. A polar surf rumbled against the ledges beneath our lodge, and the quirky melody near the window floated above it like grace notes from the forest.

Wind chimes, I thought. They weren't. There was enough light to identify the "musician" — a cedar bush with enough wingspan to attract spray flung up by the water.

I will get to the gnomes. But first you should understand the spray. It had leaped from the crashing waves and taken refuge among the branches, icing them and creating a tiny symphony in the predawn breeze.

And was there a message for us in this woodsy concert? I think so. Midwinter in Minnesota ought to be more than four months of traffic jams in the city.

I should probably explain that a day on the North Shore in winter is not necessarily an escape. Two friends, sound technicians and photographers, asked to be introduced to the winter sea.

"It's not always a performance," I said. "Sometimes it just wallows and meditates." They said performances were not part of their ticket. They wanted to see water and ice, spray and snow, and they would not turn down a certain amount of loneliness, which they said they thought was a becoming attitude for a frosty sea.

136

This I guaranteed. Like the nervous custodian of a museum, I made the introductions with care and a few twitches of hope, which I didn't try to conceal very strenuously. I didn't want them disappointed. This is a part of the world I'd like more people to explore, especially in those cracks of time—a quiet morning of midwinter—that might appall the more rational among them.

But as the morning advanced, it occurred to me once more that sometimes the replenishment we need in the outdoors does not have to take the form of a withdrawal. A reunion is better. With who or what?

When I was a child on the Range one of my aunts drove me down the toboggan chute people identify as Highway 1. It was a spectacular ride through the rimed forest and misted streams, and it came out on a wild icescape on the North Shore, filled with boulders that looked like huge white muffins and stalactites hanging over the water. She said it looked like the dwarfs had probably been playing in the ice again, making things.

I never doubted it.

For a couple of hours the clouds buried the sun Thursday and we did our dutiful clambering on the ledges and ice, uncovering no special wonders. And then the sun erupted from the clouds and poured orange streamers on the open water from horizon to horizon.

We found a cove where the water had carved miniature caverns in the shore ice. You could lie on the ice and put your head into them, and let drops of water melting from the icicles fall on your cheek.

The glazed rock was almost blinding, and it radiated warmth into our bodies. Could anybody really wonder why the ancients worshipped the sun—or doubt that these phantasmal shapes and whimsical sounds were created by something besides the water and the weather.

Gnomes, I said.

Somebody grunted and said they didn't hear what I said. I thought once was enough. But if they asked, I would have explained what—maybe I should say who—was really making music in the cedars.

Our Potholes Demand Bravery and a Copilot
FEBRUARY 25, 1986

To UNDERSTAND WHY I'm urging you to ride with a copilot if you're going to drive Minnesota potholes this year, you should know something about bureaucratic stubbornness.

I've been arguing for years that highway departments should give the public a preview of the pothole season as a means of reducing the number of axle fractures and potential hernias among the quivering motorists. The football leagues do it, and so do the fashion houses. They don't do it for those stated objectives, I admit, but custom dictates that some reasonable foretaste of thrills that lie ahead is sound public practice in America today.

I have to report with regret that no highway department has leaped at the opportunity to score with the public by holding such an open house. I had in mind a kind of statistical seminar during which the highway gurus would give such information as the diameter and depth of the biggest pothole and the length of nylon rope needed to raise victims to the surface.

In the absence of this service, I test-drove a stretch of Highway 12 to Hawthorne Avenue in Minneapolis Monday. I'm going to give it to you with no frills or concessions to frail hearts. My advice is to get rid of the shovels and concrete blocks in your trunks and load up with winches and pulleys. I would also add a miner's lamp and avalanche beeper in case you go over the rim and have to reveal your position to rescue teams. I'm recommending one other safeguard for the 1986 pothole season, which you may consider revolutionary. But it may be all that stands between you and (a) a $3,000 garage bill or (b) disappearance into a bottomless chasm.

This year, do not brave Minnesota's potholes without a copilot.

It may be expensive or inconvenient or you may get sued by your Significant Other, but the times are grave enough to demand radical solutions. By chance, I drove a few miles yesterday with a freind, who noticed the peril before I did and immediately began shouting the positions of the oncoming caverns and coolly monitoring the adjacent traffic as he did.

"You've got a pothole at one o'clock low," he said. "Medium range. A realignment job sure, maybe a displaced muffler."

I started to tilt left. "No, no, too far," he yelled. "You've got a rusty Impala on your tail and he's starting to pass."

I cut across the northeast quadrant of the pothole and felt my automobile shudder and groan. White-knuckled, we rolled silently for a hundred feet, like submarine crewmen after the depth charges. "No audible clanks," he said. "I think you lucked out. But look out, there's another at 10 o'clock. A real ugly. It looks as big as the Sea of Tranquility on the moon. It'll chew you up. But you're free to pass."

We slipped by with flutters of released tension. That pothole might have been all she wrote. If I dipped a tire there, it would have been Sam Bloom's Iron and Metal yard for sure. Without a loyal and experienced spotter in the front seat, Sam Bloom would be giving me an estimate today. I say this because you cannot possibly ride solo through the pothole season without risking either a front-end job in the garage or a sprained neck from high-speed swiveling. There is also the chance of a dislocated pelvis. If you dodge the pothole, you face the possibility of being blindsided by a Chevy van. Sappers crawling through a mine field deal with less hazard.

I was congratulating myself on having double-teamed the potholes when my buddy hunched forward to dial the radio. At that moment I plowed into a crater on Hawthorne. It was so deep, the bottom might have been radioactive from meteor fragments. My buddy hammered his head on the dashboard, and the undercarriage sounded like a train wreck.

"A $300 deductible," he groaned, "at six o'clock."

The Smallest Tug on the Line:
The Business World

TV's Paul Revere of Positive Thinking

NOVEMBER 30, 1977

MY RAMBLES PRODDED me yesterday to Studio B of WTCN, channel 11, where I struggled for 10 minutes with the smiling octopus of local television, Mel Jass.

On the station worksheet it was formally classified as an interview, but that is a perversion of the language, a sly smoke screen intended to satisfy the FCC bureaucrats. Being interviewed by Jass is like standing in quicksand up to your nose. You can see what's going on but you are really powerless to do much about it, especially to talk.

You don't dialogue with Jass. You fight him off. He once asked me a question on my attitude toward gun control and consumed the last five minutes of the show telling me why I shouldn't answer.

Yesterday, he opened with a close-up of my new book and spent the next three minutes demanding to know why I don't trade anymore at Hansord Pontiac, which, he said, is one of the world's great auto dealerships, run by a dear friend of his, Rudy Luther. I congratulated Mel on this alliance and expressed confidence that both of them should be able to survive the partnership.

And yet I don't wish to give the impression that Mel burdens me. Just the contrary. I believe unswervingly that if we had television in the 1930s and Jass was selling seat covers to America, the Depression would never have happened. Or if it did, Jass would have found a way to make us feel inspired about it: Long lines at the soup kitchen were a declaration of America's commitment to wholesome food, shut-down factories meant 30 million people had time to reorder their priorities.

Jass is the Paul Revere of positive thinking. He is television's last living disciple of the old snake oil creed that any merchandise made by man can be sold if (a) the salesman's lungs are sound and (b) he can convince the customer the product is all that stands between him and instant bankruptcy, divorce, or awful disease.

I got to the station early, which allowed me a leisurely hike through the richly-carpeted and muraled corridors of this Taj Mahal of local TV architecture. It is an impression that always jolts me, because I don't associate WTCN with mystique and glamour. It prospers by peddling the generation-before-this. If the show was a smash in the 1950s and 1960s, it is thriving today on channel 11. Its clientele is so loyal to this kind of electronic regression and low-budget nostalgia that hundreds sank into despondency when WTCN discontinued Perry Mason after 10 years of reruns. The series expired not because it didn't have the audience but because the tape was shredded.

Jass, however, prevails over even Perry Mason, pro wrestlers, pancake-mixing chefs, and the rest of WTCN's varied menagerie. He is the preserved link with television's sunrise of creation, with fuzzy, lopsided pictures on the 10 o'clock news, Hawf and Hawf, Imogene Coco, Bill Ingram, and Milton Berle. He has outlasted Dale Carnegie himself, for whom he surely ghosted the 10 steps in influencing people, if not necessarily winning friends.

I'm sure Mel Jass has hundreds of friends, but I know for certain he has a lot more gasping viewers. I'm one. Each time I see Jass deliver a commercial I decide this is the one, the all-time indispensable product without which I just can't make my way or discover the keys to contentment.

Thus prepared, I opened the studio door where Mel was rehearsing a commercial. Jass advanced invincibly. He does not greet you; he surrounds you. "You have to see this," he said. "Absolutely the greatest. No product ever invented like it. They call it Lite Bite. Only 24 bucks. Do you fish?"

"Not much."

"God, I hate this negativism. Instead of 'not much,' say 'I'd like to do more.'"

"Okay. I'd like to fish more, but not much."

"Anyhow," Jass said, "I'm doing this for Burger Brothers.

Tremendous operation, Burger Brothers. I wish I could take you to each and every store, talk to all the people. People, that's where it is. Back to Lite Bite. What you do, you put your rod in this gadget, and even the smallest tug on the line activates this buzzer and light if you're doing something else and . . . "

By now Jass had motivated himself into a froth. He called the cameraman back and was going to run through it one more time. He buttoned his plaid suit coat, this one just two sizes too large, and told the cameraman, "Make me small and to the side. Okay?" The red light went on.

"The most marvelous fishing device you ever saw, people. One tug. Crappie or muskie. It doesn't matter. And instantly you get the light and sound."

The way Jass said it, it could have been patented by Moses.

Aimlessly Adrift on a Water Mattress

SEPTEMBER 13, 1979

THERE IS NO history in my family for heroics at sea. The archives from the old country speak randomly of Balkan warriors and forge tenders. There were two stonecutters, a tax collector (now unanimously disowned), and a crowd of hatmakers, which is the origin of the family name.

The record is bare, however, of one single reference to the nautical life. Nobody fished in the Adriatic. No ancient mariners or whale harpooners appear in the genealogy tables, not a single bilge pumper or poop-deck builder.

Partly for this reason I resisted strenuously when a furniture salesman insisted that as part of an environmental change I'm making this month, I should switch to a waterbed.

"The whole thrust of your personality is in that direction," he said. "You search for exotic horizons. One of the salesman's jobs is to try to match furniture with the inner person, to harmonize the styles and textures with the longings and disposition of the customer. The reason I'm recommending a waterbed to you is that I see you as a really explorative person, in the tradition of Balboa."

I considered this thesis thoughtfully, and replied: "All I want is a good night's sleep. I don't want to cross the Isthmus of Panama or rediscover the Pacific Ocean. I definitely don't want to take depth soundings of the Mindanao Trench."

He deflected these objections with an expression of sorrow.

"Some people go through life without ever experiencing the thrill and suspense of sudden change. Somehow I didn't place you in this category. Now if you insist, I can put you on a perfectly safe and stationary Sealy Posture-Pedic, which has tremendous reliabil-

146

ity but is short on, well, flotation. I think some people just deserve to float the night away. More to the point, they NEED to. What I'm telling you is that for a few extra dollars, and just a little bit of courage, you can spend your nights subconsciously luxuriating in the surf of Bali Bali."

I asked him what happens if the surf leaked into my pajamas.

"Impossible," he said. "With the early models several years ago I know people sometimes found themselves in embarrassing situations. I know of one furniture store that got sued by a young woman because her husband's necktie stickpin punctured the mattress and flooded them both."

"What was the guy doing wearing his necktie in bed?" I asked.

"It was their wedding night," the salesman shrugged. "Their lawyer argued that newlyweds face enough risks without having to battle tidal waves on their honeymoon. The store really didn't have a defense against that and settled out of court."

No such threat exists with the King Koil Ultra, he contended.

He maintained I could spend the night in splendid languor, free from any worry about seepage, sudden gushers, or actual drowning.

And so I am here to confess that I succumbed.

Within two days I will be adrift on a King Koil Ultra, and at the moment I am in a fury of preparation that can compare only with the apprentice seaman getting ready for two years before the mast.

Although the salesman scoffed at the idea, I have stocked up on Dramamine tablets, the over-the-counter brand popular among tourists heading to the Caribbean for a windjammer cruise. My memory of a neighbor who experimented with a waterbed in the mid-1960s is vivid. He missed three work days with a condition the doctors could diagnose as nothing more or less than severe sea sickness.

I have also spent time at the whale tank of the Minnesota Zoo, to get some idea of the principles of buoyancy as they apply to water creatures in their natural habitat. I then studied sea diver's manuals to familiarize myself with the most advanced methods of staving off the bends.

In these and other ways I've tried to condition myself for the

trials ahead. I then called the salesman and said my fears had re-
solved themselves to threat of:

1. Sloshing.
2. Sliding.
3. Sinking.

"Rest in peace," he said, language with an ominous quality that
I can only assume was accidental.

"By learning how to shift body weight and move with the current, you will quickly learn how to overcome the phenomenon of
sloshing. An intricate system of baffles in the mattress will elimi-
nate sliding. You can't possibly sink if you don't capsize, and we
will give you an absolute, one-year guarantee against that."

When I left the store he said bon voyage and told me he could
put me in a fine and inexpensive barometer, which no waterbed
owner should be without.

A Star Dies Out

APRIL 2, 1982

FROM THE DAY newspapers were invented, reporters have been making the rounds with the sunrise to find out whether anything burned down or blew up in town overnight.

It is part of the newspaper's mission as a town crier, calling on the wardens of our daily lives, the cops, fire departments, and hospitals. Like the old grocery store deliverymen taking orders, the reporters used to do it on a horse. But today they use word processors with television screens and telephones. And this morning, Paul McEnroe of the *Minneapolis Star* was performing these hoary duties a few desks down the aisle when he stopped in the middle of his last call on the last day of the *Star*.

"Migawd," he said, "I just realized who I'm talking to. The coroner."

Which more or less closed the book.

The death of any daily newspaper evokes scenes and moods that seem to have been cribbed wholesale from Italian opera. The dialogue is laced with remorse and touched with bitterness and strife, and there is one thing certain about the last-act agonies: they will be both inevitable and prolonged. This puts the expiring newspaper in the novel position of being able to conduct its own postmortems and obituaries, which it has been doing with so much zeal the past 10 days that it might have died from exhaustion if nothing else.

The process comes to a merciful end today.

I think if there are any ceremonial tears today — and why not? — they ought to be for something very precious that people who read newspapers may not have grasped yet with any real sense of regret.

The disappearance of the *Star* means they have lost a choice in the marketplace, and people who peddle ideas—and mousetraps or lawnmowers—have lost a forum. An option. And that, for whatever quality and soul the *Star* carries with it to the grave, is the most crucial loss of all.

The publishers obviously didn't choreograph it that way. They had a cash interest in maintaining two healthy newspapers, and the decision to turn their enterprise into a one-newspaper operation was something from which they shrank, dating back to the days when the antitrust beagles of the government were serious about monopoly journalism.

"What kind of choice?" the critic asked. "The same guys own both the *Star* and the *Tribune*. They took directions from the same memo tubes and lined up at the same pay windows."

You might argue that in its final years the *Star* rarely showed symptoms of taking directions from anybody. That is not far from being correct. In its final years, the *Star* was nomadic and sometimes boisterous, searching for an audience, hawking extravaganzas, trying to hard to be significant and fun and what was the word, indispensable?

Different, yes. Capable of some pretty rare and entertaining journalism, yes. But lonely, yes.

For reasons the sociologists and mathematicians have been giving us to the point where the average reader or viewer wants to scream "stop," the *Star* was condemned by the times, irrespective of what was in it or the personality it tried to recreate for itself. It might have encouraged the executioner, I will admit, in its well-intentioned flailings to survive.

If, like me, you do grieve over its disappearance, I don't think we can honestly give the *Star* one full-service identity we can carry with us to the wake. It was bumptious and breezy for a while, and then it was big and important and urgent, and after that it took on some magazined slickness, and for a while it was just plain alien.

For people who work in a city room, the best thing it did was to shelter the improbable creatures like Paul Presbrey, who was a sort of crew-cut leprechaun of Twin Cities journalism. Presbrey was the *Star*'s Joe Deadline. He actually talked and acted the way they did in the Monogram movies about newspapers back in the

1930s. Presbrey used to put live pigeons in his buddy's darkroom and dead goldfish in his development soup. He once took a picture of a woman trapped under a fallen chimney and left her somewhat injured under pounds of brick, explaining, "Sorry, lady, I've got an edition to make."

He worked for years with another photographer named Roy Swan, who captured immortality about the same time when he posed a gloomy spaniel in front of a burning building to conjure some pathos and then angrily lectured another photographer who asked to borrow the dog: "Go get your own goddamned dog."

There is no point in pretending that this is an honest-to-God funeral in the traditional newspaper sense of that. Most of us will come to you in a new but recognizable garments as employees of the *Minneapolis Star and Tribune*. But some of our people won't, and that is why there is a real mourning today at the *Star*. It is because a guy like Mike Bosc, for example, a perfectly good and resourceful newspaperman, wasn't here long enough and became a victim of the numbers. Yet he belonged to the *Star*, which means he was somebody who tried to give the day a little more meaning or lilt for you, no less than a Cedric Adams did for decades or a hunchbacked little copy reader named Bill Anderson did in obscurity.

The 10 days have been a horror, if you want the truth.

The gossip of the city room spills into the sidewalks and bars and then on television and into other newspapers, and the newspaper is burying itself and recreating itself without missing a cycle. Which means it's living soap opera as well as Italian opera, and everybody's turf seems vaguely strange or threatened. And all this time the audience—people who read the newspaper—had been looking at us with something closer to generous indifference than gloom.

Perhaps that is the dash of reality the opera needs.

We want to thank you.

We want to thank you for the times you read us and for the times you brought us into your house and even into your birdcages.

There isn't all that much glamour in this business, and a birdcage is OK for a symbol of the day if you need one. We want to thank you for sympathizing with our anguish of the past 10 days and to thank you for the hundreds of thousands of dollars you have given to people who have needed. For the occasional grins you have turned on our attempts to entertain, for the solemnity you have given to brave and sacrificing people whose lives have entered yours through our news columns.

One of the rewards of being newspapermen and women is the opportunity it gives us now and then to express what is in the heart and eyes of the reader.

If we have done that once in a while, we have deserved your loyalty and your trust—for which we thank you most of all.

Only *Reader's Digest* Would Edit Isaiah

SEPTEMBER 17, 1982

READER'S DIGEST HAS made a living for decades on the premise that no great work of art is beyond redemption if you put enough editors under one roof and give them enough shears.

This, it has decided, includes the Bible.

The electrifying news today is that salvation is now accessible through the pages of a stripped-for-action "*Reader's Digest* Bible," especially edited for today's speed-of-light tempos. The announcement comes to us in the form of a promotional packet being mailed to hundreds of thousands of salvageable souls on the RD mailing list.

What we are being offered is nothing less than divine consolation and uplift with 40 percent of the Bible's literary baggage removed. It's Inspiration Lite. Less filling. They may hire Boom Boom Geffrion to do the commercial.

Consider it. You can now have both testaments at 40 percent less reading time. You can theoretically get through creation in less time than it takes to do the crossword puzzles.

It is an offer to stretch the mind. The company does not equivocate about it. In the same breathless style in which it brings out a fresh condensation of *Mutiny on the Bounty*, the company gives us a tantalizing synopsis of what's ahead for the readers.

"Saints and sinners, heroes and heroines, the atmosphere of those wondrous times, the flavor of the language, the full range and inspiration as first put down—it's all here. Send for your home-trial copy and see for yourself. If the Bible were being written today, it would read like the *Reader's Digest* Bible."

The one who deserves some understanding in this is God. No

creative type likes to be told his stuff looks better when it's shrunk by 40 percent.

I grant there is some argument about what part of the current Bible was actually commissioned by God. I further grant that no sensible person will refuse to sympathize with mankind's continuing struggle to understand all of those begats and putteths. Without having read this latest God's Word From Pleasantville, you can assume it is a smooth and readable piece of distilling and updating of the language, and that it retains (as the promotional ads insist) the best features of the Bible's Revised Standard Version.

But the bystander has to twitch a little in fear of the collisions once we're launched into this new orbital speed of reverence. This is a consumer-oriented Bible indexed under the newest techniques. It is done the same way they would steer you around with directories in the produce department at Byerly's, or the way a video store advertises cassettes of the pro football titans. It is the kind of Bible you need, *Reader's Digest* tells us, when you don't want chapter and verse but do need solace and guidance in a hurry.

"Plus an index where you can look it up. Find your favorites fast. David and Goliath. Daniel in the lion's den. Joseph in Egypt. The parable of the widow's mite. The feeding of the five thousand." Maybe in the third printing it will be down to 3,000. Anything that relieves the reader's mind of congestion. The trouble here is that once you accept *Reader's Digest*'s editors as the latest accredited handlers of the message from heaven, the old rules are off. It means all editors could claim to be inspired, a notion that will instantly put spots on the skin of anybody who writes for a living.

If I accepted that principle, for example, it would mean putting my old editor on the *Star*, Lee Canning, in the role of a man capable of improving the work of Matthew, Mark, Luke, and John. That may be possible, but Canning didn't have the kind of disposition to do it. Canning is the kind of editor who would insist that if you were rewriting the Book of Revelation it should read like a domestic argument on Colfax Avenue involving six in-laws, three cops, and the family counselor. And hold it to three inches of type, or cut out some of the in-laws.

What I'm saying is that if *Reader's Digest* makes a haul on this one, all restraints will be off the next time. If you can sell a Bible with 40 percent of the content removed, and call that a service to man's atonement, there is nothing to prevent the company from revising it again for the teenage market.

The language would not only be liberated of all begats and putteths. It would be cleansed of all words of two syllables or more. Also the beat and the idiom would have to go. This means when we got to the part in Ezekiel where the prophet calls "and he said unto me, son of man, stand upon thy feet and I will speak unto thee," in the edited version for today's high school sophomores it would have to say: "And he goes to me, he goes, 'all right, you guys,' and I go . . . "

No other language would be acceptable.

There may be perils beyond that. A magazine capable of telling us in its promotion: *"Reader's Digest* has CONDENSED the Holy Bible; its spiritual message is now in sharper focus; its age-old stories are readable at last" is capable of believing it can perform miracles. In fact, *Reader's Digest* comes very close to making that claim in this promotion.

"Somewhere in your home there is a Bible," it informs us. "It may be the family Bible, old and cherished, black Moroccan leather crumbling with age. But the binding is still sturdy, the India-paper pages still crisp."

The message is clear. *Reader's Digest* has X-ray vision.

It also has a heart of granite. That is the accusation we are going to hear from Joshua when the RD version hits the shelves up there. RD proudly tells us it has chopped out whole lists of things that aren't relevant to salvation. Among these are Ezra's men of Israel who put away their foreign wives and Joshua's long list of kings defeated in battle.

I think Joshua has a beef. Even if he doesn't, once encouraged, there will be no stopping the condensation whizzes at *Reader's Digest.* How about the 3½ days it took to create the earth?

Can you live in the belly of a sea-going muskie?

Wall Street's Stampeding Bulls
Leave Him in the Dust
NOVEMBER 19, 1982

MY STOCK HAS resisted the 1982 stock market skyrocket like a ton of zinc riveted in rock.

Everybody's stock is halfway to Mars except mine. I have drawn this conclusion from weeks of observing the graphics of the market pages, showing the latest Dow Jones averages leaping off the page above a heroic dust storm created by stampeding bulls. I have also been listening to the daily caroling of the brokerage songbirds of Piper Jaffray & Hopwood on WCCO in the morning, telling me there is practically no limit to the amount of wealth I should be accumulating in this record-breaking market.

My stock has not budged in three months.

Let me strike that for the sake of literal honesty. My stock did move two weeks ago. On the day when the stock market broke the world's record for one day's trade, ostensibly making instant maharajahs out of 50,000 necktie salesmen and pharmacists across the country, my stock dropped three-quarters.

I tell you this not in despair or bitterness. I believe certain people should not expose themselves to the lures of riches daily thrust before us by the wizards of Wall Street. It has nothing to do with the investor's poker nerves, intelligence, or the phase of the moon. Some people by background send the wrong vibrations to Wall Street. I grew up in a part of the world where people we now call analysts and financial advisers were lumped into one bag of suspicion bearing the generic label of "bankers."

It followed that anybody who seriously tried to get you to make money investing in stocks also might cheat at pinochle and probably shortweight you at the sausage counter. Naturally I outgrew these suspicions. I now trust most financial advisers and analysts I know to give me an accurate count on their strokes out of a trap. I have allowed brokers to use my car, my ski poles, and my Tabasco sauce.

My money, however, belongs to another league.

Like most people who have read about the three little pigs, I worry about the hazards of ignoring security. My investments are usually conservative. I stuck with the banks and municipal bonds until the interest rate hit 20 percent, by which time I finally yielded to my broker's screams of agony and tried the money markets. It was such an intoxicating experience I let him talk me into putting $1,000 in this small but robust Minnesota company.

The date was sometime in the middle of 1981, in a period when Reaganomics was widely being described as the Moses of American industry. "Stocks aren't doing much right now," the broker said. "We're moving into this recession, which I think will be short-lived under the impetus of the new confidence coming from Washington. The tax cuts and declining interest rates and declining inflation will come together, and this country will be moving confidently into a new prosperity in 1982. Your stock will reflect that change."

My stock was listed at 9 when I bought it. Its first response to the news was to drop to 6½.

Eventually it returned to 9. It stood at 9 last August when the market performed its well-documented eruption. For four weeks I watched the markets in total absorption. I saw ITT, IBM, CPT, and practically every alphabet combination known to computers performing all kinds of laser shows on the graphs.

My stock was still sitting in the blocks.

"It will come," the broker said. "The stock market is very volatile and is being evaluated by the pros. I think it will hold its high ground and if it does, your stock will naturally follow. Give it a couple of months."

The broker here is a man of experience as well as tolerance toward the financially retarded. Because of the ethics of the trade we have to cloak him in anonymity, but he works out of one of those noisy little second-floor cages on Marquette Avenue, which is where I found him Thursday holding two telephones.

My stock Thursday registered 9.

"What we have here," he said, "is a case where your stock will move out as soon as the business recovery takes hold. The company is well-managed and sound. It makes a form of hardware that will begin to sell extremely well when the economic upsurge sets in. I admit the upsurge is tardy. What I ask from you is faith. Also, you might look hard at those oil stocks."

The squirms began about there. Truly skilled brokers leave me hypnotized, not unlike marriage counselors and doughnut-hole makers. Once I have overcome my hereditary uneasiness in the hands of brokers, I'm prepared to accept their dogma. So faith I could give him. A thousand for Amoco is something else.

"No, no, I don't just mean the big producers. I mean I can't understand why people are so hung up on this oil glut we're supposed to have. In a few months from now, when the economic upsurge hits, that glut is going to be burned off in a hurry. Companies whose entire mission in life is drilling holes in the ground, like Apache and those, well, they ought to be moving any day now. All you need for that is a little investment chutzpah. I'll tell you how I define *chutzpah*. If a kid tries to knock off his parents for the insurance, that's brute gall. If he then asks the court for mercy because he's an orphan, that's chutzpah."

I asked him again when this economic surge was going to engulf us so my stock could head for Mars.

"I'm a great believer in the economist Milton Friedman," he said. "He's the one who said the way to economic sanity in this country is to get out of all this federal involvement. He's the one who also predicted that before we could undo the economic vices of the last 30 years, we're going to have pain. That's his prediction. People are going to experience pain."

The things they pay economists $200,000 to predict.

I told my broker if Friedman needs a testimonial, he's got it.

The Hot Competition among Caring Morticians
MAY 19, 1983

FOR THE LAST few days I have been driving to work hypnotized by the sounds of combat between some of the most aggressive morticians in Minneapolis.

It is being waged head-to-head by your friendly interers from Washburn-McReavy and Sunset Memorial funeral chapels through the voices of WCCO-AM—the only ones in town that can sound sepulchral and optimistic in the same syllable.

I don't mind confessing that the competing commercials have put me in a quandary. One day I want to be buried by Washburn-McReavy and the next day by Sunset Memorial.

I realize you can't have it both ways.

The choice was tough enough earlier this week when within a few hours I heard (a) Howard Viken give his personal endorsement of Sunset Memorial, with an enthusiasm that suggested that Viken had already given the grounds a trial run and (b) Ray Christensen pitching Washburn-McReavy with even more gusto. Because the firm has recently undergone a merger, Christensen made Washburn-McReavy sound like the General Motors of the burial business.

You almost expected to hear Mr. Goodwrench offering a discount on a valve job.

But in the last few hours I have acquired Sunset Memorial's suggested material for studio ad libs, and my indecision is now hopeless.

I was about ready to throw in with Washburn-McReavy because I had Christensen's word for it, they had 126 years of experience in preparation and burial. I don't think you can underrate that claim. I mean, in this business, time is important. What Christensen was telling me between the lines was that if Washburn-McReavy had made any serious mistakes with their clients, we would have heard about it by now.

But here is Sunset Memorial telling me how much rapture and beauty are available to me through the simple act of croaking.

"You can feel the grandeur, the peace and solitude of 100 acres of gentle hills, dignified evergreens and oaks, and eight miles of roads that tie them together. The Chime Tower summons. The chapel inspires. You begin to sense that this is where you . . . could rest most peacefully."

Those numbers are correct. Eight miles of road without a pothole.

You will not only rest serenely but be visited by more mourners, because they will not run the risk of bent frames and broken shocks or the cost of front-end alignment.

In order that none of this potential bliss should be overlooked, Sunset tells its announcers: Relate the full range of services at Sunset: The mortuary, full internment services, the modern crematory, indoor mausoleum, garden mausoleum and memorial park, even a flower shop, as well as the impressive chime tower. Emphasize the newly refurbished chapel, with its stained glass windows and vaulted ceiling, so beautiful in fact that a wedding was recently conducted in it.

At Sunset, in short, you can have it either way. They can marry you or bury you.

That did it. Sunset helpfully reminds us that "one call will do it all." I was about to call a couple of days ago, advising Sunset, "Yes, by all means, your full service plan sounds great, sign me up either in perpetuity or on the lay-away plan." And then Christensen came back some time after 7 a.m. with an all-fronts offensive from Washburn-McReavy.

"This is Ray Christensen. Many people ARE interested in a dignified, sensible, economical alternative."

I'm sorry. I flubbed there. That's the commercial for the Cremation Society, which Christensen was airing a few weeks ago. It is another disposition service Ray sold in the familiar 'CCO institutional tone of controlled exuberance. He did it so well I was on the verge of switching from restful pines and vaulted windows.

Christensen has now moved to Washburn-McReavy, and this week he made dying a positive privilege if it can be serviced by the efficient gang at W-M.

"Washburn-McReavy knows that SERVICE is a very important ingredient in the funeral business, and it maintains that service by having the finest equipment and the finest facilities anywhere. Beyond that, though, the backbone of the business, any business, is the people in it. Washburn-McReavy has an experienced staff of 60 people and over 20 licensed funeral directors. They're available 24 hours a day."

I'm a nut on convenience. Round-the-clock service is very persuasive. Mulling the options, I called WCCO's Jon Quick to inquire why we are suddenly getting all of these hot-breathed inducements from the mortuaries.

"Hospitals are advertising," he said. "other people who never did it before. Facts are facts. It's a jungle out there."

Don't tell me that, Quick. Tell me about vaulted windows and dignified evergreens. Mostly, tell me about eight miles of connecting roads without a pothole.

That may be as close to heaven as I'm going to get.

The Doubtful Paradise Wrought by Credit Cards

NOVEMBER 6, 1984

THE SHOPPERS CHARGE MasterCard company has inflicted its gold card on me, with accompanying literature that promises me a Utopia here on the glacier, smelling like jasmine and hung with bonbons.

I don't believe it.

I don't want a gold MasterCard and I don't want the pumpkin orange one, either. For the past 30 years of my life I have been dodging the promoters of so-called major credit cards, whose producers have managed to convince most of the civilized world that Americans without credit cards are economic degenerates who may steal hubcaps to feed their travel agents.

Every time I leave home, I leave home without an American Express Card. I don't say that boastfully or defiantly. I say it in evidence. It is still possible to find a room in the inn or crackers in your soup without dragging out three pounds of plastic and a referral from Karl Malden.

The role of the credit card as an instrument of convenience for the customer and the innkeeper vanished long ago when American Express and BankAmerica decided that billions were to be made if you could turn their little plastic wafers into some kind of national identity card.

Never mind your passport or birth certificate or your Airedale's registration number. Show us your Visa card and you are instantly sanitized.

The highest goal of business is to become indispensable. A radio station tries to do it by convincing us we may die miserable and neglected if we don't listen to their 65 daily forecasts on the chance that one of them may blossom into a blizzard watch. The credit card vendors do it by pretending to turn plastic into cash and by giving nonholders the aura of escapees from the mumps ward.

People who treasure their Visas and MasterCards and regard those as proof of citizenship are no burden to me. I don't pay their fee. And if using them eventually costs you a piece of your fiscal hind end, you don't really miss that until the end of the month. But I do object to being forced to take the psychological version of the fingernail test by hotel clerks primed to call in bloodhounds and the FBI if you confess to not owning a major credit card.

The room for maneuver left to holdouts against the credit card scam is dwindling. You can't cash a check 10 miles out of town, and walking around with $400 in your right sock has limited appeal. The problem is we have gotten sucked so far into the Major Credit Card Only orthodoxy that we have forgotten there were times when people actually transacted business, actually traveled from Columbia Heights to Burnsville without being forced to show an American Express card at every roadblock.

American Express wrote the other day. It was a notification. It said I was being considered for a Cardmembership in the Gold Card Club. It made me sound like a candidate for the House of Lords. John C. Sutphen, American Express's senior vice president for marketing, broke the news in a six-page letter.

He described me in terms so rare and compelling they would have made an instant convert out of my mother. John Sutphen vowed that mere possession of The Gold Card would make an eloquent impression on those I met, which almost put it in the league with the Hope Diamond and Michael Jackson's laundry ticket. John Sutphen argued that I was one of those who appreciates, "indeed, has come to expect an extra measure of courtesy and personal attention."

I believe that would have convinced my mother, and it nearly convinced me until I got to page 6 and discovered that it was going to cost $50 and who knows what else for the privilege of making life a little more comfortable for the board of American Express.

I might be willing to soften a little if I hadn't watched a hundred scenes where the major credit cards had no more clout than your fortune-teller's phone number.

It took me back to the George Wallace campaign years ago. The security agent on Wallace's plane threw out every ID card I produced until he spotted the one card he found acceptable — a pass to Ringling Bros. and Barnum & Bailey Circus.

You Don't Have to Be Famous to Be Memorable:
Extraordinary Ordinary People

A Girl from the Land of Funny Bridges

MARCH 17, 1977

STEPHANIE DEAN IS one of those people who seem to have come from a world of enchanted frogs and funny little bridges.

She is a freckled sprite, small and saucy. When she laughs it is not a careful, temporizing laughter. It is a sunburst, instantly flinging anybody within range into orbit around Stephanie Dean. Strands of hair slip out of alignment and fall over her face in impatient discord, as though pouting over their exclusion from the joke and anxious to butt in.

It is hard to imagine Stephanie being sad, although I know she has been. Like most imaginative gnomes, she has a gift for disguise. Her response to some new bad bounce is a harmless but expressive four-letter word or a party. I think most of the time she has cried, she has cried alone. To recover from this brief aberration she will usually pick up a telephone and call a friend for lunch, where any vagrant troubles for each disappear under surfs of giggles.

Stephanie and I have been lunching once a month or so for two years. I have acquired the role of confidante, foil, and anvil. Once in a great while I will advise, although I do this very tentatively and only when asked. It is the most effective defense I know against foolishness when talking to someone a generation younger.

The doctors have told her she is going blind. There was another prognosis a few years ago that was even more worrisome, but we have never talked about that and I'm sure Stephanie now simply ignores it. She has a diabetic condition that has made her world a little darker each year. At 22 she has no vision in one eye and impaired vision in the other, although she insists that has stabilized, and why argue with that? We met by phone two years ago when she was performing some service for the diabetic association. That finished, she demanded to know how the Vikings were plotting to beat Pittsburgh in the Super Bowl in New Orleans.

Lacking this clairvoyance, I arranged to have Stephanie witness the event first hand. Logistics problems developed for her in New Orleans, and I was enlisted as her escort.

A spasm of seriousness would intrude on her babblings and hop-scotching wisdom now and then, and she talked about the future. She said she had not surrendered her hopes of becoming a nurse, and marriage? Well, he would have to be an unusual person, wouldn't he?

We roamed the boisterous parlors and antique dens of Bourbon Street for hours, listened to the Dixieland combos that made her first gleeful and then pensive. We dined on roast beef in one of those continental French Quarter mansions, the Royal Orleans Hotel, and afterward rode a carriage through the streets of New Orleans at midnight.

She said she better get me home in time because she was afraid I would turn into a woodchuck or a Pittsburgh linebacker, or something dreadful like that.

Stephanie called me yesterday. She disposed of most of the world's crises promptly and then told me she wanted to talk about a fellow named Bill Scott.

She identified him as a Minneapolis policeman, 28. They met three or four years ago but, after undergoing some moderate glow, moved in other directions. A few months ago she found herself in his squad car, the citizen in the police department's ridealong program.

"We started dating again," Stephanie disclosed. "We've got the same birthday, May 29. Two Geminis. Maybe it was in the stars. He's just a terrific guy. Thoughtful, spontaneous. All those good things. We started going to ball games, movies, shows, a few parties. We also talked a lot. I think I liked that about him most. We all have superficial stuff about us. He saw through that pretty fast, but in a, well, generous way. I told him about the things I was afraid of. And he said the things that were wrong with me physically didn't matter that much, he wasn't marrying me for my eyes."

I asked Steph to try that one more time.

"We're getting married in September. Could anything be more beautiful than that?"

I said I couldn't think of one thing.

Postscript: Stephanie did marry Bill Scott. She enjoyed several years of a happiness she never doubted she would have. Stephanie died in 1982.

He Was a Miner, a Dreamer, and My Father

MARCH 15, 1978

THE SIGHT OF wind-filled schooners in his geography books sealed all further debate in his schoolboy's mind over his destiny as a man of the 20th century. He would sail into the exotic ports he memorized from the colored maps, if not as the ship's captain then at least as some kind of mate in charge of teeming hurricanes at sea.

In the mining towns of northern Minnesota in the early 1900s, the odds were rarely kind to the imagination of a 10-year-old boy.

He never saw the ocean or studied in the high school that was to have thrust him into the world with all of the required scholarship.

By the time he had finished the 8th grade, his mother and father had died and he was the head of the family of nine. His choices were foster homes for all, or the vermilion tunnels of the iron-ore mines—which required no scholarship and were not always impressed by the child-labor laws. At the age of 15 he carried his lunch pail into the red-smeared elevator the miners called "the cage," was lowered with them into the moist labyrinth of the Zenith Mine, and began working 10 hours a day.

If he ever looked on the underground mine as the dead-end catacomb of his boyhood visions or saw himself as a captive of the cold-blooded economic system of the immigration years, my father never mentioned it to me in the more than 40 years I knew him. I doubt that he felt that way. In another time and place he might have worn a tie to work or possibly commanded the ship he conjured as a kid. But that would not necessarily have made his life more fruitful. It certainly would not have enriched the worth he achieved as a human being in the 74 years that ended for him yesterday.

We kissed him for the last time on a hospital bed yesterday morning. My mother and brother must have remembered, as I did, the hundreds of times he had done the same before his daily departures for the mine. It was a ceremony that, while sincere, never really enthralled him. To be honest, my mother required it. Without knowing much about the actuarial tables of underground mining, she decided that if fate should intercede, our last sights and sounds together as a family should at least be properly affectionate. And so my father once marched a quarter of a mile back into the house through five-foot snow drifts to kiss us at 6 o'clock in the morning rather than risk my mother's retribution 10 hours later.

In the mining towns' cauldron of nationalities and immigrant ambitions, the unalterable chemistry was this: that the children and grandchildren should have opportunity to grow and achieve in places more refined and more generous than the plain frame cloisters of the mining company locations where they lived.

My father and the others adopted that as creed. They would have been the last people on earth to see their lives as something more important — as the essence of the maturing of the land and people. But they were. And it requires no artificial breast-beating or sentimentalism for us to recognize that now.

He worked underground for 35 years, in no spirit of penance for having been born in mining country in 1904 but as a career that commanded its own respect and initiative. In a way, he conducted his own small business with the paperwork he would bring home as a shift boss answerable to both the company's tally boards and the men he worked with. Away from work he fished and hunted the lake country of the great national forest, and the reservoirs of good times in it with good companions built for him as he grew older. He often expressed genuine puzzlement when a visitor from out of town would tell him it was too bad he never had a chance to build a life away from the mines and the harsh north woods.

Each time I visited in later years I marveled at his versatility of skills and his explorations, low-keyed but always precise, as a cabinetmaker, gardener, electrician, hunter, and metalworker. He worked quietly and efficiently, with a kind of control and sociability. Even in his last months, when he was weakened and tired, he produced something almost every day. And this morning in his house there are a half-dozen immaculately tilled little boxes of marigolds and snapdragons sprouting on the kitchen counter where he left them a few days ago.

Miners do not have the same relationship with the earth as farmers. For the farmer it is his life and treasure. For the miner, the underground earth might be a prison or an antagonist, but at least it is no place for things that grow and nourish. Which might explain my father's fondness for a different, life-giving kind of earth, and his gentleness with the flowers he raised by the hundreds.

He went through his tempestuous times like most, but he grew. He was tender with his family, extravagant with his energies and strength when they and others needed. He spoke harshly only of the exploiters of the land, and he refused to believe that any work or day on earth, even if it required pain, was any imposition on Mike Klobuchar.

I don't know of any person who gave more and asked less, and I'm so glad I could tell him one last time how honored I am to be his son.

Really Living a Christian Life
Can Get You into Trouble

APRIL 9, 1979

THERE IS SOMETHING unsettling to a lot of Christians in the sight of a man or woman trying to live a Christian life.

The predicaments of a Catholic priest named John Garvey, as described in a dispatch this morning from Selby, South Dakota, might offer the congregation a more pertinent introduction to the dilemmas of the Christian Holy Week today than the usual litanies offering salvation to the periodically contrite.

Such salvation is commonly sought at 11 a.m. Sunday mornings. Everything else being equal, it is not a bad hour to be saved. It is possible to drive at that hour without seriously risking six-lane neurosis, and the television is marginal, unless it is fall and they are already doing the pre-game. Redemption thus is available to us in an atmosphere of becoming calm and order, a condition made even more civilized by the post-service coffee and biscuits.

It is a long way from the fishes and loaves, but most of the worried shepherds who try to impart counsel at that hour seem to understand that few of us are capable of full-service piety, and a couple of hours a week is better than nothing.

Who's to argue? If we weren't all hypocrites, Adam and Eve would still be romping around the eucalyptus trees and the world—particularly the garment industry—might never have recovered from the shock.

The spiritual gymnastics most people try to perform, grubbing with their fallibilities while at the same time reaching for the sky, are not quite the same as the odd postures they assume in the presence of a tougher and more genuine Christianity.

The priest in South Dakota is in trouble with some of the citizens

173

because he has tried to love Indians. And he is in trouble with the feds because he declines to pay some of the taxes he believes are being used to support forces and institutions blasphemous to his religion and humiliating to some people here on earth.

The second struggle is one he is not going to win, and I'm not sure he should. Tax protest on moral grounds is an attitude that deserves our respect. But the democracy is an imperfect instrument itself and it would certainly go smash if we all ash-canned our W2s. So the tax resister must then accept the consequences of his appeal to a higher morality. And this the priest seems to have done in reasonably good humor. They have impounded his car and he is now getting around South Dakota with his thumb, a relatively suspenseful but not always reliable way to travel the prairie, black beads notwithstanding.

He does not seem as disturbed by this as by his other encounters in trying to perform the kind of witness the carpenter taught 2,000 years ago.

The priest believes we have ripped off the Indians.

Does anybody want to quarrel with that?

He believes we have an obligation in morality and justice to try to square it with them.

No arguments, again.

Money helps, of course.

All right, reverend, some money.

But what about friendship and love, the reverend asks, about joining their struggle, about trying to wear their shoes, for a mile maybe, maybe more?

What is this, reverend, some kind of cult?

The reverend is no Holy Joe or thundering avenger. And yet he might say that all this is, not matter how crude and inadequate, is an attempt to remember in the 20th century—the only one we happen to live in—what the carpenter did and said in another time.

This behavior has led to puzzlement and hostility among some of the brethren in South Dakota, or Minnesota, or Alabama, or wherever these encounters take place. Indians (or Chicanos, or blacks, or maybe Irish 100 years ago, fill in the blanks) are OK but you don't want to give their kinky mavericks all that respectability by calling them your friends.

Who the hell needs rebels?

Well, a few people, a few thousand years ago.

We dump our scorn easily and quickly on grubbers like John Garvey, who seem to be abusing the cloth they are supposed to wear so solemnly and carefully. There is something distasteful now and then about their notions of love and forgiveness and brotherhood. It is something the minister is supposed to talk about Sunday morning.

Not on a dusty reservation.

And so perhaps we can summon the willingness on this Monday of Holy Week to forgive a hitch-hiking padre for trying to be a Christian.

A Lovely Old Man's Last Song
on His Mountain
JULY 28, 1981

MOUNTAINS CAN'T SING. It is a truth of nature that arouses no dispute from either geologists with their little steel hammers or voice coaches with their metronomes. Mountains can thunder and grumble. They can roar and make echoes. But they can't make music. Nor do they have attitudes or personal quirks.

Poets and romanticists argue differently. They will see a mountain in the gloaming squall and call it sullen or hostile, or see its summit brushed gold with the first sun the next morning and call it regal or benign.

But it is made of granite and snow and frozen lava, so how can it sing or harmonize with this 70-year-old man who is moving high on its southwest skyline, smiling and humming in the wind, letting the gusts romp in his hair?

The rock is nearly vertical. It offers only a fingertip fissure for his hand and a nub no bigger than a thimble for his foot and beneath him the chasm falls 2,000 feet straight down. But Glenn Exum is singing. And although he has had two cancer operations in the last two years and has climbed on this mountain for more than 50 years, it is not a requiem he is singing.

Some of his friends called it Glenn Exum's last climb on the Grand Teton, on this thrusting, salmon-colored ridgeline of such endless virility and elemental force. He pioneered it exactly a half century ago to this very day, a college kid wearing a pair of borrowed football shoes. In time they gave the ridge his name, and he became the mountaineer-in-residence of the Tetons. He was a man of order, gentleness, and dignity. First in trickles and then in torrents, the novice climbers came to the Tetons to be thrilled or to be indoctrinated. As the leader of the guides, he did neither.

He was a mountain man, yes, but he was also a music man. He taught music in a high school in Idaho and instinctively viewed the world as a place of rhythm and harmony. He shunned strident postures and the ego hungers that so often drive climbers higher and farther, faster and more desperately.

He understood the urges. Some he harbored in fugitive spasms himself. But although he climbed the Grand Teton more than 300 times, and although others who had climbed the mightiest snow peaks of Asia marveled at his velvet movements on a mountain, mountaineering was not the godhead of his life.

His life with Beth mattered more.

His family mattered more, and his friends.

Climbing a summit, he recognized very early, did not heighten a person's worth or install him in a fraternity of the select.

Accept the gifts and the counsel of a mountain climb for what they are, he told the thousands of apprentices he introduced to climbing over the decades. It can instruct you in the durability of the human body, surround you — if you will let it — with the affection and grace that flows from a shared experience on a rope with others who come for the same gift. It can teach you that in order to deserve, sometimes you must exert.

But although sometimes a mountain may demand a supercreature to climb it, one does not have to be a supercreature to come to the mountains.

He was professorial and bright, to his closest friends even a little roguish in his campfire stories. If you could not laugh on a mountain climb, the desert might be your milieu.

More than almost anyone they had met, he seemed to his friends to have mastered the values of the good and productive life. He was craftsman, friend, a thoughtful husband and father, a man both pragmatic and philosophical, incapable of speaking harshly of another. And this was the wellspring of his view of the mountains and their treasures. They give to each in rough measure what the pilgrim brings to them.

No, they do not have personalities.

But they do, perhaps, reflect the personality of the one who climbs in them or walks in them.

Which is why any day in a mountain for Glenn Exum, rain or starlight or blue infinity, was a day of music and order.

And so it was Wednesday. His ropemates were the professional mountain men who climbed for him so many years; amateur climbers who were exhilarated not only by the mountain but by Glenn Exum's company; there were international stars and a neighbor or two from the sagebrush valley beneath the Tetons where he now lives with his wife. He could not have made a golden anniversary climb on the Grand Teton three months ago. He was weakened by surgery which, although successful, made walking itself an ordeal.

But the climb mattered, not from the demands of vanity but because the world moved in harmonies, and there was something very symmetrical and right about making a 50th anniversary climb with friends.

And when he got onto the salmon-colored rock, the decades peeled away and the pain receded. He climbed and he climbed, and he was first on the rope while the younger men gaped, and finally, impulsively, they applauded, because he climbed never in haste but always with precision and style.

And with joy. He sang, and the wind was his harmony, the wind and the mountain. When we reached the top they patched a telephone call to the valley, and he said to his wife, "Darling, we're here, at the top."

We. Not I.

There are thousands of climbers. There are not many mountaineers. This is one of the few.

She Came to the Altar in a Wheelchair
FEBRUARY 16, 1981

THEY SAT BESIDE each other at the altar, the young woman in a wheelchair, the groom on a stool he had requested so that they could begin their married life as equals.

It was not a gesture of courtliness. Their lives needed no such precious displays. They were declaring a shared emergence from a trauma of five years ago, and the special kind of spiritual intimacy it gave them.

He had lifted her from the water moments after the screams and thunder of the motor had transformed an outing on the St. Croix River into a horror.

The inboard motorboat struck her as she sat in an inner tube. The blow was so powerful and final, and the body's shock mechanism so immediate, she could not recall afterward feeling any sudden pain.

When he and others took her from the water, she was legless.

And what was she a few seconds before? A tall and athletic 18-year-old girl, an effervescent kid, chattering about summer with the young man she hoped to marry.

Then the motorboat came roaring from nowhere, and devastated her life.

"Goodbye boyfriend and marriage," one of her friends reflected a few days later. He was a nice fellow, but this was the real world, not the big coloring books with princes and vows and draw-bridges.

But five years later they sat together in white on Valentine's Day in Central Lutheran Church and listened to a minister who had befriended them talking about love and commitment.

For Kathy Tommeraasen and John Tallman, the minister said, was there really any need to dwell on commitment?

Yet they knew as the minister knew that it didn't come in any great unbroken wave of resolve, carrying them irrevocably to this hour of hymns and flowers.

They weren't always sure. She tried to track his feelings and his stamina, the line that wove from love to codes of loyalty to sympathy. In her occasional flights of resentment for having been so mindlessly crippled, she looked for signs that he might want to back away.

He did the same.

But they found none.

Once in a while they quarreled because they were both candid people, and pursuing the ideal they held on to didn't mean they couldn't be hog-headed about being right, or wrong.

They met at a Cedar Lake picnic ground six years ago, shortly after she finished high school in Golden Valley. "I melted," she said. "He was a tall and good-looking guy and I didn't think I'd have to look any further." They were both active and gregarious people, and they romped and fished and played ball together.

Her basic strength and optimism, and also her faith, pulled her out of her demoralization after the accident. The process did not happen quickly, but it happened sooner than it might for another kind of personality. She began experimenting with artificial limbs. When they married, she would walk down the aisle with John. For a while it was a scheme and then it was an obsession. But she had lost her legs above the knees and the fittings were awkward. She tried one set of limbs that made her 6 feet 2 inches tall, five inches more than her original height.

She held on to her job as a cost accountant secretary, learned to drive a car with special hand controls, learned all about the vagaries and exasperations of a world built for people who walk, and joined a wheelchair basketball team. She also refined her fishing technique, and in time was out-angling the shirt off John Tallman. He did construction and other heavy-duty work to save money for electronics school, where he is now enrolled for a career in computer maintenance.

But what was the act of walking down the aisle?

If it was a compulsion to say "I have done it," to reach a benchmark in a struggle to overcome, how did that square with a deeper ideal?

"I'll walk some day," she said. "But Valentine's Day in 1981 seemed like a good time to get started on something bigger in our lives."

The minister, the Rev. George Weinman, saw in her Norwegian family name a portrait and an understanding of Kathy Tommeraasen.

He said there was a wood called Tommeraasen that grows on mountain tops and ridges in Norway; not kindling or firewood but sturdier stuff that bent with the storms and became the hullwork of Viking ships that withstood the ocean. The couple before him, he said, knew about bending to the point of breaking, but not breaking.

That had some relevance for their lives, but perhaps not as much as his recollection of the way St. Paul defined love.

It is patient, he said. It is kind and envies no one. It is never boastful, nor conceited, nor rude; never selfish, not quick to take offense. A person may have the gift of prophesy and know every hidden truth, but if he does not have love, he is nothing.

She could not walk and she cannot move mountains, but Kathy Tallman left the altar on the arm of her husband, and at that moment no one seemed to deserve the world more.

Heaven Is an Infant's Face

SEPTEMBER 4, 1981

THE COLORS OF sunset over the Pacific poured into Debra Kramarich's eyes just hours after a surgeon's hand had freed her from a lifetime of darkness.

They came in an eruption of oranges and vermilions. For the Minneapolis-born woman of 28, standing in astonishment in the hallway of a California hospital, the sky was paved with a benevolent flame. Could anything be more beautiful?

Something could.

One day later she saw the face of her infant child for the first time.

"We just hugged and hugged each other," she said. "Until that moment my little boy's face was just a blur. Unless I put my eyes inches away from him, I couldn't see anything of him. I had never seen his eyes. I had never seen him smile. It was just heaven. I laughed and cried and just hugged him."

She is telling the world about it today, on the television networks and wherever she can, not only out of exuberance but to sound a hope for others who have given up.

She once believed herself incurably blind. In the years when she was growing up in south Minneapolis, as a student at Roosevelt High School, in her swimming classes at Camp Courage, she accepted the limits of her sightless world. She had little time or opportunity for self-serving sorrow about it. Her mother and grandparents discouraged that, and her bouncy disposition rejected it. She learned with Braille and tapes. She also learned about the casual cruelties kids sometimes inflict on each other. A few in school called her "Cyclops." She had one plastic eye; the other was scarred. Her brothers knocked out teeth and kicked some butts when they learned who was calling her names, but for a blind kid, it was growth.

It prepared her for the day last spring when a doctor in La Jolla, California, told her there was a chance she could see. A successful cornea transplant could relieve her from the condition called Peter's anomaly, with its cataracts and deformities. But if it failed, it might shut out the meager light she was able to see.

She underwent the operation May 11. And now each day in San Diego is a big new Christmas stocking of amazements and discovery.

She goes for rides on buses, "just to look into the faces of the people."

She walks into supermarkets, still faintly traumatized by her first sighted visit. "All these boxes and cans, rows and rows to the ceiling. I just didn't imagine it. The color. It was too much. I had to run out of the store."

She is going to learn how to drive. She wants to be a vocational nurse. She and her sightless husband have acquired seven foster children. The world can spin fast enough for her. She has discovered that she adores her husband even more, and in a little more than a month from now she will see her mother, Eva Lundstrom, for the first time on a visit to the Minneapolis home she left four years ago.

And there is more.

"My three brothers and sister," she said. "What a time we're going to have in Minneapolis. My sister Sandra's getting married and I'll be there as matron of honor to see it. Isn't it a fabulous world?"

Even blind, she was capable of thinking and talking that way. She was a saucy and gabby adolescent. Is that all right? Shouldn't blind kids be?

If they should, then they should also be able to plot marriage. She decided at the age of 15, the first time she "saw" Chuck Kramarich playing the piano at a gathering for young blind people in Minneapolis, that she was going to marry him.

This conviction left no instant impact on Chuck Kramarich, who was 18 at the time and grumbled something about teenagers like Debra Hermanson who talk too loud.

They had no contact for years. Debra finished high school as a "A" student in New York, where her mother worked for the Heart Association. She attended college there and returned to Minneapolis with her mother to study at Augsburg College, was married and divorced after three years, and encountered Chuck Kramarich again in Minneapolis.

"It didn't take us long to find out we were in love. He's a tremendously talented guy. His work is doing medical transcriptions for doctors, but he's good enough as a piano and organ player that he's made recordings."

There was a piano and organ store in Portland, Oregon, that offered some commercial opportunities. So they moved to Portland and sold pianos and organs. When they needed to shift geography again, they moved to San Diego, where Ryan Kramarich was born in November, a completely healthy baby.

"We didn't ask doctors whether it would be all right to have a baby," she said. "And we didn't really plan it. It just happened. We'd been thinking about adopting a blind child, but along came Ryan. I knew my condition was hereditary. But I also knew that if it's detected, it could be stopped before it damaged any organ."

It was during a precautionary appointment for Ryan that she again talked to a doctor about her blindness.

"He said there was a chance. They would need the cornea taken from someone who had just died, preferably somebody young. I called Dr. [Sidney] Nerenberg, who was my doctor in Minneapolis, and he said there had been great technical advances in this kind of eye surgery the last few years, and that I should take the advice of the doctor in La Jolla. They set a time and told me it would be two weeks. But that very day they obtained the cornea, from an 18-year-old. I felt both excited and pretty terrible, to think that a young girl had to die so that I might be happy.

"Chuck and I talked about the operation. It was scary for both of us. For him it was psychological. If I could see, would our relationship change? It worried him, and that was a very human thing to feel. I can tell you now the relationship is more beautiful than ever.

"They said I might not be able to see for three weeks, but the day after the operation the doctor removed the bandages and I saw his face. He told me afterwards I said, 'You are the best-looking man I've ever seen.' I can barely remember talking. It was just a whirl. And then that first sunset, and seeing Chuck, as handsome as I ever imagined, and finally Ryan.

"People had been telling me how he looked when he did this and that, his expressions, all those things. Do you know how frustrating it is not to be able to see them? I had one useless eye and 10 percent vision in the other. Everything was like looking at an opaque shower curtain. I could see blurs, bits and pieces. But now it was real, and it was miraculous.

"What made my sight a special gift was that my mother's second husband (Debra's father lives in India, instructing natives in boat building) died about the time of the surgery, and knowing I could see carried her through the grief. Can you imagine seeing my grandmother, who taught me so much about being self-reliant, and about the world? She said the kids who called me names in school weren't really being mean, that my blindness made them uncomfortable and they reacted in ignorance. And now I'll be able to see her."

However fast the world is spinning today for Debra Kramarich, it is spinning in harmony.

The Best Banjo-Playing Cop There Was

APRIL 30, 1982

H E WAS AN Irish cop who began each day with a song and ended it with a prayer.

Years ago they used to call people like Joe Ryan square, and later they said straight-arrow. These and labels like them are often expressed with a tweak of irony. Easy goodness is a quality often suspected and privately envied, because it doesn't happen all that often.

So yes, you would call Joe Ryan square, if you meant a man who tried to live by a creed of decency and civility. He would not object to that. He would not object if you called him Good Joe Ryan or if you called him the best banjo player on the block or the best singer who ever hauled a gun with the Minneapolis Park Police, or the smartest parliamentarian in Minnesota, or the most stubborn bowler — or a man who enchanted children as only an old man can when he deserves their love.

They surrounded him whenever he went out into his yard, constellations of noisy kids who attached themselves to Joe Ryan with their gummy hands and trusting eyes that seemed to understand a secret fraternity.

It might have been a gift with which Joe entered the world in 1898, but I think we know better. There may not be such a thing as a gift of humanity. It is a quality, rather, that needs nourishment and work, with each renewal. So that the thousand acts of thoughtfulness in the 84 years of Joe Ryan's life needed — each one of them — a small spark of imagination and spontaneity that made them real and therefore believable.

He could arrest a young thief at Powderhorn Park back in the Depression and a few days later buy him a pair of skis.

He could run outside in the early morning when he lived in St. Louis Park and photograph the neighbor's 5-year-old girl at the imperishable moment when she and her friend got on the bus for the first day, with their ID tags dangling from their necks. And 13 years later when they graduated from high school, he could give them a present wrapped in the colors of their school, with a poem for each, written by Joe Ryan.

So you might also call him the poet laureate of the Park Police, and he would not object to that.

His son found Joe lifeless in his apartment bed in Edina Tuesday. A heart attack? Possibly. Maybe Joe had done all that was in his energy and his imagination in 84 years, and there was nothing more for him. It was a day that summarized his last years. A banquet with his pals, something to eat at Pearson's Cafe. A kindness for a waitress, a parting salute to his friends there in Swedish, the only Swede words he knew. A song in the morning.

A prayer at night.

He was the last man at St. Patrick's in Edina to receive communion each Sunday, last because he was old and he had to hold on to the pew ends walking to the altar. Seeing Joe take communion was a renewal in itself for the rest of the congregation. He was a tall old guy who had lived so much and befriended hundreds, who each Sunday until she died had driven his wife to the Christian Science church across from Mount Olivet, had then gone to his own service, had organized whole regiments of young ball teams, arrested crooks, fired bullets, seen so much — and old Joe was walking as tall as he could, to be with his God one more time.

The world could deal with its crises one more week.

In St. Patrick's at the services for Joe Ryan today, a family of musicians with whom he used to play will sing "When Irish Eyes Are Smiling" and "When You Come to the End of Perfect Day," and people will remember a rather extraordinary human being.

He was something of a genius in the elemental art of knowing how to be close to people. He could do it with his chatter with a stranger at Pearson's, where he ate each day after his wife died, by going to the recitals of scores of kids just because they asked him, with his blarney but his good sense at the hundreds of PTAs he or-

187

ganized and attended, at the singalong party he gave for 150 people last year — the one the tornado broke up in Edina.

He was a cop with the Park Board. It was a sort of family thing. His brother Ed became the Hennepin County sheriff. Joe was a cop, but he never gave it the enforcer act when he didn't have to, and one day when he was acting as a sergeant-of-arms at a meeting and had to throw somebody out, he sang a nifty eight bars of "I'll Be Loving You, Always," in the roughneck's ears as he was rousting him through the door.

He left his prints all over the map of the Twin Cities. The kids had no money in south Minneapolis in the '30s so he built ball clubs and ball parks and leaned on the merchants to buy ads in the programs, and when the merchants started going under themselves he organized parties to help the merchants. He bailed kids out of jail and sometimes he had to throw them back in. When one of the incumbent thugs in the territory said he threw the last cop into the lake, Joe Ryan, who was 6-feet-2 and had bony hands, took his cap off and his badge, and said, "Try this one."

Nobody did.

He was never sure what the Lord intended to do with his life, so he tried everything. He got to be captain of the Park Police and then a security man with Prudential. He played the snares, xylophone, and banjo, ran PTAs, kid protection agencies, old people's clubs, and church picnics. In middle age he decided the town needed an expert on Roberts Rules of Order, so he went to the university extension school and in a couple of years Luther Youngdahl in the capitol asked him to lecture the legislature on parliamentary law.

He never stopped singing or being a friend. His son Tom understood that it nurtured him to be recognized, but being helpful was more important. He adored his wife, and you could barely recognize that he was so very lonely some of those days when he was his most sociable.

Sometimes the most important people on earth are the squarest guys.

Long before There Was "Peanuts," There Was Charlie Brown

MARCH 31, 1983

NOWHERE IN THE affairs of the "Peanuts" clan of Charles Schulz does a voice reveal to the pumpkin-face little man with a baseball glove: "You have cancer, Charlie Brown."

Cancer is truth and pain. The Charlie Brown of "Peanuts" is make-believe and allegory, something enchanted because he can make us smile and see ourselves in his plodding earnestness, or make us feel secretly superior. But Charlie Brown also is truth and mortality. And perhaps one of the first doctors who diagnosed the cancer of the flesh-and-breathing Charlie Brown of Minnetonka realized that and couldn't make the separations.

The doctor wept when he gave him the news.

That was seven years ago.

Charlie Brown still has cancer, more extensive than before. He also has a reddish-brown hairpiece, which he elfishly admits is intended to shelter his fugitive vanity. He has impetuous urges to tell everybody he can reach that cancer does not have to mean doom and oblivion, and he has one thing more: "I think I've finally learned to like myself."

"All the years I've been reading the 'Peanuts' strip and, in effect, looking at myself, I was never offended. I smiled with everybody else, because Charlie Schulz is a friend who had the character right. Charlie Brown is always struggling and he failed a lot. God, the things I've blown in my life. I even put stress on the first good friendship I had, with Charles Schulz. But I think for the Charlie Brown of 'Peanuts' and for me, to feel we've experienced life we've had to endure—and to love—many things."

The love, or rather the acceptance, is finally turning inward. And for this, millions of "Peanuts" readers who have never heard of the breathing Charlie Brown might want to rise and applaud.

His malignancy has spread from the prostate condition of years ago, which required radical surgery to save him, to where it now involves the liver. His present physician, Dr. Gail Bender, will not get into the morbid sweepstakes of estimating times, nor will Charlie Brown. He walks around with a plastic bag strapped to his side as a retaining pouch for body waste, as Hubert Humphrey did, and his bouts with manic-depression have sometimes curbed the treatment available to him. He deals with nausea and the other effects of chemotherapy, and now they're not quite sure why he has pain and stiffness in his left leg.

But you can still tee up the football for Charlie Brown, and no tricks, OK?

For a moment let him sidestep the medical diagnosis and remember the wistful child of fate that Charles Schulz read so well when they worked together as art instructors in downtown Minneapolis more than 30 years ago.

"My older brother was a super athlete but when I went to De La Salle I couldn't win a letter. We had athletic letters lying all around the house, none of them belonging to me. I was hungry to make friends but I didn't do that very well, either. I'll tell you how bad it was. I got into a jumping contest one time when I was in the juniors and I finished second. I thought that was just great and I had a new feeling of self-esteem. Then somebody blew a whistle and they measured again. When they finished I was back in the also-rans."

It was a destiny Charlie Brown aggressively tried to avoid. He did it first by quitting the University of Minnesota early to join the mainstream of wage earners and to certify himself as "creative" in the process. It meant progress, a status, and a faster life. And coincidentally it meant meeting a young man with a headful of cartoon characters and an ambition to find an audience.

"We liked each other," Charlie Brown said. "We did things together like skating, playing cards, going to movies, and having fun with mutual friends. But Charlie Schulz didn't like drinking. He saw me getting involved with that, and eventually we moved in different directions. Before then he told me about a character he was creating. He wanted to do a national comic strip and he wasn't sure whether it should be serious or funny or have a message or what. But he came up with something he called 'Good Old Charlie Brown.' The syndicate insisted on 'Peanuts,' and that was it. He showed me the first version of Charlie Brown, which is about what it is today, and I told him I was ticked off. I told him it ought to be closer to Steve Canyon."

Schulz's menagerie quickly installed itself as part of the American culture and eventually installed its creator in California as the head of a global "Peanuts" conglomerate. The breathing Charlie Brown himself won something, an award for design layout in juvenile publications, which became a springboard for two years at Notre Dame directing a young people's journal. From there he returned to Minneapolis to spend 20 years dealing with troubled kids as a program director with the Hennepin County Juvenile and Detention Center.

And every day Charlie Brown could look at the comics and marvel a little, because as he got older he discovered some inexplicable connection between the goofy interludes in his life and what happened to Charlie Brown.

"I've never told Schulz about it," he said, "but you can almost see something psychic going on. I remember being at a party once and being just overwhelmed by hunger. I saw this jar of nuts on the center table and I helped myself to a few. I almost gagged. I had to grab my handkerchief when nobody was looking and spit them out. Sometime later Schulz had an episode where Charlie Brown takes something to the kennel and then you hear this angry response: 'Charlie Brown, you don't even know the difference between dog food and cat food.' And then I remembered asking the hostess later that night of the party what in heaven's name was in that jar, and she said, 'My goodness, I left the cat food in there.'

"I'd never mentioned that incident to Schulz."

Seven years ago, at a time when doctors told him he might not live more than a few months without surgery, Charles Schulz called. He called again a few weeks ago. "He was just saying," Charlie Brown said, "that he's there. There's so much of the human being in him. His awareness. Somebody asked him once if he ever thought what impact his Charlie Brown would have on my life. He said, 'I think it will either make his life or destroy it.' I think it's done some of both. People ask me how it feels to be famous, and I feel foolish. How can you feel good about being famous for doing nothing, just for lending my name to a cartoon character? On the other hand, I can't deny it's opened doors. For legal reasons, Charlie has to take the position that the thoughts and acts of his characters aren't related to live people. That doesn't bother me. How could it? I'm doing a book that ought to be ready for publication soon in which I'm putting a letter he wrote to me. He thanked me for a crucifix I sent to him. He said that while we differed some on religious matters, our belief had preserved and nourished our friendship."

The breathing Charlie Brown once saw himself as ugly. He believed this because he could never find cohesion in his life, or the relationships he sought. He failed in three romances, unable to overcome his insecurity. Drinking contributed to it. But slowly he began finding worth in his work with young people. And in the last year of his employment, one of the juvenile offenders charged with a felony offered to help him up a steps when the cancer had taken hold. It was humanity stirring in a young outcast. And Charlie Brown may have inspired it with his obvious if groping eagerness to care.

Some of the young offenders became his friends.

All the friends he could get.

Charlie Brown.

The cancer began assaulting his body, but enlarging his sense of worth because he was facing pain and an unknown but he saw he could meet them. He traveled on his retirement money and he learned patience. His drinking declined. He envisioned his "life after life" and that made his pain more bearable and perhaps more understandable. He doesn't have total peace. Who with cancer does? But he quelled his resentments and his instincts to keep distance between himself and "all those other cancer patients. I did that for a while, because I didn't want to seem as much of a victim. Then I saw a little girl being wheeled in for radiation and I saw how brave she was, and that day I said, 'I'm one of them, and it's all right.'"

At 57, he lives alone today in his home. He has energy enough to ride motorcycles and do most of the normal things. His face is pallid but touched by the vibrancy of a man who has been through his battering and endured to make his final discovery of self, and to be content with that.

So that we can now all say, "You're a good man, Charlie Brown."

Postscript: Charlie Brown said he would die in harmony with his world. He did, six months later, in a Minneapolis hospice.

World's Worst Golfer Retires—
and We All Mourn

MAY 20, 1984

IT TAKES A man with an unflinching devotion to truth and history to call himself the worst golfer of his time. Such a man must be viewed with vast respect, considering the armies of potential candidates for the title.

For this and other reasons I was depressed a couple of days ago to learn of Ben Berger's decision to retire from golf.

I appealed to him to reconsider. I tried all of the strategies of the special pleader. I invoked his obligations to thousands of bad golfers who will now have to flounder in search of a new spiritual leader. Serenely, Ben turned this aside. He said that he had given his decision much and prayerful thought, and that he was aware of his peculiar duties to the bad golfers of the world, of whom I am a certified member. But at 88 and never having broken 100, he said, he was beginning to have serious doubts of seeing the dramatic turnaround predicted by his pro 50 years ago.

I accused him of impatience and waffling faith, which are the ultimate sins of the bad golfer.

Nothing registered. Ben's smile was fraught with benign and forgiving thoughts. Nobody does it better. He played bad golf that way, and how I envied that. There was something transcending about the way Ben Berger accepted futility on the golf course, an internal glow that lifted him above apology or explanation for his 120-stroke average.

All of this is now lost, and in the hordes of bad golfers on the scene today, there is not one who holds a flicker of promise of playing bad golf as majestically as Ben Berger.

Thus do the great ones recede. It is a law of nature.

Most people know Ben Berger as a philanthropist, a theater and restaurant man, a sporting promoter, a friend to former convicts, and an all-purpose good and gentle guy. For these credits he has been justly honored. But if the highest calling of humanity is service, what Ben Berger did for bad golf is unique and probably outside the reach of all emulators.

Most golfers who play at Ben's level of performance reveal some unevenness in the style and technique of their bad golf: You will get people who will routinely slice their drives, skull their approaches, and fan on their downhill lies. You will get others who shank their putts and bury their bunker shots. Practically all of these people will betray some fugitive spark of skill—a long snaking putt here and there that hits a spike mark and veers into the hole, a three-wood that catches the prevailing wind and drifts onto the fairway.

Ben's golf from end to end was virtually devoid of these redeeming moments. Ben could do it all. He could shank, slice, spray, hit short, whiff, and duck-hook. He could hit overhanging branches on his backswing and golf carts on his follow-through. On days when my bad golf is truly grooved and synchronized, I can deliver most of these shots. But I can't do it hole after hole, tee to green, with Ben's panache. One of the memorable hours of my golfing career was the day a nightclub hypnotist, Sam Vine, came out to Oak Ridge to work on Ben's game.

Vine played golf himself. In town for an engagement, he was approached by Berger's friends. They explained that Ben had carried a 36 handicap, the maximum allowed by the rules of golf, for more than 30 years. Vine was a man endowed with both professional craft and compassion.

"Show me this man," he said.

Five of us played the round: Ben, Vine, Paul Giel, restaurateur Irv Schectman, and me.

Vine said he needed material, some basic research to prepare himself before loosing his art on Ben Berger. We told him about Ben and Sam Snead. They brought the famous golfer to Oak Ridge for a charity exhibition years ago when he was in the prime of his career. Apart from being a great golfer, Snead had few remarkable qualities and practically no gift for amusement. On the first tee the starter announced Snead's foursome, including Ben, and told the golfers to play away. First to hit, Ben took his stance, waggled, and swung.

Ben hit slightly under the ball. No one has ever explained the aerodynamics of its flight. All we know is that Ben's ball wound up 25 feet BEHIND the tee. It did not hit an obstruction. It just flew backwards.

Snead looked on aghast. Nothing in all his years of roaming the world's golf courses had prepared him for Ben Berger's tee shot. When the round was over he left the course shaken and immediately went into a season-long slump, the worst of his career.

They didn't have hypnotists for faltering athletes then. Vine later worked with many. And so it was with much confidence that he undertook to reform Ben Berger's game.

After nine holes Vine was ready for therapy. After 18 holes he was calling for another hypnotist to work on Sam Vine.

Ben Berger, in the meantime, was imperturbable, slicing and dubbing, smiling and shanking, playing a kind of golf invulnerable to critics and reformers alike. He was, as the film makers might have told you, a natural.

After Eight Years of Trying,
Dick Patterson Finds Work

DECEMBER 23, 1984

HIS WORK RESUME wasn't the tidiest in town. Slash marks and strikeovers crept across its uneven type. It bore evidence that its author, no matter his other qualifications, wouldn't have made the third cut in a spelling bee.

He walked the city's streets with that resume for years. Three or four times a week Dick Patterson stuffed his references into a scruffy leather briefcase and charged at the glass-door barriers of the employment offices.

The labels on the glass doors were polite and seductive. They said "Personnel" or "Hiring Office."

Each time he saw them Patterson felt his juices rush and odd currents in his skin. There was some chemical property in that glass that dissolved his defeats of yesterday on the spot. He entered the room awkwardly but robustly. He was full of energy and drive, but he walked with a lurch and he couldn't control his hands all the time.

Almost without variation, the interviewers were friendly and solicitous.

They never told him to come back.

Some of them couldn't understand him. He knew it, and there was nothing he could do to change that. But the kind of work he was applying for didn't take a man with an orator's tonsils. The resume confirmed that. It disclosed that the applicant's job skills included washing rags, pushing carts, and putting caps on bottles.

For a time, the resume said, the applicant sorted coat hangers in a department store. Appended to it was a testimonial from his supervisor there. No other hanger sorter was as conscientious as Dick

197

Patterson. Sorting hangers, for Dick Patterson, was a job hung with the symbols of reward. It held the same allure for him as the head cashier's job for somebody else who didn't have to shrug it off when people turned and looked back at him as he walked down the street.

If he ever cried because the world's employment offices weren't programmed for people with cerebral palsy, he did it only in the arms of a friend.

Every motivation expert in the world would have been proud of Dick Patterson because he truly believed those maxims the motivators use to paper the walls of the seminar halls. If you want to be, you are undefeatable. If you can dream it, you can have it.

Not many of us dream, at the age of 55, about sorting the mail and running the office copying machine.

He was born with and maintained a normal mentality. But cerebral palsy disrupts muscular functions and impairs others, so that it wasn't unusual that despite an average IQ, Dick Patterson didn't learn to read until he was in his 40s.

He lived on government assistance but he was obsessed with wage earning as the mark of his admission card in the community. He haunted the workshops, picked up 35 to 40 cents an hour sorting things, putting labels on things.

He fantasized some. He imagined himself a businessman. He even laughed at that picture. But for years it was important for him to carry his briefcase, wear a tie, pound the sidewalks looking for work. He even had cards made. He was a genuine Dale Carnegie extrovert.

Is that all right for a guy with cerebral palsy, who washed rags and sorted hangers for a living?

He believed those maxims and each morning he would be on the street before the offices opened, convinced the world was great and all he needed was an extra edge of conviction in his voice to sell himself to a job interviewer. He learned to type with one finger, unsteady as his hands were.

He wrote for self-improvement courses on confidence and skills. But he had no illusions about running an office or keeping the books.

When he kept failing to find it, he blamed not the system, not a hard-skinned society, but himself. There was something wrong with the way he prepared himself. And in those moments he would cry in the arms of a friend.

One of those friends wrote a letter to 200 potential employers, citing Dick Patterson's drive and reliability and saying here was a man who could handle some of those lower-velocity jobs in their company.

They got one reply. Fairview Hospital asked him to come over. He was interviewed, and three weeks ago they hired him to sort mail and run a copying machine for $4 an hour.

It happened just the way the Carnegie books told him it would happen, after eight years of trying.

Never mind that he gets up at 5 a.m. to take a bus. The world is great at 5 a.m., too.

A Crusty Intellectual Is Better under the Skin

JANUARY 16, 1985

I HAVE A friend who has cancer and must make a decision in the next couple of weeks whether to face further surgery.

Its benefits are hazy and its risks are probably substantial. This he has to weigh against the distant chance that radiation might give him a longer life. And he must measure both against the prospect of recurrent and deepening pain.

He is a man who has made uncluttered thought a sort of godhead of his life and shrugged at sentiment. Romanticists he tolerates in the way grandparents put up with messy kids. Years ago he evolved a set of literary heroes, most of them clear-thinking intellectuals, some of them tyrannical, a few of them cynics. He decided he should be an enemy of sham and emotionalism. He has pursued these goals with such heat in living-room dialogue that it was not uncommon for his conversational partners to call him (a) tiresome, which they thought was a generous description, or (b) a pain in the stern, which they thought was more accurate.

We once quarreled for an hour over Crazy King Ludwig, the castle-nutty 19th-century monarch of Bavaria who built a fairy tale palace at Neuschwanstein with money ripped off from his subjects. The question was whether Ludwig deserved to be drowned, as he apparently was. Being a romanticist, I argued that justice was done. My friend thought it was a theatrical stunt and the king's critics would have been smarter trying to talk Crazy Ludwig into using the river for a hydroelectric dam.

He has struggled with alcoholism for years and he did it well. He didn't see much conflict between his AA program's ideals of humility and his smoky tirades against fools and posturers, partly because he is a kind of posturer himself.

Being a crusty intellectual and a debunker of life's follies is a handy label he has worn with a relish all of his adult life. Sometimes it gets to be a party conversational piece, and this gives him a little extra attention he doesn't turn down. When his friends haze him about it, he accepts their needles with the mock anguish of a prophet wronged by lesser minds.

There is softer and warmer stuff inside of him, but in our telephone conversation Tuesday he huffed at that kind of talk. He said he would decide on the surgery if logic dictated it. And he said he felt awkward when friends and relatives tried to express their feelings, although he appreciated them.

I don't think you can make a creed out of pursuing logic, and both of us know there are times when we must have a belief in something to make our lives sensible and even bearable. Because he doesn't know if the end is near, he seemed to be searching for a quality he could call belief, and asking indirectly what there is in his life that is worth the sentiment of those around him.

Millions of people like my friend, those who have found a semblance of peace in belief in their lives, did it by yielding their torment and fear to a benevolence they call a higher power. This is no place to be defining it, or arguing about its identity. I don't know where my friend is with faith or religion and it doesn't really matter. If he wonders why people care about him and some cry about him, he should know that what he has revealed to them in his ordeal defines him far better than the persona he created for himself.

Talking and communicating is his special glory as a thinking man, and the surgery he has already had made that a terrible caricature of his true speech. Yet he accepted that without outcry. Sometimes he has done it with a sour face and sometimes with humor but never with phony nobility. He has done his friends and wife the courtesy of never trying to be somebody more or less than who he is, grumps and all. He has been honest about his fears, but he has never railed about his bad luck nor surrendered hope.

He can believe in the goodness of his spirit, and the affection it has aroused from the little community it has built around him. It has nothing to do with intellect, but everything to do with the true test of the quality of a life. If I were John, that would be enough.

Postscript: John Locken died of pneumonia in July 1986. He had struggled for eight years with cancer, and did not yield to it.

A Hero with Knobby Knees

JUNE 27, 1985

Sauk Centre, Minnesota

WHEN THE AD peddlers for Jockey shorts look for symbols of the indestructible American male, they leave Tracy Chase standing outside with the mosquitoes.

Tracy has knobby knees, a hearing aid, and the physique of a Stearns County leprechaun. He is also 78 years old.

I don't think they could sprawl Tracy on a bearskin rug across a 24-foot billboard and sell Jockey shorts. But do you seriously believe that Jim Palmer could ride a bicycle 550 miles in six days?

Experts on longevity admit being stymied by Tracy Chase. Other men of 78 are capable of uncommon physical deeds, but most of them are driven, obsessive types consumed by the idea that age is purely a state of mind. Chase is no evangelist. He is a dumpy little man who likes to ride long distances on a bicycle because not enough women at his lodge in Sauk Centre have the energy to dance with him.

To offset this deprivation, Chase does things like ride through gales and thunderstorms, up to 105 miles a day — and then dance, if the locals can produce partners with enough adrenaline in the towns where we camp.

We will offer him our oak leaves and loving cups before leaving his hometown of Sauk Centre this morning on the last leg of our ride through the cornfields and the cyclone shelters. To prove that we love literature as well as tailwinds, we spent the final night in Sauk Centre to honor the 100th anniversary of Sinclair Lewis's birth. But it's remotely possible that Chase's notoriety might last longer than Lewis's. The first year he rode with us he wore black wingtip shoes and a propeller beanie. Since then he has acquired chic and now wears Bermudas that hang sedately below his knees.

I have run these mini-epics for 11 years and can give you testimony about things like fatigue factors and morning burnout and wounded buttocks. That a man who is 78 could absorb them every day for a week, and then plow into the nearest supper club for some serious exertion such as polkas and schottisches, leaves me ready to take gas.

"When is it going to end, Trace?" I asked.

Chase ordered me to stop moving my lips so idiotically.

"If I can't hear a freight train," he said, "how do you expect me to hear you when you're all mumbles?"

He has chosen 80 as a nice round number for his last year of bicycling 100 miles a day. "I don't want to overdo. Everybody has to make a choice. Bike riding is cutting into my dance schedule, which is tougher to keep up because my old partners keep dying off."

That is a dilemma, for sure. One of the natives of Ashby the other night recognized Tracy by presenting him with a windbreaker making him a member of the town's Loyal Order of Cooties. Chase executed his bows to his public with taste. It was like Stan Musial making one last swing around the league to accept the garlands of the crowd. We added our own.

But on this ceremonial survivors' day we also will give an honorary spatula to Scott Elden, an 18-year-old graduate of Minnetonka High School. They are never going to forget Scott Elden in Detroit Lakes, Minnesota.

The town is one of the tourist magnets of Minnesota and therefore brimming with fast-food shops. On Monday night a mob of my bike riders filled the booths in one of the factory pizza-and-burger parlors, overwhelming the young floorman who was working his first day. He was earnest but stricken, and it was clear that half the clients in the shop might have been suffering from the shafts of malnutrition before the orders began arriving.

Elden is one of those typical Minnetonka types with breeding and compassion. He also was very hungry. He walked up to the man behind the grill and said, "Can you use some help?"

"In what way?"

"There are too many people in the shop for you and the other fellow to take care of. I used to work in a grill in the Twin Cities. I can fry burgers while you make pizza."

The man said it was a deal, and I call that trust.

What about the tables?

"We have people ready to take on the customers," Elden said.

Who?

"Some of us—the customers." Sandy Vogel and Linda Semmler started circulating through the shop taking orders and, of course, indirectly handling the shop's money.

I call that more than trust. It was utter belief, fed by desperation.

So while Sandy and Linda shoveled in the orders, Scott fried burgers and the whole clientele cheered.

He might have saved the Detroit Lakes economy. Another benefit just as practical was a free pizza for Scott Elden and, evidently later, a lifetime coupon for free crawlers at one of the local resorts.

So we close the loop at Monticello today after 550 miles in six days, a few thunderstorms, a couple of near tornadoes, great outpourings of Ben-Gay, and a reservoir of memories both wacky and benign.

For all that, I've decided to walk to work Friday. Some parts of the body need more rest than others.

The Lawyers Honor a Man
Who Began in Leaky Shoes
NOVEMBER 19, 1985

HE WAS AN immigrant kid from Russia, trying to sell newspapers on 5th and Hennepin in Minneapolis in 1922, and his older competitors were beating the borscht out of him.

Si Weisman. Someday he was going to be an attorney, and wear half a dozen decorations for valor as an infantryman, and one day he would argue before the Supreme Court of the United States. But in the winter of 1922 he was wearing a raggy coat and leaky shoes and trying to stake out a small piece of sales turf in the snow to help support his mother and family. His father was gone, shot to death before his eyes during the Russian Revolution.

Such a boy was not going to run from his street corner on Hennepin. But he was being overwhelmed when a man stepped into the melee and asked what the trouble was. The other kids told him. This one was 10 years old, and to sell newspapers with a license in town you had to be 12. The kid was not only a super-aggressive competitor, but he was illegal.

The peacemaker happened to be the circulation manager of the Minneapolis newspaper the kid was selling. In his office he listened to the boy tell him how badly his family needed the money. His mother made $40 in a tailor shop, and there was nothing else unless he brought it in. The newspaper man, Harold Harlow, made him a deal. It was legal to waive the age requirement if his mother posted $100. He called a man he identified as "George." He told the kid that George would put up the money, and the boy could repay him whenever he managed it.

But now the man in the business suit saw fright in the kid's eyes for the first time. The boy asked if George were a Christian, and it mattered because he might not want to give the money to a kid who was a Jew.

Harlow never identified the donor beyond calling him George, who may or may not have existed. He said he was a Christian but it didn't matter. Si deserved the loan, and the money was his.

Weisman shared the story with his peers of the Hennepin County Bar Monday. They came to hear Don Fraser declare November 18 Si Weisman Day, which recognized something thousands of people in this community have known implicitly for years: Somewhere in this immigrant's struggle, his works, and his values is the marrow of the American idea. The making of a democratic society can be rough and unfair and sometimes brutal. But this one has come to endure because it has overridden the conflicts and grudges that boiled within its mingled people. It accepted those as facts of life, but then nourished something better, a belief in the fundamental worth of the human beings who share and create the country's bounty. This has outlasted its conflicts. But we know the belief is empty without hands and voices to stir it into our daily lives.

Si Weisman has spent much of his life doing that. He did it by bearing public witness, and then by walking into a crumbling house and offering his hand and his check to those who were about to lose it. He did it by bringing Christians and Jews closer together, remembering the day Father Tom Meagher stopped another fight on a newspaper corner in north Minneapolis and told him, "Son, there are times when you *have* to fight," and from that fight just might come friendship, and certainly respect. He did it with his rifle and bare hands in Italy and France, with a battlefield zeal that won a Silver Star, Bronze Star, Purple Heart, and the French Croix de Guerre. He was a shrewd and resourceful trial lawyer, but the beauty of his character is his innocence. Words like *brotherhood* can fall limply from the patriot's day sermon. But they have not lost their incandescence for the immigrant kid who saw his father and grandfather cut down because there weren't enough people around to defend them.

His friends brought him back from his retirement home in Phoenix, Arizona, for a day to tell him that all those years when he was talking street sense about ideals—putting faces on our slogans—weren't wasted or forgotten. From his first years in public he preached forgiveness. He also preached that if you look hard enough, the yearnings that can bring us together are more powerful than the fears that pull us apart.

Si won't be in Geneva this week for the summit meeting. But maybe he should be.

Sometimes a Nurse Mirrors the Best in Us

MARCH 11, 1986

LEAVING THE VETERANS Administration hospital Sunday morning, I mumbled a prayer of thanks.

I don't know her name and I couldn't identify her today if she were sitting across the table from me. She was busy in the few minutes I saw her, and it wasn't a time for socializing.

She attended a friend of mine who is to undergo a long and important surgery today. I don't know how nurses classify patients. They might mark John a good one because he has lived so intimately with pain so long. He must understand his thresholds, the stubbornness of his body as well as its vulnerability. Knowing it, he might be more patient and less demanding than you or me. I have that impression, but perhaps those things aren't relevant to most nurses.

I know that John has lived stolidly with multiple sclerosis for more than 20 years, that and the surgery and wheelchairs and infections and the private ignominies they have caused him. In World War II he was decorated a half-dozen times for landing U.S invasion forces from Iwo Jima to the Philippines in the face of point-blank shelling.

But he still experiences fear in the quietest and loneliest of ways, knowing he is loved by those around him but hesitant to release his fear. In that he has not been driven by some medieval code of manliness. He doesn't have to be told about the frailties of those codes. Yet he has needed the service of others so much that the idea of burdening bothers him more than pain.

Maybe the nurse realized all that.

She had to perform the earthiest of chores for him, changing and draining and doing all the homely things they must offer in Nursing 1 to deglamorize the job and to ensure that nobody walks into it with any illusions left from the high school yearbook.

From the hallway outside his room, waiting to visit, I heard more than saw. She was competent, which you expect. When she tried to humor him, she did it without condescension. When she had to heft and he had to pull or lift, and the laws of gravity seemed to be out of order, they tried to laugh together. She spoke to him with what seemed to be genuine affection, and when she had to instruct him she did it directly and economically.

When she left him, she did it warmly and quickly, and she was gone down the hallway.

You could make the point that most nurses perform their work that way, and I wouldn't argue. Good nursing may deserve no more sanctification than good policing or good counseling, insofar as it requires skills that go beyond the pragmatic ones and reach into the emotions and the values of trust. But I think the wonder of so many good nurses is that they can go on being nurses as long as they do, given the limits to the human being's stores of emotional commitment.

John spoke of his gratitude after she had gone.

His wife has been at his side daily for hours, and she has volunteered for some of the chores. But Sunday morning was difficult for him. His wife had gone to church, the operation was approaching and his anxieties—the weight of all he had been through for 20 years—had reached the surface.

And this young woman was there to convey her understanding, without having to express it.

She comforted him with her strong hands and her presence.

She also did it with her eyes, and by the spirit and friendship in her voice.

She understood that he was brave in his unpretentious way, and she expressed her respect in the small things she said and did.

She left him feeling better than he had been, which is one modest definition of the healing craft, and one she has learned so well.

A Boy Who Built a Community
He Didn't Know

APRIL 6, 1986

SUICIDE IS ONE of the ugly words in the language.

It tells of the obliteration of hope, of a pain or isolation so deep it is beyond healing and comfort. It declares the futility of struggle or reconciliation, and the powerlessness of love. Its allure, most of the time, is oblivion.

This is how we used to view the motives of suicide.

I attended a service last week for a 15-year-old boy whose body was found in the Mississippi River a few days earlier, five months after he left his Minneapolis home, which is not far from the Camden Bridge.

His mourners numbered scores of people whose dress and manner spoke the essence of middle-class middle America. They were the friends of his parents and the relatives and classmates of Brian Brodigan.

A silent question hung over the gathering. How could there be any desperation so crushing for a 15-year-old boy that it should drive him to leave a household filled with the character of middle America — its family and its learning, its gadgetry and love — and to seek relief in the dark water?

There were no judgments in the church last week, of the boy or his parents or his peers.

Nobody knew why, and it was meaningless to pretend.

Was it an irrational act in search of attention, some misguided retaliation for his mother's raised voice in a family quarrel?

Was his mind clear of the poisons so easily available to kids today, and might it have been fueled by a music that sometimes talks subliminally, or straight out, about suicide?

211

We don't know that.

I do know that three adults who attended the service spoke to me about their fears for their own children.

It is a new anxiety in family life for thousands today, chill and gray and frightening to grapple with.

If somehow he could have understood the worth he had, simply by being who he was. He was a kid who frolicked in the woods and took delight in being able to create a fishing fly. He had his quirks and loyalties and longings. He was bored by school and usually resented it when his mother tried to motivate him to reach for his capabilities. Instead, he often gave his commitments to things that asked no commitments, wounded birds, small animals that he brought home. He was allowed to keep those. They were part of Brian's world; his parents and brothers understood that.

The grownups gathered in the church could not have helped but remember themselves as 15-year-olds. They might have been rebellious and independent one hour, full of need the next. Masterful and in command of the world in the morning, vulnerable in the afternoon; people who made no sense some of the time, and at others seemed to have a focus on what mattered in life.

They were Brian. There is Huckleberry Finn in all of us. But life today is faster and more mobile and more volatile, the family more fragile. The adolescent cults of today are forged by wide-open television, chemicals, and the absorption with violence in some of our pop art. What might be normal family friction in another generation, treatable by time, now often leads to something darker—alienation, kids leaving home, threatening more.

So we were all Brian in the church last week, whatever our age. If he could have seen the warmth with which his classmates remembered him, the unconditional love his parents had always given him, the community his death had created on that day, and in future days.

He would have seen the real worth he was seeking, and had all along.

He also would have understood that the community that mourned him—those who recognized Brian in their own lives—was there when he lived.

Coping with Caesar:
Politics and Its Practitioners

Stockman Tells Us to Be Grateful for His Genius

MARCH 13, 1981

THE BRIGHT AND glib Mikado of Reagan economics is David Stockman, the budget director who is the newest television star from the Potomac.

He is usually on view on the Sunday morning public affairs shows describing the horrors that will overtake this country unless it buys the whole Reagan salvation package.

Stockman's audiences—today, at least—clearly are lubricated to listen with approval and hope. Something terribly dramatic and timely has to be done. Smoke out the panhandlers who have soiled the dollar bill and dumped on our well-documented magnificence as a people. Put a dunce cap on the federal regulators in Washington who have tied cans on the corporate knights of American business. What happened to the spirit of the frontier? Who killed Daniel Boone?

Stockman understands this and recites the creed with a vengeance. He also knows how to make the objections sound sniveling and grubby.

He calls them howls of protest, which conveys the picture of a mass baying and yelping at the public buffet when the conscientious new storekeeper takes away the packs' extra helpings of fat and sweetpies.

The truly needy, he tells us thoughtfully, need not fear.

The near needy—well, you can't cut out 48 billion from the budget and fight off the imminent Soviet invasion of El Salvador and unshackle the genius of American business and get money rolling and make it fun to belong to a country club again unless some people—including the near needy—make some sacrifices.

215

I mean who, after all, caused the 12 percent inflation and 19 percent interest that is strangling the land and making it so tough for the honest, hard-working, law-abiding citizens of America?

All right, everybody, sacrifice.

Mrs. Reagan will lead the way. She will take time out from her remodeling duties to be photographed with a needy person. So that we have no doubt about the intensity level of this scene, somebody has obligingly put up a sign declaring: "Mrs. Reagan cares about the handicapped."

Mrs. Reagan undoubtedly does. Another person who does is Lucille Anderson of Bloomington, Minnesota, who has written a letter to Governor Al Quie about her mother. Governor Quie is one of those nice and decent politicians who isn't quite sure how we're going to get out of this fix, but he certainly understands that somebody has to sacrifice. I would not call Mrs. Anderson a howler or a bayer. The lady is, however, a little hot.

"The Medicaid figures you're slashing," she writes. "Every dollar represents a person. You like figures? Sums? Let's take the sum 91. That is my mother's age. Let's take another sum. How about 58? That's the number of years she worked in alteration rooms because that is one of the few types of employment offered to women of her generation. . . . When she quit at 74 years of age it was because my stepfather had cancer of the throat and had his voice box removed. They were caretakers at an apartment building on Fairview, and she became his voice. Humble jobs, yes. But she was the very best alteration hand and he was the very best caretaker that ever was. They were best because they took pride in what they did, and never at any time ever did they ask anything of anybody.

"As little as my mother had, even after my stepfather died, even with her small Social Security, she managed a dollar for Christmas Seals and Easter Seals and even a dollar for the Humane Society. She used to give blood. She gave it until they refused because of her age.

"She is now a resident of a nursing home and receiving medical assistance. I think she suspects that she is, but she doesn't know, and I hope she doesn't find out. These people did their best to save from an income that barely provided the necessities, but their wants were few and they figured with their Social Security they would manage. Wrong. Our mismanaged government has destroyed what little security they had, so they had to seek help, and now the government is going to remove that as well."

The tiny old lady is legally blind. She can't read and do needlework anymore, so she listens to Talking Book Radio. At this point no one but the very assured Mr. Stockman can tell us where the Reagan economics will carry us, but we do know the nursing homes will have to reduce their levels of services, and I'm not sure another atomic submarine is worth that.

There is nothing wrong with raising a lot of noisy questions about what the Reaganites are up to, whatever the mood of the country or the fervor of the Moral Majority or David Stockman's projections. This is essentially a rich man's president. The focus of the new economics is ultimately to transfer substantial billions of dollars upward into corporate and affluent hands, on the theory that it will electrify the economy, produce new investments and retooled plants, and get the country moving again.

There is no assurance that this is going to happen. There is some precedent, in fact, to suggest it may not.

So we ought to listen to the Stockmans on Sunday mornings. But we ought to listen just as attentively to the Judith Andersons.

While Jeno Grilled Reagan, His Wife Stewed

FEBRUARY 9, 1982

WHILE THE FLOWER of the Wayzata and Edina gentry fidgeted and silently groaned, the volatile pizza peddler from the waterfront of Duluth confronted the president of the United States at the $500-per-person reception.

He wanted Ronald Reagan to tell him why he couldn't delay a tax cut "for us rich people."

For a moment, the only sound was a slightly muffled splat caused by the impact of Lois Paulucci's foot against the shin of her husband.

"Of all days," Jeno Paulucci grumped, "on our 35th wedding anniversary."

He was the only millionaire in the room with fallen arches from walking barefoot on iron ore chunks in his formative years.

He was also the only millionaire who spent thousands of dollars on newspaper ads telling the president of the United States how dumb it was giving immediate tax breaks to millionaires like Jeno Paulucci.

On the doubtful chance that Ronald Reagan might have missed them, Jeno Paulucci put the question again. His argument: Why rush into a tax cut with its biggest benefits for the wealthy when it means (a) killing some social programs and (b) raising the country's deficit to close to $100 billion?

The one-time sports announcer from Iowa addressed the one-time barefoot chunk-kicker from the Iron Range and, by implication, denied that it was dumb or bad economics.

"What did he tell you, Jeno?" he was asked later by an Iron Range accomplice without the scratch to buy into the reception.

218

"Well, he said they weren't cutting benefits from the poor but were cutting increases in those benefits. He didn't really answer my question."

But your wife got upset with you rather than Reagan?

"Yeah. Sure. I suppose most women would, considering it was . . . such a social sort of thing. But what the hell, I'm serious about raising those questions and I'm not letting up. I voted for Reagan and I like some of the things he's doing . . . but I came for Durenberger, not Reagan. Reagan had to make a choice between keeping one of two promises he made, cutting taxes and balancing the budget. Maybe because of the wealth of some of those advisers in his kitchen cabinet, he cut taxes. I'm asking, does he think all of us who have money and got a break on taxes are going to invest it? The answer is no, not until we can make some money. So it's self-defeating because it creates this huge deficit, which makes it even harder to invest."

Does your wife buy the Paulucci economics?

"She does. But she gave me this kick in the shins anyhow. She said, 'Jeno, can't you ever keep your mouth shut?'

"I told her, 'You've been married to me for 35 years and you don't know the answer?' "

Paulucci lived his childhood on the edge of poverty, eating macaroni and scrounging stray lumps of coal from the railroad tracks to keep the family stove going. But he flew down from his corporate aerie in Duluth on his private plane to renew his acquaintance with Ronald Reagan. They visited a year ago when Reagan attended a meeting of the Italian-American national club, of which Paulucci was unmistakably the chief executive officer. Reagan made a point of walking over to him Monday night to shake hands. There was never much hazard that the president of the United States would not remember the coal scrounger from Hibbing. Paulucci is almost impossible to overlook or forget.

The pity of Monday night, for folklore collectors, is that Reagan's schedule precluded any serious exposure to Paulucci's wisdom.

"What he should have done was say to his rich folks, 'Hey, boys, wait a year or two, will you? I'm going to balance this damned budget first.' "

Why didn't he?

"Well, sometimes rich folks get impatient. And he really believes this supply-side idea. If I had more time with him, I would have told him about this sign I've got on my office wall. It says 'Timing is everything, and not just restricted to sex.' "

It was suggested to Paulucci that he might run off a few copies of that axiom and send it to David Stockman on the chance that it might work its way into Reagan's next budget.

"Something different ought to work its way in," he said. "I'd say right now Reagan ought to put a surcharge on our income tax. Some of the things he's doing are OK. He's cutting out some greed in all those programs. He's got to keep the country strong, but there's a lot of waste in the Pentagon. I know the deputy there, Carlucci. Why wouldn't I know a guy like that? I told him, 'Hey, there's a lot you guys can cut out,' but that military spending is the Holy Grail there, you know. Reagan's got to find a way to open up jobs, and I'm going to unveil a plan for that. But if I visit in the White House, I'm wearing cowboy boots because my wife packs a helluva wallop."

Witnessing a Massacre between Commercials

SEPTEMBER 20, 1982

THE SIGHT OF people lying slaughtered in a street in Lebanon thousands of miles away came into our living rooms between football games.

They wore jeans and sandals and T-shirts, people like us.

They entered our screens on one of those lyrical fall days in Minnesota. And it had seemed altogether normal on such a day to turn on the television and join the weekend rites of renewal, watching shiny-helmeted gladiators perform their deeds for the thousandth time in our lives.

Pictures of murdered children with their faces shot off in a refugee camp do not harmonize with the serenity of a lovely day in fall. They thrust savagery into our ease without warning, intrude on the harmless hypnosis we fall into watching those make-believe battles in the arenas.

For these reasons the words and even the pictures seemed to resist an immediate surge of grief.

We have seen savagery and blood on television so many times, buildings being pulverized, human beings blown apart. We hear and see the wailing and hate; and then the silent futility hanging over the scene in the aftermath, like a judgment on the derangement of man.

We are told by some psychologists the lines have blurred between the violence of the entertainment we demand on television and the violence we see in the news, and our powers to separate them are being dulled a little more each year.

Our capacity for revulsion thins. Next month there will be something more repugnant.

And so the world's political princes, generals, saints, and reformers alike proceed with their business, recognizing— sometimes sadly, sometimes shrewdly—that public outcry commands very few divisions and the effective life of the people's outrage is very short and easily distracted.

But that is not always true. Sometimes a people's voice can take on a power so aroused and imperative that it will not be silenced, and it will stop armies and change the flow of history.

It happened in the war over Vietnam.

It cannot create peace in the Middle East. But it can expose the lunacy in which competing zealots, Israeli, Christian, and Muslim, have been killing people by the thousands under the flag of creating peace and order in Lebanon and stabilizing the Middle East.

The massacres in refugee camps by the Christian militiamen in Lebanon, exposing the blackest side of man's nature, were acts so ugly and sickening they mock any attempt to parcel out ultimate blame. The hatreds in the Middle East are as old as civilization. They are so fierce that today only a higher public conscience or the willingness of the United States, the one great power that has a moral right to intervene with its influence there, can prevent a repetition.

We are hardly pure over there. But I think most Americans would probably look at it like this:

The Israelis are powerful enough to remove themselves from west Beirut.

The mission they said they came for in their invasion has been accomplished. Our friendship for the Israelis is fundamental. The guarantee this country has given for their security is absolute. But if you are strong, and you also believe you act with reason, sooner or later you have lead. If there is a way out of the chaos in Lebanon, the United States and Israel will have to find it. We have supported Israel in its struggles as a matter of right, but that country is now run by a genuine loose cannon. Being Israel's ally and patron doesn't mean we have signed up to finesse his wraths indefinitely, or to play telegram games with him.

There was enough horror this weekend in Lebanon for the blame to be spread around. Very few hands are clean.

The scenes should tell us forever about the folly of simply being spectators, whether it is watching make-believe wars on Sunday afternoon or the ones where people wearing jeans and T-shirts like you and me are piled up on a city street with their heads blown off.

For thousands of years politicians and generals have been insisting they can save lives by building bigger and more guns, and better bombs, more than other people build.

We have bought it, because they are the experts on how to achieve peace. They prove it by being able to kill millions of people more efficiently each war.

On the same day when the newspaper told of hundreds dying in the Palestine refugee camp, it reported on a United Way organization in Texas withdrawing money from a religious charity organization because one of its bishops said we should stop building nuclear bombs.

This country is powerful enough, the most powerful on earth, to lead that cause. It still has the moral authority to do it. But more and more that must come from the churches and citizen organizations because apparently it will not come from the government. You will find some royal crackpots in the pulpit. Yet there are hundreds of others whose voices in the cause of restraining the arms madness deserve to be heard. Neither they, nor you, should be accused of being naive for saying there must be a better way than another trillion dollars for nuclear bombs we don't need.

Maybe it WAS the innocence of the day that made it hard Saturday to grasp the bestiality of what we were seeing. Defenseless people lying dead by the hundreds, herded into their hovels, the victims of political carving-up and the rages and paranoias of those who controlled their destinies.

The picture burned its way into the brain, and it cannot be forgotten.

These people had no chance to be heard about their destinies. We do.

Remembering the Legacy of Ike

JUNE 6, 1984

IN THE EARLY years of Dwight Eisenhower's presidency, psychologists and journalists by the clan were obsessed with his popularity.

It was a popularity that was enduring and deep and it seemed only marginally connected with world events or his performance in office. It was fascinating because Eisenhower in office did not seem marked for anybody's shrine of political marvels. As a beacon of style and lucidity in news conferences, Ike was a disaster. Some of his responses in front of a microphone were hard to distinguish from Casey Stengel's in a dugout. Geographically, Ike would aim an answer in the direction of Maine and finish somewhere off the coast of Madagascar.

In the cocktail parties they were fond of characterizing Ike as an amiable bubblehead, connoting someone earnest but ineffectual. Yet since the age was the 1950s, when American seemed settled into a period of comfy blandness and its military dominance was secure, it didn't much matter. They decided Ike was a father figure, and that explained the wide gauge of trust and affection the country gave him.

But if you have been reading and viewing the reprise of the hours of Normandy 40 years ago today, you probably understand the bond more clearly than the quick judgments did in the 1950s.

Ike was the face of an America whose rhythms and purpose in the greatest of its wars rang with a unity and a sense of justice its citizens believed was the soul of the American democracy. It might have been the last time America would experience that kind of solidarity. Beyond the '50s and Ike lay the tumult of class and cultural revolutions, Vietnam, and, after that, the fears and conflicts of the nuclear age.

World War II, of which D-Day was a surmounting moment, was not quite a holy war but it was close enough to forge an attitude that consumed the citizens of this country with the idea of national mission and inevitable victory. It was America in its most fulfilling hour, the one foreseen by the bleeding fifer and by Francis Scott Key in the glare of the rockets.

In our hearts, we know that this is what the unexpected national absorption with the D-Day anniversary is about.

It is more than soldiers' nostalgia.

It disturbs some of the peace activists, because to them it seems to be glorifying the ends and means of war all over again. But I don't think that is what we have seen the past few days.

We have put an aura around those years as a time of national fraternity that cannot be recaptured. We had harmony not only because it was a war we all agreed on and had to win for survival, but because the majority of us refused to see or were ignorant of the darker side of the democracy. And those who were its victims were too cowed by their weakness or the demands of the war effort to raise their voices.

That came a generation later. And out of its turmoil and street riots the country moved closer to the democratic ethic it preached. The Warren Court of Eisenhower's administration pushed the country in that direction. But Ike is not remembered as any flaming emancipator, because he wasn't.

Yet he knew how much the country could handle in social reform in the 1950s better than most of his critics. He was impressed by big-money industrialists, but he knew better than his critics the danger in letting those industrialists into the war-and-peace process. He was a soldier, but he knew the country's strength and he didn't have to peddle the humbug, rampant among generals today, that the solution to our international stresses is more and bigger tools of obliteration.

He was perceptive about the perils of military arms races far beyond most of the wisdom of the time. He knew the only sane course approaching the nuclear age was to talk, and international baiting and name calling were no answer. He knew it as a military man but also as a political creature whose instincts told him anything is negotiable, if you allow the other side some maneuver.

He led well because he was believable and honorable. The country saw that. I was in Washington on the day he was buried. I will carry to my last day the sight of old Omar Bradley, whose good sense and decency matched Ike's, holding his hand in a trembling last salute.

I think the country today celebrates its time with Dwight Eisenhower as much as it does D-Day, and realizes what it has been missing.

Cloak-and-Dagger Comes into the Church

JANUARY 20, 1985

THE PRESENT GOVERNMENT of the United States made its first bold strike for a place in history by scoring a clear-cut victory over Grenada. Some people said it would be a long time before we could match the verve and originality of that performance. But these are people with hearts of marshmallow. They consistently underestimate the government's X-ray powers to detect potential enemies of the homeland in peculiar places.

Dozens of churches in America have been giving sanctuary to Central American political refugees for several years in the fundamental belief that practicing their creed means more than singing hymns and organizing potluck dinners.

Into some of these congregations, we learned this week, the government has dispatched agents with hidden tape recorders to protect the American public from the spreading peril of compassion.

Some citizens — although evidently not a whole lot — find this undercover penetration of church councils contemptible. I don't know whether it is. Sad and demeaning may be closer. Cartoonists made a living for years attributing this kind of energetic paranoia to the Soviets and the loin-cloth emperors.

No clan of politicians has been more zealous in trying to tie itself to God and his presumed will and designs than the Reagan administration. It installed a secretary of the interior who said we should start re-exploiting public land so we could get in a few more loads of timber before the end of the world.

Orators from Ronald Reagan down invoked God, Jesus Christ,

the prophets, and miscellaneous saints to rally America on another Christian crusade against evil empires. God was conscripted into the school prayer brawl. Everybody was invited to return to the basic witness of Christianity, the one said to have built this nation's traditions.

A couple of hundred churches did return to the basic witness of Christianity when persecuted strangers came calling for sanctuary. Some of their members now find themselves under indictment, partly from the evidence of tape recorders brought into their meetings by government agents evidently posing as concerned Christians.

There is undoubtedly a law in this country dealing with illegal aliens, whose numbers are vast and almost beyond accounting. When the law has been enforced, it has often been enforced selectively, usually in response to somebody's political irritation or embarrassment. The goal of these indictments seems clear enough, to demoralize and break the sanctuary movement.

The question of offering church sanctuary to Central American political refugees has divided hundreds of congregations. To millions of people, performing an act of Christian conscience and possibly saving a life cannot outweigh what to them is the unacceptable burden of evading a law, at least technically. It is no easy decision. Good and wise people are present on both sides.

But their dilemma is only part of the equation. The government's response is the other part.

There are laws, and laws. There is, as the unquenchable Minneapolis police chief, Tony Bouza, will tell you, "all kind of idiot legislation" from which law enforcement agencies have to pick and choose.

Technical violations of the law are committed all the time, some of them by the nation's most powerful people, who later contend they were mistaken or uninformed. And nobody brings an indictment.

The sanctuaries irritate this government, which is highly irritable on the subject of Central America because it has aligned itself with policies that have prolonged the misery of thousands of the oppressed and has blinked at death squads.

The churches that gave shelter did it openly. Imperfectly but solemnly they offered the protection of their house to people who came to them in fear and estrangement. There is one kind of act of magnanimity that a hounded person will seek only from a place of God. If we will not give it there, then where?

How to Swindle and Never Lose a Perk

MAY 26, 1985

ONCE IN A while when corporate fraud gets too aromatic for even the most tolerant prosecutors, the government takes the offenders to court. Citizens gulp at the numbers that emerge in the trial or hearings. Somebody, usually the public, has been slickered out of millions of dollars in cost overruns, charges for fictitious services, or the illegal manipulation of other people's money.

Lawyers call this corporate crime.

The government often makes snorting sounds intended to convey the picture of an aroused justice eager for combat against swindlers wearing Guccis and three-piece pinstripes. It vows to take off the gloves and go after them as ardently as it goes after pimps and deer shiners.

Court judgments accompanied by large newspaper headlines sometimes follow. A company is fined. The executives solemnly deny any criminal intent and zip their briefcases. Court is adjourned and they head for the club.

Corporate crime usually means fraud, and fraud means stealing. Sometimes it reaches a scale impossible for the average, noncomputerized mind to grasp once the figures pass the tens of millions.

But the criminals almost never go to jail.

When a Las Vegas nightclub personality is convicted of a scam in which his checks flit from bank to bank, capitalizing on money he only pretends to have, he draws 10 years in the federal slammer.

When the E.F. Hutton stock brokerage does it, the executives thrust an honorable jaw to the public and sound chagrined. They pay a fine, reimburse the banks, withdraw their high fidelity commercials from television for a while, and head for the club.

Nobody goes to jail.

Later, when the dispatches told us what General Dynamics got away with, I skimmed through my large file of Crimes Against Humanity in Hennepin County. The file brought me up to date with the dark-starred burglary attempt by Craig Michael Ecklund, a man with a valiant taste for Chinese egg rolls and barbecued ribs.

One source of such food last fall was the Mandarin Restaurant on Highway 7 in St. Louis Park. Mr. Ecklund was discovered by the owner after climbing onto the roof at night and easing himself through an opening and onto the restaurant ceiling. Regrettably, the ceiling gave way, plunging the visitor into a large collection of cans containing barbecue sauce.

Before trying to repair the damage, the gentlemen did the instinctive thing and munched some of the egg rolls and barbecue ribs. The owner arrived for work the next morning to find the floor basted with tomato sauce and marinade. He also discovered about $10 worth of egg rolls missing. The police arrived in good time and were wading through the swamp of marinade when the owner surprised the defendant in a nearby shed. The man might have talked his way out of it except, in the words of the police report, "he stretched, and Officer Curley saw red sauce all over his forearm."

Caught red-armed, the defendant drew 90 days in the workhouse and another nine months on probation. Defenders of justice will not seriously quarrel with the court's decision. It seems to satisfy the hardliners and the forgiveness lobby.

So observe General Dynamics, a munitions maker whose offenses against the public were so gross that a Pentagon figure called them nauseating. It routinely billed the taxpayers for marketing and entertainment expenses intended to make it even richer and more powerful than it is, all of which fueled the climate in which the Pentagon frantically buys billions of dollars of General Dynamics' hardware it doesn't need. This corporation's excessive billing practices have been calculated and arrogant and have victimized a whole nation, to which it hasn't paid a dollar in corporate income taxes in years.

Its penalty is to be suspended for a couple of weeks and to pay a fine which it will amortize with a few months' profits. This is an organization that has been found with taxpayers' marinade smeared over its hardware and its ledgers, and nobody goes to jail.

Should we listen seriously when government talks tough about prosecuting corporate crime? And should we listen seriously when the Pentagon sounds annoyed by it?

Why? A lot of people in the Pentagon want to graduate to jobs with the companies doing the swindling.

Something More Than a Black Holiday

JANUARY 18, 1986

THE COUNTRY IS paying its respects to a national hero this week, and is doing it with less fever than a national celebration deserves.

It means we are not quite as generous as the ideals we profess. That we are better than we were is the first and immovable measure of Martin Luther King as a conscience and pioneer, and as a man who surely belongs to all times.

His elevation as an American treasure and the symbol of his people's struggle was resisted by the power structure in this country for years. The first attempts to seal his place as a historic figure were trivialized with arguments which, if they prevailed, would have devalued the transcending gift he made to this country.

Somebody said he wasn't Lincoln or Washington, suggesting he hadn't been dead long enough, as though there is a sliding scale for veneration. It was also said that no holiday had been designated for Thomas Jefferson, as though King's fitness to be memorialized should be the subject of a Hall of Fame poll.

If we acted on the slogans and ideals we have chiseled into our city hall cornerstones, the nation would resonate today with thunderclaps of gratitude. They would cut across the races and the masses and acknowledge that his voice and valor had brought his dream closer by making us see.

We hear the dutiful speeches, some of them from politicians who weren't that anxious a few years ago to enshrine his cause. We hear the songs of proud black musicians telling of their debt to King, and imploring the country to remember that this day is for everybody. Which it is.

But those are words in a song. They express a yearning and invitation for all of our people to embrace. But it is a message that still awaits acceptance in the hearts and minds of millions. We are a better and richer society today because King dreamed and led, but not all our instincts are kind. King's greatness as a human being and leader was in his being able to move the nation by appealing to the best of those instincts in both the white majority from whom he asked fellowship and the people for whom he asked decency.

He met vested power with an admission of his weakness: that he had no fires to light in the street nor righteous terror to wage.

He marched among the institutions he sought to change not to dismantle them but to bear witness to a wrong. His was not the only way that persuaded or forced us to yield some of our bounty and privileges to black people. But King's was the most enduring way because it exposed to the glare of our conscience the sham of our conduct against the nobility of our words.

No one should ask the impossible in the recognition of King today. He is first a hero to his people. The rest will come in stages, and perhaps not as grudgingly as some black people fear. Because of the way human beings are constructed, it is easier in 1986 for whites in a football crowd to give the embrace to a Walter Payton or William Perry than it is for white people on the streets or in the country to extend the same embrace to the memory of Martin Luther King. Payton and Perry give them identity in the arena. King made us think about our inhumanity. His legacy is that in doing it, he brought us together, and more of us will see that each year in a dozen ways.

I think white people would serve the spirit of King's day not so much by congratulating the country on the progress it has made, but in recognizing how casually we can renege on the commitments he inspired. Affirmative action was right. We owed, and still do. The cities can and must be restored, so that we can put millions of alienated young black people in jobs. We can serve the day by recognizing that the most urgent business of this country is still here on earth and not in the bankrupting folly of trillion-dollar "Star Wars" gadgetry.

A Few Mental Burrs Short of Absolute Ecstasy:
The Human Condition

An Old Man Calls on His Lady

JUNE 3, 1977

UNFAILINGLY, HE WEARS a white shirt and a tie, a limping old man calling on the lady he loves.

He fell a few weeks ago. It meant the walk to the bus stop from his small frame house in south Minneapolis took longer for an 84-year-old man. It didn't mean he would have to stop seeing the lady, or that he could. He has not missed a day in the four years since she entered the nursing home.

They never married. Neither had success in previous marriages. They met 35 years ago when he was 49 and she 46, at a time when both had pretty well abandoned any idea of romantic love as a reasonable hope, or need, for their middle age.

They traveled together at times, had dinner, strolled the side-walks, talked a lot, and, as they reached old age, found the rewards of mutual need and absolute trust that define love for the emotionally-scarred human being where often the poets fail.

It was a kind of permanent courtship. They lived apart, but saw each other almost every day. An illness that followed his military service in World War I confined Andy to a career of handiwork around stores. In the 1940s he adopted a boy who as a teenager was bright and animated and full of potential growth, but who died of leukemia at 17.

He met the woman he called Zel about then. His talkative energy and quirky curiosities amused her first, and then became very important to her. She was restrained, quieter. One of his whimsies was his insistence on attaching personal qualities to the old Ford automobile they rode around in. He bought it when it was a year old in 1957, and called it, naturally, Henry.

237

He pampered it almost as much as the lady, and it became indispensable four years ago when she went into the nursing home at the age of 77.

His visits became an unchangeable part of the daily environment at the David Herman Health Care Center in south Minneapolis, as predictable as the lunch hour they invariably followed. There has never been an interruption. Winter storms and heat waves have been no impediment. If he was sick himself, he made no announcements. Some time ago he piled up his car, got it repaired, and continued his daily visits with Zel. A few weeks ago he crashed the car again, wrecking it and cutting himself. But he showed up at the nursing home, a grudging convert to the limited joys of daily bus riding for a Ford-lover.

He long ago became one of the regulars among the nurses, aides, and attendants at David Herman. The appearance of Andy in the early afternoon was a declaration that another day had progressed in more or less good order, and the world was in reasonable harmony. He was there again today, and so will he be tomorrow. He may bring oranges, bananas, whatever Zel has requisitioned for today. Possibly flowers. Always zest and laughter. And neatness, dignity, his white shirt and tie. The lady deserves all those things, he tells the attendants.

If he has suffered much in his own life, the aftermath of his Army service, the death of the adopted boy, his recent injuries, he reveals little of this to the friends he has made at the hospital—and probably even less of that now to the lady. He has become her guide in the nursing home corridors, delivering travelogues, her errand boy at the commissary, buying crackers and nuts, and still the man who courts her daily.

They talk about whatever she wants to talk about. If sometimes in her pain she is cranky, he holds her hand, says something sympathetic, but then grins and tries to talk her out of it. If she is tired and would rather rest, he sits, and before he leaves he will talk about the excitements of tomorrow.

"There are a lot of ways you see and experience what most of us call devotion," one of the attendants said, "but this fellow seems to give it a deeper meaning. He isn't solemn all of the time or even most of the time. He tries to make her laugh and do things, and he is always there. It's really one of the most beautiful love stories you could see, and it doesn't matter that one of them is 84 and the other is 81."

But perhaps it matters very much.

A Professor Rejoins the Learners

OCTOBER 20, 1977

HIS GOATEE ANGLED trimly from his reddened face and this, together with the smock he always wore lecturing, gave John the look of an amiable revolutionary about to conduct a short course on bomb throwing. He spoke with a kind of muted, tenderized hoarseness that suggested a man who had battled for years with northern blizzards or unruly customers in a fish market or what—

Or booze.

John was the hospital seminar's resident authority on booze. His students were an unremarkable cross section of the community, 20 or 25 of them, sitting at chairs with writing flaps. These performed a dual function. The more studious used them as a platform for taking notes. The less studious used them as a buffer to avoid concussions when they fell asleep and dropped their heads.

The scholars included three or four factory workers, housewives, a minister, drifters, a couple of secretaries, a truck driver, three or four salesmen, a displaced cowboy, and a journalist.

Most of them enrolled in the course without much exhilaration. You might call their presence there a triumph of the benign coercion of the Hennepin County court system, which never came right out and told these suspected alcoholic drivers to get educated or get jailed. But it didn't really offer much choice, either.

I'm not sure about John's academic background. His rhetoric was smoothly structured, and his mind adroit. But unless Harvard conducted an extension course in Sweeney's Bar, I would have guessed John managed to evade the Ivy League in his youth. He was somewhere in his 50s and his credentials were flawless. In his more active days he had been a drunk, vagrant, panhandler, and booze-tank regular at city hall.

Somebody persuaded him to try a better way, pointing to the limited virtues of getting greased three nights a week and the unpromising future in waking up with a blank brain and palsied fingers.

John stopped drinking. He not only performed good works for himself but for others less perceptive in finding a track out of the jungle. He became an authority on alcoholism, certified by the institute's gold seal and applauded by even the most exacting professionals.

Nobody I've ever heard on the subject of alcoholism was more persuasive than John. He would stand at his blackboard with white and yellow chalk. He would make precise and terrifying graphs showing the deterioration of the human brain under the prolonged assaults of alcohol. He would describe symptoms with both the emotional power of the trained platform stylist and the credibility of one who had experienced them and now understood.

And yet he was chatty and gentle. Nobody knew much more than John about the fallibility of the human being, his vulnerability to the seductive force of self-deception. Hypocrites, he said, we all are or have been or can be, and never as surely as when we turn to booze or other chemicals to soothe the pain or fly from the truth or just hunt for a more exquisite excitement or plain old good vibes.

He had been dry for years, he said, but he never lost the realization that each day he would have to do it all over. And he knew all of the mental tricks and rationalizations of those who pretended it was different. Prestigious universities and successful psychologists often consulted John, asking him to share his presentations and to advise with them with their own training programs.

Not all of his students had been falling-down, drunk-tank types of boozers, but practically all of them had the genuine potential.

The first day I heard John was the day of my last drink four years ago.

He telephoned not long ago, bombed out of his head. We talked and talked, and he said all of his knowledge and his perception crumbled one day before the old tyranny reawakened. He said he would try again.

He will.

And he thought some of his old students, and possibly people who should have been his students, ought to know that sometimes will and brilliance aren't enough to face the power of it. And it is at times like this that the combined strength of other fallible people is the best defense. It is called AA, and it is still the best way for most.

How Not to Organize a Tryst with Your Wife

FEBRUARY 2, 1979

WHAT MODERN MARRIAGE needs most, two sex therapists instruct us in the current *McCall's*, is more dating, preferably the kind that finishes with pillows and purrs.

They don't mean extracurricular trysting in strange beds.

The trouble most couples dig for themselves, argue Drs. Shirley and Leon Zussman, is assigning low priorities to sex in their daily lives—a proposition that may surprise locker-room attendants who have to listen to the jocks' daily accounts of their latest devastations.

"We have time for work, movies, TV, chores, dinner parties, cleaning the house, mowing the lawn—but often we are too busy or too tired to make love," the therapists lament. "Sexual activity between partners is not always honored as an activity that is planned for, for which time is set aside, or that even takes place at times when both partners are relaxed and rested. We believe it is essential for couples to plan special times to be together for the sole purpose of enjoying each other's company. We suggest actually making a date, as you would to go out to dinner or play tennis or golf."

I share this thesis with you today because of a response I have received from a 36-year-old mother and supermarket checkout cashier in St. Louis Park, who reads the magazine and left it open to the Zussmans' article at a time and place almost impossible for her husband to avoid.

Two days later, her husband telephoned her at work in the morning, announced his schedule for the next eight hours and then, lowering his voice to his best boulevardier baritone, said, "How about a date after dinner tonight?"

"The rest of the day I was just flying," my informant confides. "I got our daughter recruited to some hastily organized slumber party engineered by my best friend. We had a quiet and uncomplicated dinner with lots of bright conversation, and it was just mutually understood that we would let the evening's program take care of itself along the lines the doctors suggested, with no unnecessary intrusions from the outside world. So I took the telephone off the hook and left a note on the door saying, 'Gone for the night. Back tomorrow.'

"One of the things the therapists recommended was to do some low-key planning for the excitement ahead by giving your mind and muscles every opportunity, relaxing yourself mentally and physically. So I took a leisurely bath and was toweling myself when I heard low moaning sounds from the bedroom, interspersed with some medium-core four-letter words.

"I found my husband in his Viking gym trunks and T-shirt, lying on the floor and twisting in terrible pain.

" 'My back,' he groaned. 'I think I've broken it.'

"It almost panicked me. I didn't have the faintest idea what all this meant and I asked him what happened.

" 'It's those goddamned sex therapists,' he said. 'They said get ready by doing some yoga or something. What do I know about yoga? I tried some side-saddle hops and five deep knee bends. I was going to finish with ten sit-ups. The sit-ups were what did it.'

" 'Did what?' " I asked.

"My husband was bitter. 'These people were going to make me the world's greatest lover,' he said, 'and they not only killed me for bed but for the bowling league tomorrow. How the hell am I going to be the world's greatest lover with a slipped disc?'

"I asked him if Ben-Gay would help.

"My husband said he was way past Ben-Gay, and he refused to make love in a wheelchair.

"With tenderness and liniment I got him in reasonable shape in a half hour. The night looked like it might be salvaged. I put on one of Jackie Gleason's old dreamy-music albums and, remembering what the therapists said about setting a mood, I asked my husband to think of a movie where we sort of recaptured the early thrills. I thought he was going to remember *Love Story*."

"And what was the name of the movie he gave you?" I asked.

"*Tora! Tora! Tora!*

"It was all downhill after that. The next day I found out my daughter came down with a bad case of flu and had to go to the hospital, and my best friend was trying to get me all night on the phone."

I asked her what was her strategy for the weekend.

"Saturday night we're having all of the relatives over," she said. "Sunday night he's taking heat treatments for his back. I think I'll finish reading *McCall's*."

Please Don't Tell Me You Feel Fine

FEBRUARY 1, 1980

I HAVE BEEN temporarily exiled onto the untouchable list of one of my telephone regulars, an office receptionist from Hopkins. My offense occurred early in our last conversation. She called to complain about a television commercial and asked how I'd been. I said I was fine.

Lord, how I wish I could now recall that odious word.

It triggered the woman into a harangue of denunciation and grimly couched pity. "Why don't you just come right out and say how you feel?" she demanded.

Not wishing to aggravate my sins, I quickly reorganized and probed my conscience to produce a more acceptable reading. But I was forced to express regrets.

"I can't do it," I said. "I do feel fine. I would like to tell you something different, but that is a fair evaluation of the state of my mind and the condition of my pancreas this morning."

My explanation infuriated her. She accused me of copping out and covering up. She said my telling her I felt fine violated every modern principle of free and open exchange between two up-front people.

Its infamy went deeper than that, she said.

"As a response to a sincere question, saying that you're feeling fine is a meaningless, rhetorical hash or, worse, it's a prophylactic dodge. It's a throwback to another time when people either were afraid to express themselves honestly or were too careless or callous to discover those feelings. Why shield yourself? If you feel really good, why not articulate that in a way which leaves the other person with no doubt about the level of your happiness this morning."

I said I didn't know what more I could do than apologize. "Tell me," I said, "how are you today?"

"I'm Super," she replied. "Just Super."

I examined this report with envy and mystification. "How can you say that?" I asked.

"With complete candor," she said. "That's exactly what the world is to me today. I am confident and enthusiastic. My health is excellent, my bills are paid, and all my plumbing is in order."

I said I would be the last to want to intrude on this swelling euphoria. But I had to admit my own life met most of those requirements at the moment and, while I felt fine about it, I just could not claim to feel Super.

I fanned again. There wasn't much I could say to appease the lady and I felt miserable about it.

"Saying I feel Super is an affirmation," she said. "It's positive and it's forthcoming. It puts me right out there with a declaration, yards ahead of your faint and passive 'fine.' I don't want to hear that. It's like an X instead of a signature. It has no character or texture. Tell me you're lousy or tell me you've got a hangnail or tell me you're feeling marvelous or that you're lazy or slow, but don't tell me you're fine."

"Should I hang up?" I asked.

She wanted to know where I had been the last 20 years, whether I had ever attended a Dale Carnegie course, a Mary Kay seminar, or a "Dare to Be Great" rally. Those were some of the launching pads of the new consciousness, she said, and scores of her friends were now responding. "I have a friend," she said, "who when you ask her how she feels replies as if she is a meterologist. She gives you how she's feeling in terms of the weather. I think that's original and exciting. She will tell you she feels clear and sunny, or partly cloudy. Sometimes she will say she feels breezy and once in a while she tells you she feels like hail, which I think is tremendously expressive."

"Is she ever an occluded front?" I asked.

"I also have a friend who, when you ask her on the phone how she feels, will say something like, 'Just wonderful.' Now my question to you is, why not say something like that the next time you feel OK."

Here I objected. "I just have never experienced many moments in my life when I felt purely wonderful," I said. "People who have felt this way have my unabridged awe. Even in my moments of highest pleasure and achievements, there have always been a few mental burrs to keep me short of absolute ecstasy, such as, 'How am I getting down?' or 'What's it going to look like at the end of the month?' So while I have felt fine hundreds of times, I have almost never felt completely wonderful. I'm sorry."

"But that's it, that's it," she exclaimed. "That's honesty. The next time somebody asks you how you feel or to describe the experience, tell them, 'Almost wonderful.' "

I have been slapped for less than that.

Why Was She Wearing Her Ski Pants So Low?
FEBRUARY 4, 1980

A WRENCHING SAGA from the snow slopes is before us today, weaving together the dramatic properties of a pretty skier, a pair of runaway skis, and a set of bib overalls at half-staff.

I offer it for your attention only after grueling research to verify its principal elements. The primary sources for it are eight Lutheran skiers, members of a weekend party. I have accepted the basic thrust of their account because all of my instincts tell me you cannot bring together eight Lutherans from Edina who are unanimously wrong or imaginative.

With this as a working hypothesis, I've concluded that the events gathered here are truly reported and, furthermore, they constitute a clear warning to mothers: Before you send your daughters onto the treacherous slopes in bib overalls, be certain they understand *all* of the potential hazards, including the one posed by the limited availability of rest rooms.

My chief informant is an Edina woman who is a commercial artist, renowned among her friends for her qualities of stability and calm. She is a careful narrator, without a shred of showmanship. She deserves a respectful hearing, and I know with your fundamental sense of fairness you will grant it. She believes the distressed heroine of the incident may live in Minneapolis and should be treated with both sympathy and pride.

"She performed with tremendous bravery, according to all of the accounts," the lady said. "Only bad luck wrecked her chances to get the skis under control. What happened was that this young woman was taking a lesson for intermediate skiers with a small group at one of the popular resorts. They were on top of an instruction hill, away from the more congested runs, when she developed a need for the rest room.

"They were at a point in the lesson where the instructor didn't want to send her down the hill. The facilities were a long way off and it was only a small class, which meant it was more or less dead time for the rest of them. So he told her to go into the bushes.

"She didn't object. It looked like the easiest solution, and there was a lot of privacy because they were isolated on this instruction hill. She went into the thicket and first had to take off her jacket and then, of course, unstrap her bib overalls.

"She had completed all of the necessary things and was just preparing to stand up when her skis began inching forward. She didn't realize until then that the ski points had swung around to the down-slope position. And it didn't take her any longer to see what a precarious position she was in. She was moving through the thicket, in the sitting position, with her bib overalls down to her knees and her poles long gone."

I intervened in the narrative, ashen with foreboding. "In this position," I said, "she had no way to protect what so badly needed protection."

"None," my informant confirmed. "Within a few seconds she had emerged from the thicket and was now careening down the open slope, her overalls around her knees, the straps flying behind her, unable to navigate to the front and exposed to the stern."

"How terrible," I commiserated.

"Exactly," the commercial artist agreed. "She tried really heroically to get the skis under control. But she had built up too much speed to do any effective edging and the snowplow technique was out of the question, her knees being wedged that way by her low-slung overalls."

"But why didn't she stop herself by just sitting down?" I asked.

My informant dismissed this proposal with a sniff of impatience. "The condition she was in?" she asked. "How would you like to sit down, charging down ice and snow with your pants around your knees?"

I apologized for not thinking it through.

"For three or four hundred yards she sped down the hill that way, between and over moguls, around light standards. Finally she hit a big mogul, flipped, came down on her leg, and banged her ankle. That stopped her, but it also broke her ankle.

"The hill patrol came with a stretcher and got her to the hospital emergency ward, where she underwent surgery that evening and was quickly back in good spirits. The next day in the hospital she happened to meet a young man who was hospitalized overnight. He was wearing a ski sweater and a big bandage on his face. She asked him what happened.

" 'You'll never believe it,' he said. 'I was skiing yesterday and suddenly this weird sight flashed in front of me. Some woman was sitting down on her skis with her jeans down, flying out of control down the slope. I was so startled I lost control myself, smashed into a tree and broke my nose.' "

Never drop your guard, outdoor lovers. There is peril where you least expect.

Trying to Stay Healthy Could Kill You

JANUARY 9, 1981

I BELIEVE IT is merely a matter of time until researchers discover that mother's milk is a long-range contributor to lumbago and eating whole-wheat bread drastically expands our exposure to gout.

No other conclusion is available to the jittery citizen accosted by the latest finding from the relentless hawkshaws of the science laboratories at the University of Maryland who have discovered a probable connection between decaffeinated coffee and cancer.

The report leaves me traumatized.

For 15 years I have been drinking decaffeinated coffee as an act of faith in the essential good works of the central nervous system if left unmolested, and to avoid bubbles in the lower tract.

I have done it to promote the quality of life, to make myself more congenial to my neighbors and creditors, and to live longer so that I can pay more taxes to finance scientific research.

Drinking decaffeinated coffee has become a cornerstone of my daily exertions. It has given me a sense of time and place. When new waves of research punctured most of our illusions of the good life and dissolved practically all of the joy from food, drink, labor, and sex, drinking decaffeinated coffee stood there as an obelisk of hope and stability.

The Maryland agents have now determined there is a risk of people contracting pancreatic cancer if they chronically drink decaffeinated coffee. They also found some linkage between cancer and the consumption of wine and exposure to dry-cleaning chemicals, but it is the caffeine connection that puts me on the floor today, burbling in total futility.

I thought of calling my doctor but reconsidered. The guy has been on decaffeinated coffee himself for 12 years and he may be in no better condition today than I am.

You do understand the awful symmetry of these research disclosures of the past 15 years.

As late as 15 years ago I was smoking three packs of cigarettes a day. I did it for all the orthodox reasons — companionship, confronting tension, reward, because I was a sucker for the tobacco ads, and because I envisioned myself as Buck Jones gunning a rustler every time I lit up a Marlboro.

The doctors eventually persuaded me that cigarettes cause cancer, heart disease, nicotine hangover, emphysema, yellow fingers, and halitosis.

I believed, and still do.

I quit, cold potato. I threw out all the cigarettes in the middle of a drag in August of 1965 and none has corrupted my gums since then.

But smoking cigarettes had become an inextricable part of the morning machinery. I would arrive at the plant, install myself in the office behind all of the gadgets of the writer's dodge, light up a cigarette, and begin the day.

Abandoning cigarettes created a vacuum, a psychological no-man's-land. They had to be replaced.

I experimented with the usual substitutes. I tried chewing pencils but learned this was a potential cause of lead poisoning. I tried munching jawbreakers but dropped that because the high sugar content was fattening and a potential cause of heart attack.

I began consuming vast volumes of straight coffee but learned quickly that the caffeine in coffee presented horrors so extensive that I might not last another year.

Caffeine was described as a potential cause of heart trouble. It was a stimulant and, therefore, aggravated problems of the nervous system and also produced a day-long case of the yips. In addition, it was a diuretic. If you took too much caffeine you were either scaling the walls or exhausting the plumbing or being measured for the cardiac ward.

I gave up straight caffeine and switched to decaffeinated coffee.

For years I was satisfied with the office Sanka, which issues from machines and has the general texture of thinned crankcase oil.

But it was a salvation. It relieved me of fearsome hazards to my health and filled the psychological void created by my abandonment of poisonous cigarettes.

I then learned that a change of pace was desirable from time to time, and so I moved to Brim.

Brim was excellent until Seymour next door here informed me that sometimes Brim gave him bubbles.

From there I moved to Taster's Choice. I have been living thus in this palace of straw, which today is blown all to hell by my discovery that decaffeinated coffee may give me cancer of the pancreas.

Does anybody have a jawbreaker?

The Wisest Grad May Not Be the Richest
JUNE 1, 1983

COMMENCEMENT SPEAKERS WENT through a painful period of disrepute not so long ago. This was in the 1960s and early '70s, when the revolting young scholars preferred graduation exercises dominated by rock blasts or ukulele solos.

Values changed in the later 1970s and so did the atmosphere of the commencement. Nothing happened in the 1970s. Choked by the price of gasoline, the world sort of stopped. Graduation exercises became a languorous contest between the senior class and the commencement speaker to see which could fall asleep first.

But today the commencement speaker is counter-attacking with all flags flying. They don't bring him on to warm up the crowd before the band gets there. He is allowed once more to sit on stage in passable dignity instead of squatting in the drum section. All of these recycled courtesies are being thrust on the graduation speaker because suddenly he is relevant again.

Advice is back in.

The scholars now tune down their transistor radios in the back tiers of the risers. Practically no one drags on grass between the valedictorian's remarks and the introduction of the speaker.

It isn't because the speakers have smartened up and learned how to doctor the amplifiers. The kids are no cabbageheads. They are looking at the classifieds, and they know the work market better than Reagan's speech writers. What they want from the commencement speaker today is not eloquence but hardcore job leads.

The commencement speaker finds himself in a dilemma. He wants to be positive, under pain of being accused of damaging the business climate. Unfortunately, he finds himself under duress. In

255

the old days the speaker simply advised the graduates that no goal was beyond reach: They could be president. The problem there is the recent record of the presidents. Kennedy was assassinated, Johnson abdicated, and Nixon was thrown out. Ford spent his tenure bouncing golf balls off galleryites, Carter was ignored, and Reagan was shot. No self-respecting speaker urges graduates to become president anymore.

They could become computer programmers and analysts. But at latest count there were 60 million U.S. citizens under the age of 14 who are skilled computer programmers, most of them in kindergarten and nursery school.

The graduates could become teachers. But the birth rate is going down and we have Reagan's word for it that the country is not getting value right now out of its education system—which the administration appears intent on dismantling because it gets in the way of the ultimate goal of a warhead in every garage.

The speaker could urge them to get into mass communications. But you may have to win a beauty contest to get on the air in the future, and if you prefer print journalism you may need professional counseling rather than references.

Does this mean gloomy destinies for the graduates? No, not at all. It just means a little more suspense. And it excuses me for borrowing from a few thoughts I shared not long ago with a senior class that wanted to know if it was still all right to look at life as adventure and a form of seeking a summit.

You can beat that metaphor to death. It still has validity, but it is deceptive. Goals, yes. But an actual summit attained may not be the ultimate test of the search. The journey itself may matter more. What does it make of us? Does it deepen us, gentle us, make us more human, quicker to smile at our pretensions, quicker to recognize them, slower to be annoyed by those less nimble than ourselves?

In our urges to make it at the pay window or in our relationships, or to meet the demands of ego or peers, will we dull the humanity inside us, and squander the chances to elevate our lives by failing to enlist the goodness that is in us? And worse, by failing to see the goodness in others?

If we are going to make young adulthood a climb, isn't it better to see it as a quest that brings discovery rather than as a struggle that brings a prize? If we all had one gift to give, I would give curiosity. From that flows discovery. And I think the surmounting discovery is that no matter what our material success, our lives will be hollow without the recognition that the most profound moments are the ones when we serve, when we meet a human need, when we accept or extend love.

The rest will pretty much come to us as we deserve. The bounces usually even out, and the ones who make it financially or aesthetically are simply the ones who work hardest for it, the ones less prone to invent alibis, to blame the angle of the sun or the disposition of the boss. Brilliance is not required. Durability is.

So it does matter how we experience the road. I felt that a couple of years ago, riding a bicycle through the western prairie with my daughter. It occurred to me somewhere in Wyoming that I had climbed the Matterhorn six times, flown planes and balloons and explored caves, skied the wilderness and slept with the wolves. I had been thrilled and scared, lifted and blessed. I had experienced treasures of the spirit and of nature I never imagined possible; and yet none of them equaled the quiet pleasure I felt traveling the highway with my daughter, looking over my shoulder and seeing her enjoy the breeze, the open road, and even those abominable sounds coming out of her transistor radio.

Love, yes; but also the intertwining of a service. One meeting the need of the other. That is the most enduring treasure. Young people might smile at the middle-aged father recounting that as the final truth of the adventure. But I know as they get older they will experience it, and understand.

He Caught Her Dress in His WHAT?
DECEMBER 18, 1983

IF YOU DISCOUNT all of the war stories about the perils of overeating in the next two weeks, I want you to burn the name of George Monaghan into your vulnerable psyche today and ask yourself a question: Is there another zipper lurking somewhere as treacherous as George Monaghan's was at the movie, and if so, could fate strike again?

The answer is yes. There is no evading it. If it happens, my ardent hope is that you will be able to avoid arrest, divorce, or a bolo punch to the kidneys.

None of these calamities overtook George Monaghan, but all were at least theoretically possible.

I will introduce George. He is a colleague, a good and esteemed one. George is a man of middle age, sometimes visible with a tuft of a goatee, a creature of quiet speech and droll manners. He is one of those likeable and inquisitive people who derive much joy poking into the world's odd crannies. Learning about the life cycle of the cockroach may not ignite you, but George will detect something there that is valuable and possibly vital. Such people frequently find their steps dappled with the banana peels of life, and there we begin the drama.

He had gorged himself at dinner before the movie. He admits it now, and it surprised him, because George is a man not only of moderate build but also of generally moderate habits.

"The movie was *The Sound of Music*," he said. "It happened some time ago, but I remember that and I also remember being so uncomfortable after eating so much that I just had to adjust my clothing. I unbuckled the belt of my suit, loosed my waist and lowered the zipper."

Please note that George Monaghan's actions to that point were nothing original or controversial. Millions have done the same. The theater was dark, and George, sitting next to his wife and another small person, was the soul of discretion. An adroit turn of the wrist, and the deed was done.

Sometime later George heard a stirring in the seats nearby and, seeing the party next to him about to leave well before the end of the show, stood to let his neighbors pass. As they were, George briskly redid his zipper. It just seemed like the proper thing to do.

The tall woman who was passing him at that moment came to a halt. It was an involuntary act. The woman wasn't curious.

She was stuck.

George had zipped her dress into his fly. There they stood in the darkness, undeniably meshed.

They became aware of their impasse at about the same time. George quickly tried to lower his zipper. It would not yield. He tried to pull it up. Nothing budged.

He tried jiggling, although that is not his nature.

All this time the tall woman stood viewing George's feverish movements in a mood of volcanic despair. Yet she did have quality. She did not erupt. Instead she whispered, "Don't tear the dress, whatever you do."

It was George's fervent wish not to. But what was the man going to do? You have accidentally zipped the nylon of your sleeping bag, or the fabric of your jacket. Every time you do it there is a siege of panic and you feel trapped and powerless.

Now try to imagine the predicament of George Monaghan. He has zipped himself into the dress of a strange woman in a darkened theater, while his wife is sitting there pondering both the odds against this insanity happening and the escape routes.

"I suggested to the woman that we should at least go into the aisle," George said. "It was better than doing nothing." Together they sidled into the aisle. Pausing there, George tried the zipper futilely. The woman seemed to want to help, but under the conditions, there wasn't much she could do that looked appropriate.

Preceded by the rest of the woman's party, they made their way toward the lobby, trying to maintain a low profile despite their unusual gaits.

The manager met them in the lobby. "He tried to help," George said, "but it was one of those things you sort of have to do on your own. I felt terrible. Nothing like that had ever happened to me."

George was magnificent under pressure. In three minutes of hard maneuvering he had released the woman. The only damage to her nylon dress was a tiny wedge torn in the side. She disappeared hurriedly.

"It's funny what people associate with movies," George said. "Some of my friends tell me every time they go to a movie they thing of the shower scene in *Psycho*.

"Every time I go to a movie I think of my zipper."

It is a tough heritage, but George is a survivor. He has seen no reruns, however, of *The Sound of Music*.

How to Excel by Being Dull

DECEMBER 21, 1983

ONE OF MY correspondents, at the brink of burnout after futilely chasing the frontrunners in neighborhood trends for 15 years, has abandoned himself to the highest reward of the liberated man — a life of dullness.

He tells me he has become a full and defiant convert to the cult pioneered by Joseph L. Troise, whose book, *Dare to be Dull*, is the bible of men who are devoted to the creed that uninteresting men make the difference today and may eventually take over the world.

"How can you be defiantly dull?" I asked John L.

"By being proud and up-front about it since that unforgettable day when I stopped my silly and destructive attempts at denial," John L. said. "For years I lived a life of shallowness and deception, trying to impress my friends with the naked brilliance of my after-dinner conversation and my prowess in the world. ·

"I'll give you an example. When friends came over I used to alternate the background music on my stereo between Mick Jagger and Linda Ronstadt early in the evening, switching to Hindemith and Bartók at dinner to demonstrtate the wide horizons of my good taste.

"Now I put on the collected works of Florian Chmielewski."

Anxious not be unkind to the polka-thumping politician from Sturgeon Lake, I asked John L. if listening to Florian's polkas is a symptom of militant dullness.

"Who said anything about Florian's music? I put on his collected speeches. I also put on New Balance running shoes on the first tee at the club. I don't think you can be evasive about dullness. The only way you can harvest its true enrichment — which means you can free yourself of the awful goad to make captain of next year's block party—is to plow into it full bore.

"I think the tragedy in America is that literally millions of American men are latently dull but have yet to be discovered. I want you to help in this much-overdue process."

John L. said I could speed the emancipation of countless men by creating a Minnesota version of the standard Joseph Troise multiphasic test to measure their real, if hidden, capacity for dullness. He said one good way to get into a positive frame of mind about it is for the individual to look at his personal life and ask himself what he does, and compare that with the far more gratifying things he *could* be doing.

"What you do," he said, "is climb mountains, bicycle 100 miles a day, ski, jump out of airplanes, fight with politicians, and sleep with the wolves. What this is going to get you is knobby knees, a splayed rear end, and probably rabies. You are capable of much better than that, and every time you tell me snowstorms are invigorating, I know it."

Shamed by John L.'s ringing summons to dullness, I have developed his test. Please answer all questions fearlessly, or do it for the man in the house.

1. Do you ask the waitress if Happenings coupons are exempt from figuring out the tip?

2. Do you interrupt your mate's playful attempts at sex before breakfast to listen to the snow emergency announcements?

3. Are you thrilled when Greg Coleman punts out-of-bounds on the 15-yard-line?

4. Have you bought season tickets for Mayor Donald Fraser's next inaugural address?

5. Do you believe peat will replace Hiawatha and hockey sticks as Minnesota's next great resource?

6. Do you think the Republicans would ever recover if the Democrats reduced the state income tax surcharge?

7. Do you think the Democrats will ever reduce the state income tax surcharge?

8. When you take your spouse to a second honeymoon in the

Radisson South, do you order a waterbed, a mirror on the ceiling, or a Sony TV with Spectrum cable?

9. Have you guessed a date in the office pool on when the 1968 Volkswagen will fall through the ice on Medicine Lake?

10. Do you plan to show up at the next performance in Orchestra Hall wearing Gore-Tex® wind pants?

If you answered yes to at least five of these questions, I'm told, you qualify for a heady life of aroused dullness. Those who have answered yes to three show promise. If you took Spectrum cable instead of the waterbed or ceiling mirror for No. 8, you will probably get Frank Viola of the Twins balking the runner to third. Which means you have freed yourself from all of the shackles of pursuing superficial excitement. Next, you can opt for Cal Griffith doing the Lite beer commercial.

He Is Cowed by an Assertive Woman Driver
DECEMBER 10, 1983

THE PLACE TO examine the most awesome impact of the women's movement is not in the bureau of statistics or the voting booth but on the highways.

If there are women in the audience, please accept this as the spotless truth: What follows is spoken without heat or disapproval. I believe the woman I met on Interstate Highway 35W two mornings ago was animated by the highest impulses of competence and order. Moreover, she had style. She did not raise a hand or digits once in the universal signal of contempt.

I didn't say she lacked aggressiveness.

Let me back up right there. I didn't say she lacked assertiveness.

I am going to back up again. What she didn't lack, friends, was rail-to-rail belligerence.

Being belligerent in itself need not be a negative quality. Sometimes it can serve a constructive purpose. The lady's purpose was to tell me that as a driver I was a dawdler, inferior technically, lacked freeway smarts, and was lousing up her morning. She may have been right.

She tried to convey this idea for 10 miles from Bloomington to downtown Minneapolis. But I began getting the general drift before we reached the marges of Richfield, when she pulled even with my car and released some incendiary language that made me instantly grateful that I never learned to read lips.

I share this episode with you because I'm certain that we are in the midst of some social phenomenon out there on the throbbing asphalt. What we have, in fact, is an eruption of equality. For more than 50 years, hawkishness, arrogance, scorn, and snarling four-letter words were considered the perks of male drivers. The privileges are now being divided. The democracy has fulfilled another dream.

She entered my life someplace north of 82nd Street, driving a beige Escort and inching up on my rear bumper. She had flawlessly coiffed butter-colored hair and an expressive face, very scenic when she was someplace in middle gear temperamentally. I had the distinct sensation, drawn from the fact that she was flashing her brights in my rearview mirror, that she wanted me either to improve my 50 miles an hour or to disappear into another lane. Neither option presented much promise. I was locked in by automobiles on each side and by a Ramcharger in front of me. What I did was to ease the throttle, thinking if I could create some distance between the Ramcharger and me, the impatient Escort might be able to slide in between us.

I made that maneuver inspired by the purest fellowship of the road. I'm sure you must see that. Unluckily, the woman misunderstood. She thought it was the crudest kind of spite.

Well, it certainly was her prerogative, and, as the experts on fingerprints would say, I can identify with that. So she gave me some more lights. She then gave me horns, and a few teeth. As she passed me somewhere beyond Diamond Lake Road she also give me the tip of her tongue.

If there were another way to say it, I would. A few minutes later, by the blind destiny of the traffic flow, she found herself running behind me in another lane just on the outskirts of downtown. In my mirror I could see her going through some stricken vibrations that I'm sure were meant to say: "What have I done to deserve this klump in front of me?"

When we got to the light at the freeway exit on 9th Street I found her idling in the lane next to mine. Devoured by curiosity, I opened my window and sociably motioned her to roll down her passenger window. She did, surprising me. Her voice gave off faint scents of sulphur. "What do you want?" she said.

"I'm just dying to know your occupation," I said. I had been sorting out the possibilities. When we passed Richfield I thought she might be a drill sergeant in the reserves. Later I switched to truck driver and from there to traffic cop and professional wrestler.

"I'm a dentist," she said. "And I'd love to do one of your cavities, Eight-ball."

Up window.

It could have been worse. She might have been the county assessor.

The Hardest Part Is Saying You Love Him

FEBRUARY 22, 1984

THERE IS SOMETHING in the male condition—in spite of the best intentions and wisdom of our tutors at the counseling tables—that makes it a struggle to tell a friend how much he matters. The masques and distance and the stern suppressions nursed by centuries of role-building are slowly peeling, but women still do that so much better, and perhaps it is they who should be the tutors.

So when I fumbled with my feelings he was generous not to smile in recognition of the irony of it: that he would have done it just as ineptly. He lay on a hospital bed in St. Paul, sifting out the preliminary diagnoses from the doctors. It was solemn news, but he has lived through so much injury and internalized grief, so much psychological horror, that he could accept it without anguish, and, in fact, with a willingness to look for a treatable future.

He is the kind of person who years ago, stretching back to childhood, had all legitimate excuses to fly apart and to find oblivion. He fought that off with his intelligence and the insistence of his instincts that the human being who valued his time on earth could outlast defeat.

Ideas have been his blood. Books were first his gurus, then his sanctuary, and finally they became his career. They have never been his escape, because the clickings and wheelings and spasms of the human mind have always fired his explorations, and the work of a James M. Cain or James Michener or Antoine de Saint-Exupéry helped him explore some of the lonely and fragmented alleys of his own life.

I don't know many people I admire more. It is not so much the friendship, although when I saw him in the hospital Tuesday, being courteous with his visitor and trying to be informative about his condition and his hopes, I told myself what enormous richness there is in that. He is one of those people who may have entered your life, a person who has seen too much difficulty to bring joy, but who brings something better: truth with himself, a tolerance and trust in you. A comfort to sit with and talk, knowing the mutual privacy and good will that will govern the conversation. It is the kind of friendship that can accept long lapses but needs no reaffirmation or validating. We have played a few games of tennis each month for more than 20 years when he has been able and, because we are children of the same generation, plow afterwards into a dialogue of feverish reminiscence. We talk about a hundred things, about Fred MacMurray's insurance salesman in *Double Indemnity*.

On the heavier days we could lay out the selected gray laundry of our fallible lives. We found ourselves long ago on the same rough frequency in how we look at the world, at some of its nobilities and some of its more stubborn shams. We also discovered the same rough weaknesses and capacities for conversion. In the process we have cleansed most of the remorse or the anger of the moment, but mostly we have shared the bewilderment—and that more than the others became the agent of a self-needling amusement that was always the best way to end our conversations.

The finest people you meet are the ones whose lives and values teach you something that deepens you as a human being by giving you a glimpse of a spirit that truly endures. Whole sections of his childhood are gone to him, blotted out mercifully by a power who can define? He went through spinal ailments, other body ruptures, later a treatment-induced addiction to codeine and after that, alcohol addiction. He lived with literal and emotional nightmares for years and yet when he faced the moment when he must cut off all his escapes and delusions, he chose sanity and pain.

His refusal to return to the darkness of nine years ago, beyond the control of his intellect and nerve, led him to accept a spinal tap one day without anesthetic. And every time I would encounter a great athlete and be tempted to call him brave, I would remember

Bob struggling to hold his sanity, and I would remember what constituted authentic bravery.

And he has never stopped working, reading, growing, and advising us as a thoughtful critic. He has never stopped being a good father, and a friend.

And I love him.

Postscript: Bob Sorensen died in May 1984. He was 54, the victim of cancer. He was widely honored and respected as books editor of the Minneapolis Star and Tribune.

The Red Dirt Ennobled Their Faces
OCTOBER 25, 1984

I DON'T REMEMBER his face, but I do remember his forearms. They were big and hairy and they separated me from three of my best front teeth in a high school football game in northern Minnesota nearly 35 years ago.

He's a Minneapolis businessman now. Because our tracks carry us in different directions, we haven't met for years. He telephoned on the pretense of talking about the election. The discussion was perfunctory and not especially profound. He drifted through this and that for a few minutes, and then confided that his father died a few weeks ago. He wasn't morose about it. His father was an iron miner who lived into his 80s. He was a pensioner who seemed comfortable in the last years of his life, satisfied materially and lifted by the knowledge that his kids had achieved and were well off.

The son was groping for a response to his father's death beyond the natural grief that had subsided. He asked what he could do in memory of his father's sacrifices for his family as an immigrant iron miner.

I never met the one he called "the old man," but I knew hundreds like him. They were my relatives, my neighbors, and my gruff tutors when I was a kid. To earn money for school, I shoveled iron ore at their sides in the dripping red tunnels of the underground mines. At lunchtime in the little wood shack 1,500 feet beneath the surface, they would rummage through their lunch pails, wrap their ore-smeared hands around a pork chop sandwich and talk. Some of them were vulgar and a few were silly, and their giggling voices

270

gave me an odd kind of shiver, as though a colony of comics had been turned loose in a tomb. They spoke in broken English or in their native Yugoslavian, Finnish, or Italian. The collision of their languages heightened the alien vibrations in the shack.

It was a place where I saw my first pornographic pictures, and where I first learned something about beauty.

Most of the men ate without speaking. Some of them chewed absently, some reflectively. They worked in grime and never very far from the threat of caving earth. They were human moles. When poets celebrated the dignity of man, they might not have been thinking very hard about underground miners. Their faces were smudged from rubbing the rock wall when they set a drill bit or a dynamite stick. The seams in their faces were streaked with ore dirt. They had the caricature look of actors painted by a deranged makeup artist who ignored the rims of white skin under their mining helmets and lathered the rest in red.

But they didn't make the sounds or strike the postures of martyred men. They and their wives came of their own accord. Nobody would erect any monuments to their fame or their work, but there was something deeper that absorbed them. One of the miners wore a long, coffee-strain mustache in the old-country style. His black eyes roamed the walls fiercely enough to split the ore unaided. But he motioned for me to come to his bench, and he talked about his son and "big university." The glare vanished, and he shook his head in wonderment. *His kid*, going to the big university.

People ask now and then what to see if they visit the ore towns of northern Minnesota. I tell them to look in on the museums and the abandoned pits, but to find a place, a barber shop or a saloon or maybe a lodge hall, where they can look into the faces and hear the voices of another and earlier America now almost gone.

The immigrants still come to this country. But the ones I remember came at a time when the hungers of their ambition for their children fused with the restless yearnings of the young country and produced something marvelous. It was a country that demanded and abused, inspired and rewarded. It did all of those things to the immigrants I remember. But before they worked their last they engraved for us a truth: that much of this country's greatness springs from the struggles of its people, the ones it first exploited, and then needed.

That their children recognize it is their best memorial.

Shifting Gears with a Maestro's Baton

NOVEMBER 15, 1984

THE FRONT SEAT of the car is the utility room of America, adaptable to almost all urgencies and arts. Some people make love in it and others plot the overthrow of the office manager.

I conduct.

I have never carried this confession to a psychologist. I have also never carried it to Neville Marriner, the world's busiest orchestra conductor. Marriner is usually 35,000 feet over the Grand Banks of Newfoundland and therefore unavailable for consultation. This is a pity, because I have seen a very common flamboyance creeping into my style, and it is threatening me with exposure on the freeway.

Like most of you, I use the front seat of the car to act out my fantasies. To the relief of my relatives and my lawyer, I have never fantasized myself as a hot-blooded lover or a Hindu levitationist. Conducting is something else. Of all the big-visibility performers in town, the Kent Hrbeks, Tommy Kramers, and beluga whales, Neville Marriner is the one who earns my rankest envy.

It ripples the glands to imagine all that power and virtuosity, instantly obedient, at the flick of a fingernail or the vault of an eyebrow.

Lately I have been doing the Rachmaninoff Second Symphony in the front seat of my car, and Wednesday morning it led me into the terrible embarrassment of a public lecture.

Like most outstanding artists, Marriner is a cinch to scout. That is important because the hack conductor needs every edge to get through three symphonic movements without being reported to the cops in St. Louis Park. Being English, Marriner is an enemy of the passionate-windmill style of conducting. This again is helpful because while I conduct with more verve and frank emotion than Marriner, what profit is there for art if you go wild and punch out the windshield?

Marriner's best moves are a series of little frontward pigeon steps when he wants intimacy with the orchestra, and the underarm scooping thrusts he makes when he wants more body. The pigeon steps would mean hitting the brake at 55 miles an hour and incurring a $5,000 case of whiplash. The underarm scoops, though, are built for front seat conducting, where the cardinal rule is to keep the hands below the dashboard unless you want to wind up in a psych ward.

What happened Wednesday was that I slipped the cassette into the tape deck and brought in the opening largo of Rachmaninoff's Second Symphony somewhere along Highway 18 on the way to Highway 12. This may not strike you as an appropriate place for languorous music. But I have analyzed my conducting style and decided what I do best is summon dreamy violins. For this I need space, because as any conductor can tell you, bringing in rapturous violins takes a right hand that floats in suspension and fluctuates slowly with the nuances of the music. If I did that in crowded traffic at Turner's Crossroad, somebody would be sure to mistake it for a crude gesture.

Where I lost it was on Highway 12 just short of the underpass coming into town. By then I was totally engulfed by Rachmaninoff's smothering melancholy. I breathed hard over the cruise control, pleading for more intensity from the bassoons. When the galloping finish finally came, I charged into it, stabbing at the heater and the glove compartment to evoke drums and cymbals all the way from Dunwoody Institute.

It was my bad luck that a car in the adjacent lane pulled into the meter stall behind mine when I made my first stop. "I was watching you," he said. "Was it Rachmaninoff?"

"How did you know?" I said, startled.

"I could tell by your tempo back there when we passed the Highway 100 cloverleaf. You were awful when you got to the fugue."

274

I asked if he played for the orchestra and was crushed by the answer. He said he lays tile for a living. He said he conducts all the time in his car, but even laying tile he had better moves than I showed him.

I told him to try me with Beethoven. I could blow him out.

The Computer's Sobbing Victims
MARCH 28, 1985

OUR SURRENDER TO the home-computer tyranny has been eager and total. Because it is, no one hears the cries of the victims.

I'm a victim, and I'm crying. Nobody has appeared at my door with sprays of lilies and violins. Worse, no one comes up with a solution when the whole oversold 21st-century gadgetry breaks down in a whimper of futility.

Do you want to know the most maddening part of the computer cult? It is not the domino factor of escalating bills. Those are the ones you pay for new wonder toys to avoid the dread stigma of being exposed as the owner of obsolete equipment. No, the worst part is the sweet serenity on the lips of the bright young salespeople when they tell you that they can't solve your problems and that the situation is quite impossible, something the manuals say can't happen.

"We can't fix it," the voice said to me amiably. "It isn't like radio and television stuff. We can't go in there with a long-nose pliers. The problem isn't mechanical. We've checked out everything. The programming is flawless. The computer has everything it needs to know to act exactly as the manual says it should act. Since there is no reason for your computer to act the way it is, there is no known cure. Try love."

How I envy that sublime calm. It makes me feel guilty for being so jugheaded not to appreciate the basic principle of home computers: People who make them and sell them never claimed to understand them. We are just beginning to realize that a high percentage of computer systems now being sold to the innocents eventually reveal symptoms of brain and nervous disorder, or at least the electronic version of it. Because the computer programmers cannot give therapy to the computers, they compensate by giving therapy to each other.

I found myself in the middle of this engrossing exercise a few days ago after working for weeks with a computer programmer building a list of names that could be transmitted from the computer onto mailing labels. The company I bought the gadgetry from is reputable and sound. Its shops teem with scrubbed, highly motivated young people talking bytes and Ks with that marvelous fraternity of initiates who want the whole world to tap into their wisdom. It's almost impossible to avoid being swept into the contagion. They said cassettes could do it. I just had a few hundred names. The system had to store them someplace and then put them onto the little printer I bought at the urging of a salesman who seemed genuinely stricken at the thought of anybody going through life without a printer.

My home programmer was a young woman of unflinching competence whose fingers flew across the keyboard and created miracles on the screen from her goody bag of software. She also revealed maternal values, tapping the word processor with much tenderness when it performed well, speaking a soft, clucking language to it. She assigned the software, worked up page after page of operating instructions, described the process as completely simple and glitchproof, and left me to my devices.

In two weeks I filled a cassette with names, thousands and thousands of bytes. Then I filed each section of names on the tape again to avert some accidental wipeout. So I had it in duplicate, and it couldn't have been more careful or more professional. And when I tried to run the names back from the cassette to the computer, the computer announced sadly: "Names end in odd sizes." Further the computer spoke not. Paralyzed by some nameless neurosis, it just wouldn't go.

The computer programmer came with her first aid equipment. She tried for three hours to reason with the software and the computer. She called fellow wizards all over town. They uttered hushed, arcane sounds. Nothing happened. She called the shops downtown. The wizards there didn't know. She called the factory a thousand miles away, the inventor.

And in the middle of their high-tech ganglia, in the fortress of the computer age, nobody could tell her why the system wouldn't work. They ran tests and programs, psychoanalyzed the software, and announced: "It's perfect. It just won't work."

Don't get rid of your Smith-Corona or your stapler.

Mothers Are Convinced You Are Starving

JULY 9, 1985

WHENEVER I VISIT my mother, it is an unbreakable rite that I have to carry a cardboard survival box out of the house and pack it in my car before returning to the treacherous world beyond her kitchen range.

It is a box filled with life-support systems, mostly caloric. Since I entered adulthood, my mother has convinced herself that I live under the constant threat of starvation.

Years ago I began calling her attention to the basic mathematics of the drive from my hometown in northeastern Minnesota to Minneapolis. Barring forest fires and tidal waves from Lake Superior, a reasonable riding time is six hours.

She believes this is time enough to expose me to 15 varieties of grief and hardship, beginning with fainting spells from hunger and including attacks of pneumonia, double vision, and hives.

I have never asked a nutritionist to analyze the energy concentrated in one of these cardboard boxes. I believe Napoleon's army carried less into Russia. My mother is 79 years old, but nobody has accused her of harboring a one-track mentality about the hazards available to her two sons once they are beyond the reach of her kitchen and medicine cabinet on the Iron Range. Several years ago she began supplementing the usual vats of home cooking with jars of vitamins and Rolaids.

One year in winter I found two wool blankets and a booklet on how to cope with hypothermia.

A year ago I found a compass and a police whistle.

My mother is a tiny, guileless woman who nonetheless owns the fastest hands in the north as a packer of cardboard boxes. There is a predictable rhythm to her work. She began Sunday morning, for example, by suggesting that I might look better five pounds heavier. She thought that at 160 pounds I seemed on the verge of shriveling up.

"You told me the same thing 10 years ago," I said for the record. "I weigh today what I weighed in 1965. What are you putting in the box?"

It was encased in aluminum wrap and it was firm and a foot and a half long. She identified it as a roll of strudel pastry the people on the Range call potica, with a soft *c* and 15,000 calories in a roll. It takes two days to make and would outsell penicillin and Chinese jade on the open market. It is marvelous and beyond duplication anywhere on earth.

I thanked her and said a half roll would do. This she slid into the box beside three cans of icebox cookies, a half-dozen frozen pasties, and a dozen of Zupancich Bros. best homemade sausage.

"How long will it take you to get to Tower?" she asked.

"It's 15 miles from here. Why?"

"It's Sunday and the stores might be closed. I better put the other half of the potica in the box."

I closed the lid before she could. "I'm driving a car, not jogging," I said. "What's in the little white jar?"

"Vitamins for the hair. You should hang on to what you have."

She wanted to know if I had enough air in my tires. So I recited my checklist. I said I had an oil fill and a filter change in Duluth and I was carrying a full tank of gas to guard against the possibility that every service station from Canada to New Brighton might be closed.

I reopened the box and examined the contents. There were enough cannisters and bottles to give a man stranded in the Yukon equal protection from malnutrition, heartburn, falling hair, and rabies. With satisfaction I noted that she had slipped no extra contraband into the box, so I hauled it into my trunk.

Before I turned the ignition key she handed me a can of cheese balls.

Safely home, I stashed it all in the refrigerator and the cupboards. The aluminum wrap felt a little bulky, so I opened it.

It contained not one but two halves of apple strudel potica. It was the craftiest job yet. She could have gotten past customs.

The World Exploded in the Front Seat
DECEMBER 10, 1985

I REMEMBER ONLY the impact. There was thunder in my ears, and it was shocking. My one sensation was the violence, of being thrust uncontrollably across the highway. I remember feeling bewildered and disoriented.

And then my car was spinning. There was a second sound, a crumping, and my car came to a stop near the edge of the highway.

Upright in my seat, I could see a station wagon stalled broadside on the highway. It was steaming and the door on the driver's side was battered. Inside, a middle-aged man was hunched forward in his seat.

I left my car and ran to the station wagon. The man was unconscious, his face gray and inert. I reached in through the open window to touch his face and to ask if he could hear me. After a few moments, he began exhaling air in short, hissing sounds. His lips began a rapid quavering. I was going to loosen his collar and breathe into his mouth, but I shouted again, louder, and he opened his eyes. I said help was coming and that he must not move. He spoke groggily of the pain in his shoulders, and a few minutes later the paramedics were there.

By then people who had stopped at the intersection rushed to the station wagon, offering assistance, and to a white convertible that was lying in the snow in the median between the east and westbound lanes of Highway 7 in Hopkins. There were three young people in the convertible. I could see the face of one, blood streaming down his cheeks.

A Monday afternoon in the car, tending to some routine business. And then a rending and grinding, and blood. Two of the cars were demolished, and the third appeared to be.

It's not relevant or proper to probe the cause of the accident here. I don't know all of the details, and they may or may not reveal fault among those involved. A half hour after the accident, all five of us were under care in Methodist Hospital, the middle-aged man for multiple fractures.

I share the incident with you for this reason: Seconds before I opened the door to my car, I felt an irrational impatience. Something was restraining me, and time was important.

It was then I felt the seat harness.

It probably saved me. At this exact and uncanny moment, something else occurred to me as I was unclipping. Three days before, I had talked to a young woman from Coon Rapids, Holly Lovik, as part of the research of a column that appeared in Sunday's newspaper. In it, I confessed having been a recent convert to seat belts a year ago, after driving more than half a million miles under foolish and needless risk.

She and her husband were wearing seat belts Monday morning when their car collided with a snowplow. Doctors needed 160 stitches to close his scalp wounds. But those who examined his flattened car said he would have been decapitated without the belt.

I don't know whether my car was hit once or twice. I do know that when it stopped I was sitting erect and clear-headed. There was an ache in my right arm, but it didn't seem serious and later the X-rays revealed no fracture.

The man in the station wagon was wearing a harness. I don't know how he could have survived without it. The convertible in which the young people were riding was 14 or 15 years old, and, according to the Hopkins police, not outfitted with seat belts at the factory.

Once in a painful while, the journalist finds himself in a personal crisis that tends to reinforce what his professional eyes have told him about the quality of paramedic service in this community, the emergency hospital services, and the competence of its law enforcement people under duress.

My memory isn't at all crisp on every detail of the accident, but what I found unforgettable was the laconic comment of a member of the paramedic team: "I've never yet unbuckled a dead man."

The other thing I found unforgettable was spinning out of control on the highway, not knowing what had happened, being held upright by straps I had buckled in five minutes before.

Why Are We Cleansed by a Walk in the Woods?

MARCH 30, 1986

I LUNCHED A few days ago with a man who is seeing the first streaks of sunlight after a long night of personal and business calamities.

He is a man of action and off-the-wall urges. He is also a good fellow whose leaping enthusiasms are sometimes unready for his mixed judgment and brittle emotional bones. If you read horoscopes you would probably identify him as an Aries.

He said he had called because Easter was approaching and he wasn't sure of his location spiritually. It coincided with the surges of life and warmth in the outdoors, and it was as though on this one weekend somebody had thrown a switch and an invisible organ responded with the sounds of revelation. He could feel the expectations rising in him amid all of the signs of renaissance around him, both the ones he expected to see in his church today and those in the woods beyond his house.

I told him I thought he had the world pretty well balanced up. I congratulated him and asked, reasonably enough, why he was telling me this.

"I feel like a hypocrite," he said. "I want to believe, in the way people conventionally believe when they go to church on Easter. I want calm and belief in my life because I need that badly, but I'm not finding much of it, and the only place where I consistently find it are the times I get away from the turmoil and come close to nature."

I said theology was heavy stuff for lunch; so was therapy, and both probably should be left to the scholars. I suggested spinach salad for the time being. I thought we could probably reach some sort of spiritual clearing by planning a hike together for June. But because we had both prowled the hills for recreation, and because we understood the other's impulses, he persisted. He wanted to know what it was we found in the hills that he couldn't find in church.

What we found there, I said, was certainly available in the other. The comfort we search for in a church sometimes makes demands on us intellectually and requires a kind of compliance — and humility — that some are not temperamentally willing to make. So we sometimes make finding God-in-church a struggle with our intellects. It confronts us with dilemmas of conscience, in which the old religion mixes with the new consciousness and gets us to thinking about the church down the block. If I were a preacher, I wouldn't relish a Sunday sermon.

But most of us have a second chapel in our lives, where there are no walls or stained glass. It is a place where we sense something divine in a personal way so intense we feel a reconciliation we have never felt before.

I don't think there is any contradiction between this, the idea of a higher being reaching us through the miracle of nature, and the kind of intimacy with a personal God so many millions of us have tried so hard to achieve in church, synagogue, mosque, and shrine. Sometimes it is easier to find God in a maple leaf. There is more to the woods than trees and mushrooms.

Human beings have tried for thousands of years to discover tangible proof of some higher and benevolent being in their lives. The search has led us into impenetrable thickets of theology. But there are days in the middle of the forest when it is less complicated, when the mysteries and the dilemmas are peeled away, and when we may be closer to the discovery than we realize.

If God is peace, why should it be so hard to understand what it is that stirs us with gentleness and thanksgiving on the forest trail?

The woods seem incorruptible. More than that, we feel a kinship, and a sheltering, and we are cleansed. We may be alone, but we do not feel alone.

Why do we struggle so hard, at a moment like this, to understand what has happened to us, and what or who has touched us?

The Train to Shangri-La

MARCH 16, 1986

THE YOUNG WARRIORS in short pants will go through their exertions in the Minnesota boys' high school basketball tournament again this week, and I will offer them my sympathies.

The teams don't travel to the tournament by train any more. We may have been the last.

I express sympathy because the train made the tournament something more than Shangri-La, that slice of our-guys-in-lotusland it has never quite lost. Several years ago the tournament's architects converted it into a sort of anarchy of equality, which makes it impossible now for the casual bystander to know who is playing where and why.

But the immensity and voltage of the show are still there for the gaping adolescents who are part of it. And if you agree with that, imagine putting a train ride into it as the chosen vehicle of their delivery to the halls of immortality. Nobody on our team called the train the Orient Express, although that was the mood of suspense and exotica it invited. They put us on the train at the depot in Ely and it was a track straight from the ore pits and the tamarack stands into Babylon, from the Moose Lake Road to Hennepin Avenue.

We didn't call it the Orient Express because they didn't give names to the trains of the Duluth, Missabe and Iron Range Railroad. They were more practical about how they designated trains. If you want something touched with the aura of forbidden excitement and romance, how about L-45?

No doubt it was an express. Once it got past Tower-Soudan, the passenger train from Ely to Duluth assiduously avoided all towns over a population of 10. So it highballed through the spruce swamps and we felt like royalty. Never mind that they sidetracked our flyer at Wales Junction for a 126-car ore train. We used the time to memorize a few more stanzas of *Beowulf*.

We had a coach, Ed Buckley, a massive, cigar-smoking Buddha who held the overall portfolio of truant officer, parental surrogate, and jailer. Ed played football with Bernie Bierman at Minnesota after World War I and he was our guru about the corruption lurking in the streets if we strayed from the Curtis Hotel lobby. But he said nothing about our reception when we got to the Great Northern Depot.

For one night we were the only team in town. The high school league was paranoid about blizzards marooning teams from the remoter outposts, so it mandated a Monday departure for all teams 250 miles or more from the city. We walked out of the terminal — and were ambushed by flashing red lights. Most of us thought it was a pinch. We had faces dominated by dark and guarded features that sprang from the Balkans, and we tended to squatness and emphatic jaws. "Geez," my roommate said, "I think they're going to frisk us."

Ed Buckley calmed us. "It's a police escort," he said. "You guys rate sirens. The whole town is wild, and they love you in Minneapolis."

Well, it was exultation. We waved at the curious and somebody threw roses at us. For the next two days the newspapers were saturated with our pictures. And after we squirmed by Crosby-Ironton and Hutchinson in the first two rounds, we were hounded in the lobbies and elevators by packs of oglers.

They filled the fieldhouse with a record crowd to watch these squat and loveable creatures from the subarctic battle Minneapolis Henry and the 6-foot-10 Jim McIntyre for the title. Six bands besides ours played the school song and our team charged into the arena on a crest of adrenaline. It was so heady that our first guy out of the door for warm-ups dribbled down the court to the edge of the circle and fired at the basket. The ball soared 25 feet over the blackboard and into the second deck.

We didn't get a whole lot closer the rest of the game, but I'll never forget that train ride.

They should do it today, although I'm not sure you'd get the same effect from Amtrak.

When Small Towns Suffer, We All Do

JUNE 29, 1986

ONE OF THE young men on my bicycle tour ran short of money in the town of Chokio, west of Morris, and needed substantial equipment repair. With practically no documents or negotiable plastic, he went to the village bank for advice.

The bank manager listened to his story. He said there were bank policies that prevented him from remitting money on the one card the bicyclist carried. He then walked to his desk and wrote a personal check for $50 and gave it to the stranger in town, a man he had known for five minutes. "You can repay it," he said, "when you get home."

Chokio is a community of 559 people whose lives have been bruised, financially or emotionally, by the farm depression. It is a rural town like hundreds of others, its architecture sturdy but unremarkable, its timetables and rhythms tuned to the sun that nourishes the corn and soybeans of the surrounding farms. The Indian language gave it its name, which rhymes with Ohio. Chokio means *halfway*—between what and what is in some dispute. It doesn't advertise its civic charms much. It hasn't raised a billboard 50 feet tall outside of town on Highway 28 telling the traveler that when you're in our town, you're a neighbor.

In most towns like Chokio, that is understood. It explains why a man in a troubled farm village would write a check to a vacationing visitor in need, without considering the irony of it.

A day later 200 of us made an unscheduled rest stop in the 90-degree heat in the town of Grove City, northwest of Litchfield. We parked in the shade of the huge oaks in the yard of a Lutheran church. It stood beside a small cemetery whose lawn was freshly trimmed. Because the church was unoccupied, there was no one to ask for permission. But the watering hose was irresistible, and we took turns spraying each other and filling our bottles. In a few minutes the police drove up and welcomed us to the church. They said there were showers down the road that they would glad to open for us, and a mile back on the highway a farm family waved in dozens of the riders for water and snacks.

None of this is exactly unprecedented. But if you have experienced the middle American countryside often enough in this way, I think you must realize the priceless quality it brings to our lives and how close all of us are — despite our urbanization — to the soil.

Human nature is pretty much the same around the globe. So we don't have to attribute to rural folk any soapy nobility. But what they have to give us isn't much available in the city. The city is sound and power and turmoil and excitement. It is rushing and congestion and a hundred things to do.

The small town is patience and belief in the soil and a lot of harmless gabbing and listening. It is a place where the years seem to tie together with some sense of order and replenishment, where there is something from the past that teaches and deserves honor, and where the family is the deepest and richest soil of all.

It is the primary source of whatever permanence and stability remain in our lives, the kind of living most of us have experienced at one time or other. The small town, and the countryside that feeds it, may not be where many of us could or would live year-round. But a day or a week there will nurture us with the loveliness of the greening country, and make us feel a little more human because it reawakens our trust.

Because of that, what happens on those uncluttered streets, when a bank closes or when a little business makes headway, should matter as much to two million here in the cities as it does in the cornfield.

There is country soil in the blood of everyone. It is why we should not be surprised to see grown men and women frolicking in the water on the lawn of an unattended country church. For a moment, it seemed to belong to all of us.

290